Officers found the body under a board and a streak of lime. It was wrapped in plastic and badly decomposed. A short distance away in some scraggly piney woods, they located and disinterred another plastic-wrapped nude body.

By the time the twenty-seventh body was unearthed, police officials had had enough. They announced that all the bodies that were going to be found under the shed floor had been recovered. The job of identifying the remains had already begun, but ten years later authorities would still be trying to learn the names of some of the victims.

Experts estimate that the perpetrators of more than 40 percent of the murders committed in the United States are escaping justice. A staggering number of these elusive killers are serial killers.

Who are they, and why do they kill?

SERIAL THRILL KILLERS

SERIAL THRILL KILLERS

Clifford L. Linedecker

KNIGHTSBRIDGE PUBLISHING COMPANY
NEW YORK

Published in the United States by
Knightsbridge Publishing Company
255 East 49th Street
New York, New York 10017

ISBN: 1-877961-56-6

Designed by Stanley S. Drate/Folio Graphics Company, Inc.

10 9 8 7 6 5 4 3 2 1

First Edition

◆ CONTENTS

INTRODUCTION

They are nightmares become reality—savage, remorseless assassins who butcher for the sheer pleasure of killing. Self-appointed death angels, they select their victims from among the weak, unprotected, unwary, and convenient.

They are serial killers.

Some experts use terms like *recreational homicide* when describing the crazed acts of the men and women who kill once, then again and again. For them, taking a life—sometimes after submitting a victim to terrible torture, rape, and other perversions—can be a means of relieving tension or simply a way to fill the long hours on an otherwise boring evening. It can be a completely casual, random act perpetrated on a victim selected by the merest chance or accident. Stabbing and strangling are favorite means of murder for serial killers. They're more personal than guns.

Victims are likely to be prostitutes, topless dancers, hitchhikers, transients, runaways, the very young or the very old. Serial killers look for the helpless. One highly respected crime consultant describes them as the most cowardly of criminals. They are excited by power, domination, the ability to control, and the opportunity to play God by choosing who will live and who will die.

Psychologists say serial killers are more difficult to explain than mass murderers, who suddenly slaughter a number of people in a single orgy of violence. Mass murderers are often set off by a personal trauma such as loss of a job, a missed promotion, a divorce or other romantic rejection. The victims may be people close to them or total strangers.

Unlike the case with most murders, the victims of serial killers are almost always strangers. And their murders are carefully crafted, carried out—and covered up.

Most of the 20,613 homicides committed in the United States during 1986 (the last year for which figures were available at this writing) involved relatives, friends, associates from work, or other acquaintances. But a disproportionate number of the approximately 30 percent of those homicides that were still unsolved a year later are believed by law-enforcement authorities to be serial murders.

Ted Bundy, who admitted only hours before his execution in Florida's "Old Sparky" early in 1989 that he murdered twenty-three young women (he never confessed to the three Florida slayings he was convicted of) and is believed to have taken the lives of many more in a terrible bicoastal spree of kidnap, rape, and murder, is the archetypal serial killer.

Not only was he intelligent, smooth, and charming, but he always selected victims from among young women whom he had never met before. Murderers who have had no previous contact with their victims until their single fatal encounter can be extremely difficult for law-enforcement authorities to track down.

As recently as 1966 only 6 percent of U.S. homicides investigated by police produced no known motive. By the early 1980s, unknown-motive homicides had soared to more than 20 percent. The percentages are still climbing.

There are more than thirty-five thousand known murderers in U.S. prisons, including approximately fifteen hundred on death row. But criminologists believe that many more than that are prowling the streets because they were never caught or never convicted of their crimes. And some experts are estimating, as well, that the perpetrators of more than 40 percent of the murders committed in the United States today are escaping justice. A staggering number of these elusive criminals are serial killers.

Who are they, and why do they kill?

In the past decade, these questions have provoked increasing concern on the part of criminologists and law-enforcement authorities. National, state, and local studies have been funded and staffed with some of the most knowledgeable and respected experts available from universities and police agencies.

They have come up with a plethora of conclusions, recommendations, suppositions, and theories. Serial killers, they tell us, suffered head injuries during childhood. They were bastards, came from broken homes, or were the products of one-parent families. They were beaten by alcoholic parents, their mothers were prostitutes or overbearing, and their fathers were weak or unaffectionate. They were sexually abused as children, or exposed to violent pornography, or victimized by drugs.

It's true that some of these factors exist in the background of some serial killers. Bundy's mother spent her pregnancy in a home for unwed mothers, and shortly before his execution he blamed pornography for inspiring his violence. Margie Velma Barfield (whose outrageous crimes are chronicled in chapter 8) was a prescription-medicine junkie and claimed that when she was a teenager she was raped by her father. Carroll Eugene Cole (chapter 5) blamed his bloody rampage against female barflies on traumatic experiences in his home life during his childhood and adolescence.

Millions of other people who never kidnapped, raped, or murdered, however, can point to similar unfortunate incidents and circumstances in their lives. The sad truth is, no one has yet come up with a valid explanation for why one person becomes a serial killer and another, with similar life experiences or background, does not.

But the experts know that sex and power are prime motives.

Although many criminologists believe that most serial killers are primarily sadistic sexual psychopaths, in the broad sense of the term they are not insane. They know exactly what they are doing.

They're clever, and they tend to plan their crimes and their cover-ups carefully.

An FBI study of thirty-six convicted male serial killers found that most were either psychopathic or sociopathic personalities who felt sexually inadequate or had previous unhappy experiences with women. There are others with different personalities and different motives, of course. There are killers like James and Susan Carson, Donald ("Peewee") Gaskins, Rudy Bladel, and Velma Barfield—all chronicled in this book. None of them fit the description of sexual psychopath, but their motives were as darkly sinister, and they were every bit as deadly as more widely known, sexually motivated butchers like sadistic homosexual John Wayne Gacy, Jr., Boston Strangler Albert DeSalvo, and Bundy.

Whatever their motives, they are a special breed of killer, and their number, as well as the dark roster of their victims, is rapidly increasing.

Today, law-enforcement officers track them with computers, specially trained experts lecture at police seminars focusing on their crimes, and extraordinary efforts are made to coordinate investigations by police agencies from a bewildering variety of jurisdictions.

The U.S. Justice Department's Regional Information Sharing System sponsors seven Regional Crime and Information Centers around the nation to gather data on violent crimes and organize conferences for police officers.

The FBI operates the Violent Criminal Apprehension Program (VI-CAP), a computer-assisted system that correlates crime information from records of homicides reported by many of the nation's seventeen thousand police agencies. It also assists investigators by making available the services of a special Behavioral Science Unit at the bureau's academy on the Marine base at Quantico, Virginia. The unit helps develop psychological profiles of serial killers and provides other information.

VI-CAP was instrumental in linking a Tampa, Florida, man arrested on an apparently unrelated rape charge in 1984 to a particularly grisly crime spree that had baffled police for months: a series of murders of prostitutes, topless dancers, and other young women in the Tampa area. Bobby Joe Long was ultimately given two death sentences, pleaded guilty to seven other slayings, and while in prison admitted to a tenth.

Incredible as it may seem, however, even when serial killers are caught and convicted, they are often paroled. In Canada, they are sometimes granted daylong leaves from maximum-security prisons and allowed to roam old haunts where they previously terrorized, raped, and murdered.

Savage killers like John Gacy and Wayne Clifford Boden (chapter 10) became model prisoners. Beating the system can be an entertaining and exciting part of the game for serial slayers.

Bundy took great pleasure in obstructing the system. The smirking multiple sex slayer escaped from a Colorado jail, staged an outrageous comic-strip courtroom marriage, boasted that he fathered a child in a prison visiting room, won three stays of execution, ran up a taxpayer bill of six million dollars for legal expenses, and made a string of judges and attorneys look like pitiful circus clowns during an exhausting decade-long encampment on Florida's death row.

When he was at last executed for the murder of a twelve-year-old girl he raped, tortured, and dumped in a pigsty, the public was so fed up by the legal highjinks that they congregated outside the prison by the hundreds to dance, chant, and burn sparklers in celebration of his death. Private citizens were sending a blunt message that the men and women in the ponderously muddled justice system didn't seem to grasp: Dealing with serial killers isn't a silly game for a few venal lawyers and misguided do-gooders to play out in the nation's courtrooms. Punishment should fit the crime!

Capital punishment does indeed prevent serial killers from ever killing again. No one has ever provided any valid evidence that serial killers can be rehabilitated. But murderers who are executed can never escape or be paroled, only to hunt down and slaughter new victims.

A society that refuses to execute its most monstrous killers is making a dangerous statement: that it will not protect its own citizens, and that there is nothing so sacred that it is worth defending at the price of life.

Some behavior is simply so vile and disgusting that the interests of justice cry out for and demand the ultimate penalty.

SERIAL THRILL KILLERS

1 ◆

ROMEO MARTY'S MINI-MAUSOLEUM

Harrison ("Marty") Graham (1987)

Rotting garbage, broken wine bottles, abandoned hypodermic needles, even smears of excrement piled in the street by both dogs and humans are a sad fact of life in the festering North Philadelphia slums. And residents were unhappily accustomed, as well, to putting up with the junkies, prostitutes, thievery, and 'vicious domestic quarrels settled with knives, fists, and guns that were an integral part of daily life in the black ghetto.

But the nauseating odor seeping from the crumbling third-floor apartment finally became too much for neighbors near the dilapidated three-story row house on North 19th Street to bear. And if the situation weren't aggravating enough already, blood had dripped from the apartment into the second floor.

It wasn't the first time there had been trouble over the sickening stench coming from the apartment. Neighbors had in fact called a day earlier, and the landlord had checked out and then dealt with the complaint: The husky, broad-shouldered tenant of the apartment was ordered to leave. He agreed to get out, but left an inside bedroom door nailed shut. He explained that he wanted to protect personal property, which he planned to return for.

Evicting the tenant didn't solve the problem, however, and by the next day—a blisteringly hot and muggy Sunday morning in early August—the odor had become intolerable. This time a relative of the owner climbed the worn stairs to the third floor to investigate. He cupped a hand to shield the light from his eyes and peered through a keyhole into the gloom of the offending apartment.

Then he clattered down the stairs to summon police.

Even before climbing to the third floor, past the trash on the stairs, the missing plaster, the peeling paint, and the yellowed urine stains, the first police officers to arrive at the scene recognized the smell that had the neighbors upset. It was the cloyingly sweet odor of death.

That stench wasn't an uncommon phenomenon in the crumbling old neighborhood a few blocks west of the campus of prestigious Temple University. Violence, as well as the runaway abuse of alcohol and narcotics, takes a heavy toll of lives in all big-city slums, and the City of Brotherly Love was no exception.

The row house on North 19th Street seemed to be an especially good bet for finding a body, because the third-floor apartment was notorious as a shooting gallery where junkies could go to inject heroin or smoke dope. And junkies often overdosed, causing panic among their friends, who were likely to leave the bodies where they fell in the rush to get away and avoid a brush with police.

Police had been to the building thirty times in eleven years, to investigate a variety of complaints including drug abuse. But if officers expected to find a victim of an overdose they were in for a shocking surprise. The filthy two-room apartment had been turned into a macabre garbage- and trash-filled ossuary littered with rotting corpses.

The condition of the apartment was almost too squalid to believe. It was infested with fleas and roaches, and a jumble of torn mattresses, stained bedsheets, old clothes, crumpled panties, stubbed-out cigarettes, and rusty food tins were tossed willy-nilly on the bare wood floor. A grease- and food-encrusted hotplate was set atop an empty wooden packing crate, and there was an old sofa with the springs popping through the cushions. An ugly bloodstain smeared one wall; crude drawings of female heads were scrawled on another.

A sprinkle of syringes, needles, bottle caps, and other drug paraphernalia protruded from the knee-deep refuse, and a fly-covered bucket partly filled with a foul slime of human excrement that writhed with fat, ugly maggots festered in a corner.

A police patrolman stumbled across the room and removed his hand from his mouth and nose long enough to push open a window and get some fresh air into the stench-filled apartment. It was difficult to comprehend that humans had lived there. But there was no doubt they had died there.

A husky policeman put his shoulder to the door to the bedroom and shoved. The ten-penny nails bent and ripped from the frame as the door popped open, and the musty, sweet odor of decomposing bodies settled over the police officers like a shroud. Five cadavers, in various stages of decay, were arranged haphazardly in the cramped and dirty room. Two of the corpses were propped against walls, and when investigators lifted them they found others underneath. A sixth cadaver, still relatively fresh, was found wrapped in a sheet and blanket in a tiny closet.

"It was amazing," a shocked homicide detective told journalists. "It was bodies piled on top of one another—literally."

One of the corpses was nude, another nearly so. Two of the bodies had mummified. Two could be identified as black females, but the others were in such deplorable condition that authorities couldn't immediately determine their gender or race or how they had died.

One set of remains was so badly decomposed that there was little more than a skeleton with a fuzz of flesh and hair hanging on it. Doctors suggested that it might have been in the apartment for several years.

Police confessed that they wouldn't be able to determine if foul play was involved until autopsies could be performed to determine cause of death.

A crowd of men, women, and youngsters gathered to watch the activity as police and officers of the medical examiner's department trooped in and out of the charnel house, first with handkerchiefs crumpled tightly to their mouths, then with gauze surgical masks. The onlookers slumped languidly against police cars and ambulances, sat on stoops, or gathered in little knots and leaned against the dilapidated red-brick row houses nearby, idly commenting on the possible identity of the cadavers being carried from the building in body bags, and the whereabouts of the big, muscular man who had lived in the apartment.

Only a few blocks away from the scramble of police squad cars and ambulances clogging North 19th Street, the life of the ghetto went on as usual. Hookers in tight hot pants and flimsy shirts or blouses strolled provocatively in high-heeled tackiness along the refuse-littered streets, and dope dealers stood attentively at curbs like darkling sentries, offering easy and rapid drive-up service for a stupefying variety of illegal drugs.

On some corners drug sales were so open and so brisk that dealers set up card tables to display their wares. In other areas sales were more clandestine, and users stuffed their money through mail slots, then waited a moment before their drugs were pushed outside through the same openings. And yet other locations were so heavily fortified with cinder blocks and metal bars that narcotics-squad officers referred to them as "gate houses."

But after the grisly discovery on North 19th Street, the major attention of police—in that neighborhood, at least—was on the bodies, and the former tenant who had so recently vacated the apartment.

Alerted by relatives who said they hadn't seen her for about a year and feared that her body might be one of those carried from the fading red-brick build-

ing, detectives began tracing the movements of a
twenty-seven-year-old North Philadelphia woman
named Cynthia Brooks.

And they concentrated on learning everything
they could about the mysterious man who had
somehow managed to live in the apartment amid
the overpowering stench from the piles of garbage,
human excrement, and decomposing corpses. Most
of the neighbors knew him simply as Marty, a dark,
muscular black man who looked big enough and
strong enough to qualify for a job as a lineman on
the Philadelphia Eagles professional football team.

Some of the people police talked to described him
as an easygoing, friendly fellow who was quick to
help out when someone had a bit of carpentering or
car repair to do. In fact, he sometimes picked up a
few dollars as a handyman, they pointed out.

As the investigation broadened, however, police
began to develop a more ominous picture of the
former tenant. And after sifting through a bewildering roster of nicknames and aliases they came up
with Marty's true identity.

He was twenty-eight-year-old Harrison Graham, a
hulking, slow-witted giant who played and talked
with hand puppets. His height and weight exceeded
six feet and two hundred pounds. Graham was
known for an insatiable appetite for cheap wine and
dope and an eye for good-looking women. And his
main sources of income did not include his handiwork as a Mr. Fixit. A neighbor complained that his
work was in fact sloppy and that Graham was always
borrowing his tools, then breaking them because he
tried to get jobs done too quickly.

Most of Graham's income was from a three-hundred-dollar monthly Social Security disability check and from fees he charged dopers for the use of his apartment as a shooting gallery. Although his low-level involvement in the neighborhood's thriving narcotics trade was common knowledge on the street, a quick check of the police computer turned up no traces of an arrest record. There was no indication that Graham had ever had any trouble with the law.

He was a party man, an insatiable ghetto Casanova who trooped into his apartment with shopping bags full of wine and dope and a steady stream of young women. Since moving into the apartment six years earlier his habits had seldom changed. Near the first of every month, when his Social Security check arrived, he would bring in the women and the booze, and the loud parties would start. Marty's apartment became known as the place to go for drugs and sex.

Before moving into the ninety-dollar-a-month apartment, Graham had stayed several blocks away with his mother and his girlfriend, Robin DeShazor. But his mother got fed up with their heavy drug use and threw them out. She blamed Robin for luring her son into the dope scene. An attractive twenty-six-year-old who had once had aspirations of singing and modeling, Robin lived with Graham in the apartment for two or three years, then just dropped from sight. Graham said they broke up and she moved out.

But there was no shortage of available women for the good-looking, muscular Lothario. And there were plenty of things for him to do, like working with drug dealers. Robin's mother told a reporter that Graham worked as a runner for neighborhood narcotics bosses, collecting money from buyers on the street, then going to his apartment, digging into his cache, and lowering the dope on a rope through a window.

A onetime drug user said he had gone to the apartment often to buy narcotics from people there, and that sometimes fifteen or twenty men and women would be jammed into the cramped spaces shooting dope. Business was so brisk that people would often be lined up on the sidewalk and street waiting to get inside.

Sometimes big trucks were parked along the curb in front of the building to block the view of police driving by in patrol cars, and neighbors complained that the apartment was known all over the city as a shooting gallery and source for narcotics.

An eighty-seven-year-old woman who lived a few doors away told reporters that she patrolled the area in front of her home with a sawed-off pool cue and sent at least one junkie to the hospital with lumps on his head. Neighborhood-improvement activists said they had been trying to do something about the dope dealing in the apartment for years.

Robin's mother made regular visits to the apartment for months, trying to talk her daughter into leaving because of the drug activity. But Robin wouldn't listen. Her mother had good reason to worry. A high-school dropout, Robin was an epileptic; when she was fourteen she gave birth to a daughter. A few years later she was treated at a university clinic for narcotics abuse. She married briefly, then separated. Finally she met Graham and moved in with him.

There were ugly warning signals indicating that

Graham wasn't the good-natured doper, boozer, and harmless womanizer he seemed to be. A neighbor was startled one time when she went upstairs to investigate screams coming from the apartment. She was confronted by Robin, naked and shrieking at the top of her voice while her husky boyfriend held her by the hair with one beefy hand and used the other to batter her with his huge fist.

Another neighbor who remembered Robin and two other women named Renee and Mary told of hearing screams one time and looking up toward the apartment. Graham was holding Renee by her feet and dangling her from a third-floor window. After a while, he pulled Renee back in through the window. The neighbor never saw her again.

She did see a notebook that the illiterate handyman had filled with crudely drawn pornographic sketches and proudly showed to her. The drawings were of male genitals, and of naked women. Ominously, some of the women were depicted stretched out under a male foot.

And many young women in the crumbling neighborhood made a point of giving the ominous row house on North 19th Street a wide berth, not only because of the dope dealing but also because of stories that Graham had beaten and raped or tried to rape several girls who made the mistake of visiting his apartment.

As homicide detectives issued an all-points bulletin to pick up Graham for questioning in the baffling case, other officers, along with members of the fire department and the Philadelphia medical examiner's office, began carrying the cadavers, body parts, and litter from the apartment.

At the morgue, the remains were sprayed with disinfectant to kill harmful bacteria, insects, and eggs before autopsies got under way by a veteran team of pathologists and investigators in a specially ventilated room.

Police technicians also obtained fingerprints from the three cadavers that were in the best condition by injecting chemicals under the flesh, causing the ridges on the fingertips to stand out. Copies of the prints were sent to the police administration building (known in Philadelphia as the Roundhouse because of its unique architecture) to be checked against their records. Additional copies were later forwarded to the Pennsylvania State Police headquarters in Harrisonburg and to FBI headquarters in Washington, D.C., for comparison with state and national files.

Efforts to identify the remaining cadavers would be concentrated on the comparison of teeth with dental charts of missing people and on close inspection of bones for telltale fractures or other identifying marks and configurations.

Only two articles of clothing seemed to offer good clues: a woman's demin skirt and a gray sweatshirt. The sweatshirt was decorated with the design of a rose with red petals and green leaves, and the French words *Pour Toi* ("For you"). The uniquely decorated piece of apparel was taken from the corpse of a small woman who would have weighed about 110 pounds and had several teeth missing.

A public-assistance card found in the littered makeshift mausoleum also pointed to the possible identification of one of the bodies as the woman the neighbor had known as Mary. The card carried the name Mary Mathis. The thirty-six-year-old licensed practical nurse and mother of five was estranged from her husband and hadn't been seen for a long time by friends or members of her family.

A day or two after the discovery of the bodies, Mrs. Mathis's husband identified the skirt and the rose-designed shirt as his wife's. A fingerprint check confirmed the identification. Mary Jeter Mathis, a woman who had had a loving family and a bright future before turning to drugs, was one of the dead.

Investigators checked into the possibility that inspection of welfare rolls could turn up medical records leading to identification of additional bodies.

Early Monday morning, the day after the initial discovery, police found the shinbone of a human leg and the bones from two feet under a rotting foam-rubber mattress on a second-floor roof a short distance from Graham's apartment window. Firemen with ladders checked roofs of other nearby buildings, and police fanned throughout abandoned apartments and dark basements in the vicinity. In one of the basements, search teams found a skull, torso, and other remains wrapped in a brown blanket and tied with an electrical cord. They appeared to match the remains found on the roof.

Police spokesmen revealed that the body count had risen to seven, and they were still searching.

A high-school youth told investigators that he had seen Graham digging in a vacant lot several times. The boy said that when he asked what was going on, Graham replied that he was burying dogs. Police inspected the lot, then brought in a backhoe and hand tools to dig up areas where the earth showed signs of being disturbed. More bones were recovered, and momentarily investigators feared that the death list was about to climb again. But closer observation quickly disclosed that the bones were of animal origin. Graham had been telling the truth about the dogs.

But investigators wanted to talk to him about the bodies in his apartment, and the remains found on the roof and in the basement. Two days after the first grisly discovery was made, a warrant was issued for Graham's arrest on a charge of corpse abuse. Some authorities were speculating that the case might involve a combination of natural deaths, or deaths from accidental drug overdoses, as well as homicides. But whatever the individual or collective cause might be, they pointed out, Graham was in serious trouble for living with the corpses and failing to notify authorities so arrangements could be made for proper care of the dead.

It had been nearly two weeks since the missing man had cashed his last Social Security check, and investigators were almost certain that he was broke. Plainclothes and uniform officers checked out soup kitchens, churches, and the homes of relatives— anywhere the fugitive would conceivably go looking for a handout.

More than one thousand copies of Graham's photograph were distributed to patrol officers and police in special units including the Highway Patrol, Burglary, Sex Crimes, Stakeout, and Narcotics divisions.

The citywide search for Graham had barely gotten under way when a young woman contacted police and told them that Graham had been her lover for a few months. She detailed a squalid romance marked by long sprees of drinking, doping, and sex. She said that during one lusty sex session, Graham confided to her that he had killed Robin. When she refused to believe his story, she said, he took her to the rooftop, pulled up the mattress, and showed her Robin's body.

Their romance ended at about four o'clock one morning when they quarreled and Marty chased her downstairs, swinging at her with a machete. Graham retreated after she was able to flag down a nearby police patrol car.

When investigators located a report of the incident, they learned that a patrolman had followed the woman upstairs to the apartment, where she had accused Graham of hiding a body. Graham denied there was any body there. Nevertheless, the officer dutifully poked through the piled garbage and trash in the apartment, peered into the closet, and even climbed to the rooftop and gingerly lifted the mattress to check underneath. He didn't find a body. The incident was written off as a minor disturbance.

After the discovery of the seven corpses a few weeks later, however, the bizarre case attracted a storm of publicity in the local and national news media. Philadelphia was already reeling from shock after the disclosure, barely three months earlier, of another house of horror in the city's squalid northside ghetto, where a red-bearded schizophrenic with a long history of mental problems had operated a torture chamber and sexual abattoir.

Forty-four-year-old Gary Heidnik was eventually convicted of murdering two women, then grinding up the body of one of them and mixing it with dog food, which he fed to famished prisoners he kept

shackled in the basement as slaves for perverse torture and sex orgies. He was sentenced to death.

Philadelphia had had more than enough of abused
and murdered women, and residents responded to
the search for Graham with scores of telephone tips
to police. Dozens of sightings of the suspect were
reported. Police in squad cars were dispatched to a
restaurant in North Philadelphia when a waiter reported observing a big man who looked like Graham
loitering outside. Officers talked with a big man
there, but it wasn't Graham.

And when they investigated another call a couple
of hours later from a staff member at the James C.
Giuffre Medical Center in North Philadelphia about
a suspicious-appearing broad-shouldered man stalk-
ing the corridors, it, too, turned out to be a false
alarm.

Another restaurant worker who had sometimes
given Graham handouts of chicken wings, candy,
and other food scraps when the handyman was broke
and hungry reported seeing him walking in the Center City area of Philadelphia one night. But if the
pedestrian had indeed been Graham, he was gone by
the time police arrived to check out the report.

Graham was known to be a dedicated walker. He
had no car and couldn't drive anyway, and he didn't
like taking public transportation, so he walked. He
was a familiar sight both in the North 19th Street
neighborhood, and miles from there, strolling along
the street, muttering to himself or chatting content-
edly to his hand puppets, appearing as if he didn't
have a care in the world. Graham was suddenly

famous, or infamous, and almost every day police checked out tips of sightings, always with disappointing results.

Then, on a warm early Sunday afternoon exactly a week after the horror on North 19th Street was unveiled, the fugitive's mother telephoned and said he was with her and wanted to surrender. He claimed the bodies were in the building when he moved in, and he hadn't known that authorities were looking for him.

As officers pulled up to the curb of a North Philadelphia street corner in a patrol wagon, Graham meekly submitted to arrest and allowed his hands to be cuffed. He said he had been living in a couple of abandoned houses in the neighborhood. As investigators had suspected, he was penniless and had been eating in soup kitchens.

He was transported to the Roundhouse. During an exhausting interrogation session that lasted hours, Graham at first denied that he was responsible for the deaths, then reversed himself. He said he was sorry and wanted to get his life straightened out. He confessed that he strangled the victims, all women, with his powerful hands when having sexual intercourse.

"They are girls I had in my apartment," he said. "I got high with them and had sex and strangled them while having sex."

Graham explained that he prepared himself for the fatal sex sessions with a devil's brew of prescription stimulants and painkillers washed down with huge amounts of booze. He didn't know or couldn't remember the full names of two of the women he killed but provided detectives with nicknames. The suspect said he picked the two women up on the street and lured them to their deaths with offers of booze and drugs.

He also picked out pictures of Mrs. Mathis and of his longtime girlfriend, Robin DeShazor, from among several photographs shown to him, and identified them as women he had strangled. He confirmed that Robin was the first victim of his sex-and-murder spree. He said he strangled her the previous winter, then pushed her body out his window onto a second-floor roof. Later, after the woman he had shown the corpse to threatened to notify police, he carried most of the remains—including the head and torso—to the nearby basement. But he left Robin's feet and shinbone under the mattress. All the victims were either girlfriends of his or other women who frequented his apartment.

Graham said he didn't mean to kill the women. He would fall asleep after frenzied bouts of drugs and sex, and sometimes when he awakened he would find his partner dead. He knew that his lovemaking was rough, and other girlfriends had complained about being choked while having sex with him.

During one homicidal binge two women were killed on consecutive nights only a few days before the bodies were discovered in his apartment, according to the chilling confession.

The suspect said that he picked up a woman he knew on the street as Cookie and took her back to his apartment, where they guzzled a potent combination of bourbon and Thunderbird wine. Then they had sexual intercourse and Graham passed out.

When he woke up, the woman's body next to him was heavy and cold. "I accidentally strangled her while having sex," he said. Police believed that the woman Graham knew as Cookie was Mrs. Mathis.

The night after Cookie's death, according to the confession, Graham picked up another woman he knew as Barbara and took her back to the apartment for booze, sex—and murder. "She had some vodka and orange juice and I had some 'bird, so we went upstairs and got high," Graham confessed, according to later testimony of a police officer. "We drank and talked and that led to the same thing as Cookie— sex. And that led to the same thing as Cookie—I strangled her."

Police said Graham recounted that he left the bodies of both women in the front room until neighbors complained about the stench and he was ordered to get out of the apartment. It was then that he carried the bodies into the rear room and nailed the door shut, officers quoted him as saying.

The brawny suspect seemed to be doing his best to cooperate, but his memory was understandably spotty. He explained that he routinely started his day with up to ten pints of cheap wine or a case of beer, and topped that off with whatever whiskey or other hard liquor he could get his hands on. If cocaine or other drugs were available, he jolted his system with those as well. Then it was time for sex.

Graham explained that he littered his apartment with the bodies of his ex-lovers and friends because he didn't know where else to put them.

Authorities charged him with seven counts of murder, and seven counts of abuse of a corpse. There was no bail on the murder charges.

Spokesmen with the Philadelphia Medical Examiner's Office announced that in addition to its official identification of Mrs. Mathis as one of the victims, it had identified four other young North Philadelphia women as well. Cynthia Brooks's family's agonizing yearlong search for her ended when one of the bodies was identified as hers. The others included Patricia Franklin, a twenty-four-year-old mother of two; Sandra Garvin, thirty-four; and Barbara Mahoney, twenty-two, the woman strangled the night after Mrs. Mathis's murder. All were black and had lived in or frequented Philadelphia's sprawling north-side slum neighborhood. Despite Graham's confession to Robin's slaying, her identification was not considered official until a few weeks later, when confirmation was made through dental records that matched teeth in the skull found in the basement.

Police said they were still checking missing-person reports in efforts to identify the other remaining victim. She was described as a black woman, between twenty and thirty years old, about five feet, nine inches tall, and with curly hair.

It would be twenty-four weeks after discovery of the remains, near the end of January 1988, before she was finally identified as Valerie Jamison, the mother of two school-age sons. Her parents reported that the twenty-five-year-old woman had been missing since the previous April, when she dropped the children off at their home. An alert forensic investigator with the medical examiner's office had realized that she matched the description of the lone unidentified victim from the North Philadelphia death house, and matched bones in her back with X rays of the woman obtained from a local hospital.

Autopsies disclosed that small bones in the necks of two of the women whose bodies were recovered from the house had been fractured, indicating they died of strangulation, just as Graham said. The Jamison woman was one of those. The other victims had apparently been dead longer, and their corpses were in such bad condition that it was more difficult to determine the cause of death. But there were no signs of gunshot, stab wounds, or bludgeoning, indicating that strangulation or drug overdoses might have been the cause. Police and pathologists knew only too well that more deaths in the North Philadelphia slums were caused by violence and drug overdoses than by heart attacks.

The Philadelphia Medical Examiner eventually ruled that all seven women were victims of homicide, even though the condition of the other bodies prevented the examiner's office from determining the exact cause of death in five cases.

During the preliminary court hearings, after Graham's legal counsel questioned the murder charges in the five cases where cause of death was not resolved, a judge upheld the medical examiner's determination. The jurist ruled that the general circumstances in which the bodies were found indicated that homicides had occurred.

Graham was a well-behaved prisoner and cooperated with authorities, as well as with doctors who conducted psychiatric examinations. A psychiatrist and a psychologist appointed by the court studied Graham and described him as a mentally retarded, drug-dependent psychotic who was not capable of assisting attorneys in his own defense. He was found to have an IQ of only sixty-three, indicating that he was mildly retarded.

But another panel of psychiatrists reported that

although he had major personality disorders, he was mentally competent to stand trial and assist in his own defense. Graham was scheduled for trial.

The suspect's court-appointed attorney, Joel S. Moldovsky, worried that evidence likely to be introduced by the prosecution would be so ghastly and horrifying that it might prevent jurors from reaching a fair decision. Consequently, after conferring with his mother and with his attorney, Graham waived his right to a jury.

A little more than a year after his arrest, Graham went on trial before Common Pleas Court Judge Robert A. Latrone. The courtroom was packed with spectators, and court officers turned away dozens of people who didn't arrive early enough to claim one of the scarce seats.

The defense team contended that Graham was retarded, psychotic, and not guilty by reason of insanity. "I'm looking to save my client's life," Moldovsky told journalists.

Graham, who had worn a soiled T-shirt and ill-fitting blue jeans for earlier hearings, pulled a red-and-gray knit sweater over his prison blue shirt for the trial itself. At times he followed the proceedings closely. At other times he seemed to be distracted and more interested in playing with his puppets.

The most dramatic testimony came from a young woman who appeared as a surprise prosecution witness and said she had lived with Graham for three years.

Paula Renee Pinder said she met him in 1984 after agreeing to go to his apartment to exchange sex for drugs. The twenty-six-year-old woman said she moved in with him, but life with the lusty handy-man wasn't easy.

She said he regularly put his hamlike hands around her neck and squeezed while they were making love. At least three times, she said, he choked her so hard that she lost control of herself and urinated on the mattress.

"This one time, I thought I was dying," she told the hushed courtroom. "Everything was getting darker, and the air was getting less and less." She claimed earlier in statements read to the court that it seemed her lover liked to hurt her when they were having sex.

The witness said that even after she quit living with Graham, she continued to see him in his apartment, and noticed particularly nasty odors that smelled like something dead. She thought it might be a dead rat, but Graham told her the odor was from the bucket he used as a toilet.

She said she didn't believe him, and that the smell appeared to be coming from the back room that he had boarded up. She said that when she asked him about the room, however, he ordered her not to try to look in there because she wouldn't be able to handle what she might see.

Miss Pinder also testified that her former lover told her that he killed Robin because she was seeing other men and spending his grocery money on parties. "One time he told me that if I ever hurt him like Robin did, I would wind up like she did—dead," the woman testified.

She quoted him as telling her that he once became so angry at Robin that he smashed her head through a window glass. Sometimes when he beat Robin, the witness said she was told, blood smeared the wall so badly it had to be painted over.

Graham was clearly upset at the appearance of his onetime sweetheart on the witness stand, and he muttered audibly during her startling testimony. And when she said he admitted having sex with Robin's corpse after killing her, he yelled: "Oooh, you still lyin', girl."

After Miss Pinder's testimony had concluded, Moldovsky told the press that he believed it would be helpful to his efforts to prove the insanity defense. "A witness like this shows the abusive, bizarre, gross, inexplicable behavior of someone strung out on drugs and alcohol," he said.

The defense had surprises of its own, and presented shocking testimony from a jailhouse informant who claimed that convict Anthony Oglesby was rewarded with money and sex for testimony against Graham. (Oglesby had testified earlier that he witnessed Graham choking Cynthia Brooks and Sandra Garvin and said he also saw the decomposing remains of Mary Mathis in the apartment.)

Alexander Peterson, who was serving time at the Northeast Correctional Institute for rape convictions, insisted that Oglesby told him he provided evidence against Graham and testified as part of a deal with authorities, who paid him a small amount of money and arranged a sexual reunion for him in a motel with his wife. Peterson refused to change his story, despite spirited cross-examination by Assistant District Attorney Robert King and angry response by police who labeled his accusations hallucinations and fantasy. And at one point, the judge complained about the trial being sidetracked over what he termed "mini-issues."

Moldovsky had yet another surprise, and in closing arguments suggested that the dead women may have merely died of accidental drug overdoses. He even suggested that the murder scene might have been tampered with by relatives of the landlord. But the defense attorney also made it plain that he wasn't abandoning the insanity issue.

He described his client as a "dumb, passive conduit" used by women. And he further suggested that Graham was a naive man who may have also been the fall guy in a scheme to cover up deaths in a building that was widely considered a shooting gallery for drug abusers.

King labeled the defense attorney's suggestions as fantasy, and argued that the prosecution had presented a strong case based on solid evidence that proved Graham's guilt. Pacing back and forth in front of the bench, the prosecutor derisively declared of the defendant: "He accidentally strangled seven women. Do you believe that? How can you believe that?"

Graham, the prosecutor insisted, was a serial killer, someone who knew what he was doing.

Throughout the closing arguments, Graham sat quietly at the defense table, fiddling with four small brown monkey puppets with false fur. He sat them on the top of the table, patiently arranging and rearranging them, in circles and in lines, sometimes facing one another and sometimes face to back as if they were in marching formation.

Judge Latrone deliberated for six days, then an-

nounced a verdict finding Graham guilty of all seven
counts of first-degree murder. He was also found
guilty of abusing the corpses of each of the victims.

Graham waived his right to have a jury recom-
mend his sentence. "I want you," he told the judge.

King advised Latrone that the state would seek
the death penalty during arguments at a sentencing
hearing. Moldvosky said he would plead for his
client's life on grounds that Graham had no previous
criminal record, was mentally and emotionally disturbed, and had a lifetime of traumatic experiences.

After listening to arguments, Judge Latrone announced a seemingly complicated sentence that
spared Graham from execution but will keep him
behind bars for the rest of his life. The judge ordered
both a life sentence and six death sentences. But the
complex order calls for Graham to first serve seven
to fourteen years in prison for abusing the corpses of
the victims, then a life sentence for one of the
murders, before any of the death sentences is carried
out.

If the life sentence is ever commuted or if Graham
receives parole, he will then face execution in line
with the death-penalty rulings in six of the murders.

The judge explained that he chose life in prison
instead of the death penalty for the serial killer in
the first of the murders—Robin DeShazor's—because of mitigating circumstances. Graham had no
previous criminal record.

2 ◆

MYSTIC MURDERERS WHO KILLED FOR GOD

James C. and Susan Carson, a.k.a. Michael and Suzan Bear (1981–1983)

James and Susan Carson were convinced that they had been chosen by Allah to do His work, so they became hit men for God.

Followers of a bizarre Muslim cult of their own twisted design, they roamed the West Coast for three terrible years, mingling with leftover flower children, street people, and dopers—killing on what they believed to be orders from Allah.

When their bloody odyssey of death was ended at last, they called an outlandish press conference at Sonoma County Jail, where they'd been imprisoned, and announced their motives for the perplexing blood spree. Pronounced James Carson: "Koran law says, 'Thou shalt not allow a witch to live.' Witchcraft, homosexuality, and abortion are causes for death."

Curiously, none of their known victims were either witches or homosexuals, nor were any of them involved with abortions. But there was little about the blood-crazed, self-described Muslim warriors that made sense.

Even their star-crossed first meeting was strange. James, having broken up with his wife, teamed up on a double date with a former college pal from the University of Iowa. They were smoking pot, dropping acid, and listening to rock albums when he slipped into the bedroom with his buddy's date. He moved into her unfurnished Scottsdale, Arizona, townhouse the next day, and she responded by giving him a new name.

James Clifford Carson didn't suit her. Hereafter, she would call him Michael, after the mighty angel that fought Satan and his demons. Even his friends began using his new name, and much later law-enforcement authorities and journalists would follow suit.

She had experience changing names. Her own name had been Susan Thornell Barnes until she and her teenage lover of the moment took some magic mushrooms one night. She awakened to find that she had painted red triangles throughout her house and signed the psychedelically inspired artwork "Suzan."

Most of her life, up to the last year or so, had been insipidly conventional. The pampered daughter of a wealthy newspaper family, she married well, had two children, and occupied her days with country-club activities, jogging, and tennis.

But by the time she met Michael, she was thirty-five, and her life of tedious gentility had turned to a madcap existence of hallucinations, outrageous sexual escapades, and vandalism that alienated her from family and friends, and entangled her in agonizing brushes with psychiatrists and the law. She had split up from her husband years before, and eventually even her grown children decided they had endured all they could take and walked out on her.

Suzan's new lover and soul mate had also been a privileged child. Except for his earliest childhood in southeastern Kansas, most of his growing-up years were spent in Tulsa, Oklahoma, where his father was an executive with an oil company and so highly thought of that he eventually went to Washington, D.C., as an adviser to President Richard M. Nixon.

A long-lasting childhood illness that weakened his bones helped convert the boy into a reader and budding intellectual who developed sympathies for atheism and Marxism and founded a chapter of the antiestablishment Students for a Democratic Society in his high school. Neither the radical political and religious philosophies nor the DS found much support among his Oklahoma neighbors. And he strayed further yet from the rock-hard patriotism and devotion to family and church of most mainstream Oklahomans when he became entranced with the hippie life. He began smoking dope, traveled to the Haight-Ashbury district of San Francisco, joined in anti–Vietnam War demonstrations, and at the University of Iowa promoted Robert Kennedy's presidential hopes.

Now he was thrilled with his new woman, as well as with his new identity. He was bowled over by her intellect, her beauty, her lovemaking, and her encyclopedic knowledge of the occult. She seemed to know everything about astrology, meditation, ESP, astral travel, and the cosmic supernatural struggle between the forces of good and evil. And even though she could hardly read, because of dyslexia, she was incredibly bright. What others might have perceived as hopelessly freakish and off-the-wall, Michael considered charmingly spiritual.

When he returned home from his job as a waiter one day to find she had cut off her hair, he was understanding. After all, not only was Suzan nine years older than he, but she had been enlightened. She was a natural mystic.

After experimenting, since his days as an atheist, with Buddhism, Judaism, and mysticism, he had become a peculiar sort of Christian. It seemed that together they might be able to sort out their joint spiritual karma. She began to confide to her soul mate about visions, and conversations with a huge, nude figure of Allah. After a short time, Suzan and Michael became Muslims.

Nudity was an obsession with Suzan, and it got her into trouble. Michael was eager to share all of her experiences, and they lived together naked in the townhouse until they left Arizona for a trip through Europe. They had returned home only a few days when she stepped out of the house nude. A neighbor called the police, and a little later Suzan was dragged naked from the townhouse, handcuffed and screaming. Six months later, after completing a six-month probation on the nudity charge, she and Michael left Arizona for the West Coast.

The stage was being set for murder.

Like the onetime Oklahoma boy James Carson, Karen Barnes grew up as a down-home girl surrounded by loving family and friends who shared typically wholesome middle-American values. She was a Georgia farm girl, a fetching strawberry blonde with a vivacious, trusting personality. She was also adventurous and bored with small-town life. And after an experience as an extra in the Burt Reynolds movie *Smokey and the Bandit* when she was seventeen, she set her sights on living the exciting and glamorous life of an actress. So she hopped a bus for Hollywood and stardom.

Karen didn't become an actress, but she did find her way from Hollywood to San Francisco, where she fell into a 1960s hippie time warp. The naive teenager with the fetching Georgia accent was quickly up to her pretty neck in the ugly world of dopers, thieves, and down-and-outers. Her friends were leftover hippies, strippers, punkers, winos, and drug dealers. By the time she met the Carsons, she had changed her name to Keryn and was one of the pathetic young burned-out street people living a hand-to-mouth existence in the Haight, subsisting on whatever money they could pick up from welfare, drug dealing, thievery, panhandling, or sex.

She collected welfare, did a little topless dancing, experimented with tarot cards, ouija boards, and witchcraft, briefly followed various gurus—and did a lot of dope.

Suzan and Michael drifted into the Haight, easily melting into the hippie subculture, where they were accepted as the dope dealers they were and developed a reputation for handling some of the best marijuana available. They also developed reputations as mean-spirited, religious wackos with a predisposition to violence that alarmed even the most laid-back and devoted leftovers of the Love Generation.

But Keryn was attracted to them immediately, and when they wandered into the city on their periodic visits, she shared her apartment with them—or, if she was living with friends, dragged the strange couple along so they could crash for a night, a week, or a month. Early in 1981 the Carsons spent several weeks with Keryn, and had barely dropped from sight before the landlord and a plumber found her blood-crusted body.

She was crumpled in a corner of the tiny kitchen of her cramped two-and-a-half-room apartment. Her skull had been smashed with repeated blows by a heavy object, and she had been stabbed more than a dozen times in the neck and face. One of the stab wounds had been inflicted directly into her open mouth, and her jugular vein was ripped open. Curiously, in view of the savagery of the assault, someone had pulled a frayed quilt half over her, and placed a pillow under her head.

Keryn was fully clothed, and there was no indication of sexual assault. Her purse was lying nearby with nineteen dollars inside, seemingly ruling out robbery as a motive. The Spartan furnishings of the apartment didn't appear to be the type that would attract a thief. There were no signs that any electrical appliances had been present in the modest home. There wasn't even a light bulb.

A few candles were scattered around the rooms, and the odor of incense still lingered. A few pillows, quilts, the stove, and the icebox accounted for nearly all the furnishings. It seemed to be a typical hippie pad. There was even graffiti. It was crude and child-like, but in two locations—on a wall and on the icebox—the name "Suzan" had been scrawled.

Friends of the twenty-three-year-old victim provided the name of Suzan's companion and rough descriptions of the pair. Michael had long stringy hair and a beard, and his clothes were ragged and dirty. Suzan also had long hair, habitually wore sweaters or blouses and long skirts, and had the wild-eyed look of a religious fanatic or madwoman. Both had the bony, haggard appearance of wanderers who were strict vegetarians and often subsisted on handouts or leftover food scraps scavenged from garbage cans. In physical appearance and behavior, they were like scores of other hippies and transients who drifted in and out of the Haight, however, moving up and down the coast, venturing inland a few hundred miles or leaving the area altogether, depending on their whim of the moment.

People like the couple described to police usually didn't bother with such documents as driver's licenses or Social Security cards and seldom held conventional jobs. They were almost impossible to trace. And there was no hard evidence that they were involved in the killing, only the suspicions of some of Keryn's friends.

One of the hippies police talked to was a gentle, long-haired young man named Randy Jacobson, who had fried his brains long before with acid and a devil's cornucopia of other psychedelic drugs and street potions.* They also talked to Jacobson's girl-

---

*Three years after police talked with Jacobson, who was so good-natured and loving that his friends called him "Cosmic Angel," he also disappeared. Although his girlfriend and others

friend. Suzan and Michael had stayed in the couple's apartment for a while, but spent much of their time chanting as they worshipped Allah. And they talked about a holy war against witches, whom they insisted all deserved to be put to death.

Keryn had been the first victim of the holy war launched by the self-styled Muslim warriors. Yet she had also almost become another Muslim wife to Michael. But Suzan had balked.

Ignoring the warnings of more perceptive and suspicious friends, Keryn nevertheless listened seriously to the dope-dealing couple's garbled and paranoic diatribes on good and evil, the approaching Apocalypse, the great Satan Ronald Reagan, and holy wars. She crashed with them at the apartments of friends, shared dope with them, and hitchhiked with them to Los Angeles and Arizona. But they parted ways in Arizona, and Keryn hitchhiked back to San Francisco by herself. Michael and Suzan followed.

Suzan was still seething at the near union of Michael and Keryn, and was convinced that the pretty young hippie girl was an evil witch who was draining her energy and psychic powers. And Keryn had cast a love spell on Michael.

Both the Bible and the Koran admonished, "Thou

---

searched desperately for him, he wasn't heard from again until the summer of 1985, when his remains were recovered along with the bodies of other men, women, and children in rural Calaveras County. Law-enforcement authorities blamed the grisly murders on a pair of ex-Marine Corps buddies, Leonard Lake and Chitat ("Charles") Ng. Lake committed suicide, and Ng fled to Canada, where at this writing he was fighting extradition proceedings initiated by the state of California, where he is named on several murder charges.

shalt not suffer a witch to live," she reminded her soul mate.

Michael and Suzan had holed up in a cheap hotel just outside Oxnard, north of Los Angeles, to escape a blinding rainstorm when Allah used three lightning bolts to pass on the death message, they believed. As each bolt flashed in the turbulent sky, Suzan told her fellow Muslim warrior, the command was repeated: "Kill Keryn."

The assassins were hiding in her apartment smoking hashish and marijuana when she returned home one cold, damp night in early March. They angrily accused her of witchcraft and raved for hours; then after Keryn curled up in the kitchen with a pillow under her head to sleep, Michael smashed her skull with a heavy frying pan.

Alarmed at her death rattles, he grabbed a paring knife from a counter and plunged it into her throat and face.

Then Michael and Suzan gathered up their dope, packaged it into handy tinfoil packets, and walked out into the busy Haight.

Flushed with pride and righteousness after Michael's first kill as a Muslim warrior, but fearful of retribution, they hitchhiked out of the Haight and up the coast to Humboldt County, the marijuana capital of the Western world. They went to work there at an isolated forty-acre pot farm a short distance from the town of Garberville. There they clipped and manicured freshly harvested simsemilla, the potent form of seedless marijuana that is among the most highly prized cannabis in the world. They watered the growing plants and harvested them when they were mature, hanging them upside down

to dry so that the powerful sap would work its way
to the choice leaves and tips.

They didn't know if police were looking for them,
but it seemed they had the best place in the world
to hide out. The marijuana farm would have been
almost perfect for them if it had not been for a
young long-haired beer guzzler. He was a friend of
the owner and claimed to be a carpenter who was
building a two-story chalet on the property. But he
spent more time working his way through six-packs
and slipping girls into the compound than working
on the cabin. Suzan and Michael talked halfheart-
edly about killing him, but instead they left, with
several pounds of dope.

Moving up the coast, they stopped in Portland,
Oregon, for a while as Michael worked on a book,
Cry for War. He wrote furiously, blaming most of
the world's ills on bankers, the Vatican, and power
movers. Suzan helped him, dictating long, rambling
sections developed from her visions. Homosexuals
in San Francisco were slated for live cremation.
President Ronald Reagan, former President Richard
Nixon, Vice President George Bush, California's
"Governor Moonbeam" Jerry Brown, British Prime
Minister Margaret Thatcher, the Ayatollah Kho-
meini, and Charles Manson were listed as targets for
assassination by the ambitious Islamic Hashshashin.

In the spring they packed up their dope, made
photocopies of their book, and began hitchhiking
south to northern California's picturesque Big Sur
area. Just south of Santa Cruz they caught a ride
with a construction worker who was a weekend
hippie and took them to a tree house he said they

could live in for a while. But they didn't get along, and he sent a roughneck with a gun to kick them out. The gunman, who lived nearby in a tent, beat up on Michael. Bloodied and shaken, the Muslim Hashshashin fled to a motel. Suzan was furious and demanded that Michael get revenge. She instructed him to fashion Molotov cocktails from soda bottles and gasoline. Michael slipped back to the tree house in the early predawn darkness the next day and set it afire. Then he firebombed the construction worker's cabin and the gunman's tent.

Not only did they get away with the caper, but while they were hiding out in a boarded-up cabin, Suzan found a rusty .38-caliber revolver and a box of ammunition. Michael spent the day cleaning the weapon, while Suzan sewed him a holster to wear just inside the waistband of his pants.

Now that they were armed, and well fed from food they found in the cabin, they hitchhiked to Los Angeles. But they soon turned back to Humboldt County and the comforting security of the pot farm. They arrived just in time for planting season, and their old boss was so happy to have the unanticipated help that he put them up in an abandoned Volkswagen camper. The carpenter was still there, and the chalet was still unfinished.

This time the marijuana farmer asked the couple to help plant seedlings and irrigate the young plants. And he gave Michael a .22-caliber rifle and a .30-30 with a four-power scope and instructed him to use the weapons to keep poachers away. Again, they could hardly have been happier. The only problems were the carpenter—and a friend of his, a newcomer they hated even worse.

Clark Stephens was from San Diego, and he was a regular user of heroine, cocaine, pot, and just about any other drug he could get up his nose, take into his lungs, or inject into his veins. Nobody else was around but Suzan when Michael ordered him off the property at gunpoint. Stephens refused and cursed Suzan. So Michael shot him. The first time Michael squeezed the trigger of the old revolver, it misfired. The second time, a bullet smashed into Stephens's mouth. He was slammed backward onto the ground, and Michael walked over and calmly fired another shot into his ribs. Then he sent a third bullet crashing into his victim's brain, just behind the ear, execution style.

Michael gathered up the spent shells, and Suzan helped him drag the body up a hill. Then she returned for some kerosene and they drenched the corpse, lit a match, and tried to burn the body. After more than an hour of watching patches of flesh burn off, and adding more kerosene when the fire went out, they were still left with a telltale, though blackened and badly damaged, corpse. So they covered it with rocks and chicken manure brought up the hill for fertilizer.

Later that day when the pot farmers and druggie friends of the owner gathered in the unfinished chalet to booze and dope, they couldn't figure out what was keeping Stephens from joining them. He had left his pickup truck in front of the chalet.

A few days later, Michael and Suzan left for a little village in Oregon that was filled with hippies and dopers. But they were soon broke, and Oregon was too cold for them, so they turned south again.

They ran out of rides just outside Garberville.

Their worst fears were confirmed when they learned from one of the young dope farmers they had worked with that gossip was going around that they had murdered Stephens. There was even talk of going to the police, an unusually desperate move among the suspicious pot farmers and distrustful antiestablishment hippies and survivalists of Humboldt County.

Before Michael and Suzan could get out of town they were spotted by their old enemy, the carpenter. When a sheriff's deputy stopped a few minutes later and asked them how to get to the chalet, they gave him false directions and sprinted into the woods. The next morning they were holding a sign marked "L.A." and hitchhiking along a highway deep inside Trinity National Forest when a caravan of police cars passed by, then pulled to a stop a short distance up the road. They tossed the sign away, dropped their backpacks, and scrambled down the mountainside into the woods.

A couple of the lawmen dashed a few yards after them, yelling for them to stop. Running as fast as she could, Suzan turned to look at her pursuers and slammed into a tree, knocking herself down. But she was back on her feet in seconds, scurrying down the mountainside.

The policemen roared with laughter when Suzan hit the tree. They couldn't figure why the two dirty hitchhikers were so frightened. The posse, which was on a search-and-rescue mission, had only stopped for a break so some of the search team could urinate; they had no idea why the couple would take off like they were running for their lives.

The motive of the two spooked hippies began to fall into place when the lawmen inspected the abandoned backpacks. In addition to a large stash of tightly pressed marijuana, they found a box of ammunition for a .38-caliber Smith and Wesson, a copy of *Cry for War* that included passages calling for the assassination of President Reagan, and a driver's license. A California State Police computer check of the name on the license revealed that the owner's billfold and license had been stolen several months earlier. Suddenly, the fugitive couple wasn't funny anymore.

Law-enforcement officers streamed into the area, searching on foot, with dogs, cars, and a single-engine airplane. Luck was with Michael and Suzan, however, and they managed to elude the posse. But they became separated and lost track of each other.

They were high in the mountains and it was freezing cold. Deep drifts of snow were piled up in most areas, but Suzan made her way to a boarded-up deer hunter's cabin, where there was temporary shelter and food. She was lean and scrawny, but her early years of jogging and tennis, and more recently her self-inflicted Spartan lifestyle, provided her with surprising stamina and resiliency. She barely took time to warm up and eat before she was out of the cabin again, beginning a torturous trek back to civilization. One after another, she climbed up one mountain, then down to the next.

Michael also hiked up and down mountains, traveling almost exclusively at night, until he passed through Humboldt County to neighboring Mendocino County. From there it was a simple task to hitchhike to Los Angeles, where he easily and inconspicuously melded into the smelly mélange of university longhairs and aging hippies.

Incredibly, he was hitchhiking in Alhambra when a sleek little sports car squealed to a stop beside him. It was the car owned by Stephens, the druggie he had shot in Humboldt County. And the driver was Stephens's friend, the carpenter. The men took one startled look at each other; then the driver spit in Michael's face. Snarling that Michael was in trouble, the carpenter speeded away.

Michael hurried away from the highway, but got only a couple of blocks before a policeman in a city squad car pulled over and, with gun drawn, forced him belly-down on the street. Michael was frisked twice, but the revolver he had hidden in the silk holster Suzan had sewn inside his pants was missed. While he was being transported to a local lockup, he sneaked the weapon out and carefully slipped it behind the back seat of the squad car.

Yet, being able to get rid of his gun undetected wasn't Michael's only lucky break. The California Highway Patrol had gotten the carpenter's telephone tip about a murder suspect hitchhiking in the Alhambra district, but when local officers contacted them the dispatcher said that the CHP had already been in the area and cleared. The local policeman mistakenly interpreted the dispatcher's message as meaning the prisoner had been cleared of suspicion and could be released.

A few miles away, police in the suburb of Monterey Park were searching for a long-haired rapist whose description resembled Michael's, and he was booked by police there as a rape suspect. He identified himself by an alias, the name of the man whose stolen driver's license had been left behind in the Trinity Mountains. After police showed Michael's mug shot to the rape victim a couple of hours later, he was cleared as a suspect and released. Courteous police even drove him to a freeway ramp where he could continue hitchhiking. It wasn't until the work shift changed later that afternoon that an officer found Michael's fully loaded, five-shot revolver behind the seat of the squad car. By that time he had melded back into the easy anonymity of the quixotic mix of races and lifestyles that make up the heterogenous population of southern and central California.

But despite his phenomenal good luck, Michael also made a stupid mistake. During interrogation, he had carelessly given police the name of Suzan's ex-husband in Scottsdale, Arizona, as a reference. It was a slipup that would later provide investigators with vital information about their suspects.

Suzan emerged from the mountains in Humboldt County, and like Michael, she hitchhiked to safety. They found each other at a cabin they had previously discussed as a safe house, in the picturesque little northern California town of Sonora.

A few days before the lethal lovers were united, Stephens's pathetic remains were recovered by police in Humboldt County. A dog from the pot farm had been found mauling the skull. After that, investigators merely followed their noses, tracking the sweet, cloying smell of death to the grave. Animals had dug out the charred body and eaten most of it, but police were able to recover bits and pieces of bones and clothing. Then they found a billfold. Inside there was a photograph and written identification of the owner: Clark Stephens.

Humboldt County Sheriff's Department investigators in Eureka were furious when they learned that one of their prime suspects in a grisly murder had been in custody, only to be released because of careless police work by their big-city brothers in blue. But at least, thanks to the mug shot taken in Monterey Park, they now had a photo of him. They also had a revolver he had apparently been carrying. And they had the name of Suzan's ex-husband in Arizona.

Humboldt County Sheriff's Detective Rod Lester flew to Scottsdale to talk to the ex-husband, and suddenly everything began to fall into place. Lester left the upscale residential community with the true identities of Susan Thornell Hamilton and James Clifford Carson. The sheriff's department also picked up a copy of Susan's arrest record, as well as copies of her fingerprints and her photograph.

California's Bureau of Organized Crime and Criminal Intelligence and the U.S. Secret Service entered the investigation when they learned of the threats against the president and other politicians in Michael's manuscript.

Michael and Suzan camped in the safe house only a couple of days before they resumed their seemingly endless crisscross trek through California and Oregon. They walked and hitchhiked from one hippie commune to another, stopping in secluded gold-mining camp towns that had been worked out one hundred years earlier, and in bustling, modern cities including Portland, Berkeley, and Los Angeles.

They were thumbing along a highway near Bakersfield, California, in early January 1983 when thirty-year-old Jon Hillyar picked them up and drove them in his pickup truck to Santa Rosa, about seventy-five miles north of San Francisco. Suzan decided before they climbed into the truck that Hillyar was a powerful and evil witch. And it was their duty as holy Muslim Hashshashin to kill him. They all stayed together at the home of one of Hillyar's friends, where Michael and Suzan smoothed out the details of their murder plot. They would carry out the assassination the next morning, using another handgun Michael had stolen during their wanderings, when Hillyar drove them to a busy freeway ramp to drop them off so they could catch a new ride.

Hillyar and his riders were almost to the freeway dropoff site when Michael pulled his gun. Hillyar snatched it away from him. Suzan was sitting between the men as they fought for the weapon, and the truck lurched along the highway, careening madly from side to side until Hillyar slammed on the brakes. He and Michael tumbled to the pavement.

Michael screamed at Suzan to stab Hillyar. Hillyar yelled at a youth watching transfixed from a nearby fruit stand to telephone police. Suzan had two kitchen knives hidden in her boot, and she plunged one of them into Hillyar's back. It broke off, so she grabbed the other one and went for his eyes. But the desperate man clamped his teeth down on her finger and bit as hard as he could, almost severing it.

The struggle with Suzan gave Michael an opportunity to wrest away the gun. But Hillyar scrambled to his feet and lurched back to the truck. Michael fired two shots. The second one grazed the dope dealer's head. Michael and Suzan grabbed his legs and dragged him into the grass alongside the road.

There, Michael fired two bullets into his head, execution style.

But this time the holy assassins had picked the wrong time and wrong place to kill. The bizarre death struggle had taken place at midmorning, only a few yards from a busy highway intersection, in front of at least one eyewitness. They realized that at best it would be only minutes before police were on their trail. With Suzan driving, they speeded north along busy Highway 101.

Minutes later they had turned west off the highway. As they had feared, they were soon leading a string of pursuing squad cars in a wild dash through small towns and past rows of grapevines. They were headed for a shimmer of comforting hills and forests a few miles away, where they might have an opportunity to escape on foot into the wilderness.

Suzan was driving with all the skill and daring of a Hollywood stuntwoman. Then she turned onto a gravel road on the outskirts of the small town of Calistoga, at the north edge of Santa Rosa, and they found themselves in a dead-end parking lot. She braked furiously, spun the steering wheel, and the pickup slid across the lot into a ditch. As three squad cars squealed to a halt around them, Michael and Suzan leaped from the truck and dashed into a vineyard. Police had spotted Michael's gun in his hand, and squeezed off several shots after yelling for the fugitives to stop. Michael dashed toward the nearby Napa River. Suzan disappeared into high grass. The police officers radioed for reinforcements, including a helicopter and a dog unit.

A California Highway Patrol officer and a husky Napa County Sheriff's Department deputy nabbed

Michael and disarmed him as he was wading across
the river. A minute or two later Suzan was captured
as she tried to cross the river a few yards down-
stream.

They were locked up in the Sonoma County Jail
in Santa Rosa on murder charges. Michael identified
himself as Michael Bear, and promptly went on a
hunger strike. Suzan refused to give police any name
at all and was booked as Jane Doe. She also refused
treatment for her finger injury, but after several days
managed to get a letter delivered to Michael. At her
prompting, he ended his hunger strike.

Reunited at a preliminary hearing after weeks
apart, they hugged each other and giggled like high-
school freshmen throughout the proceeding. And at
every opportunity they spouted slogans and drivel
about their Islamic mission and their holy war
against witches. Bail was established at one million
dollars for each murder.

It was difficult to carry on a holy war from prison
when the big-city press didn't know about the warriors' exploits, so Michael wrote to the San Francisco
Chronicle's popular columnist Herb Caen complaining about the lack of attention. Friends of Keryn
Barnes read the column and notified San Francisco
Police Inspector Carl Klotz. Michael Bear Carson,
and his wife "Suzanne," as she was identified in the
column, sounded like the religious weirdos suspected of murdering Keryn.

A little more than a month later, Klotz and other
officers met with Michael and Suzan to listen to a
long-winded account of the grotesque holy war. In
accordance with the couple's trade-off demands that
the big-city press attend, television and newspaper

reporters were also present for the freakish recitation at Sonoma County Jail.

Michael admitted beating and stabbing Keryn to death with a frying pan and paring knife because she was a witch who had cast a hex on Suzan and was sucking her vitality and beauty away. Michael's memory was phenomenal, but he insisted that he had stabbed the girl only twice in the neck, not more than a dozen times as indicated by the coroner's report. Although the mystery of the additional stab wounds inflicted on Keryn's body was never officially cleared up, detectives had heard enough to realize that Suzan was fiercely jealous of the pretty hippie girl. But Suzan screamed an angry denial, backed up by Michael, when a detective asked if she might have inflicted some of the stab wounds.

Both admitted their part in the murders of Stephens and Hillyar, however. The men had to die, they insisted, because they were evil witches who had sexually abused Suzan—a devout Muslim wife. Stephens called her nasty names; Hillyar brushed his leg against her during the pickup-truck ride to Santa Rosa. Suzan giggled about ordering Hillyar's death.

Asked about some especially grisly decapitation murders that occurred in San Francisco's Golden Gate Park at about the time Keryn was killed, both denied they had anything to do with them. They admonished that they were prepared to talk only about murders in northern California, a statement that left the interrogators wondering whom else they may have slain in southern California, Arizona, New Mexico, Oregon, or other states they wandered through during their queer nearly three-year odyssey.

At the conclusion of the exhausting interview, which meandered through more than six hours, the reporters returned to San Francisco with headline stories. Klotz and his partner returned with enough solid information and evidence to justify warrants for the arrest of Michael and Suzan for Keryn's murder. Bail was established at one million dollars each. Keryn had been dead more than two years.

Murder charges were also filed against the couple in Humboldt County for the Stephens slaying.

Michael and Suzan's trial in San Francisco was so queer, filled as it was with outlandish references to the mystic and psychic worlds, that at another time in history the defendants might themselves have been accused as witches and faced burning alive or being crushed under stone slabs.

A university parapsychologist testified for the defense that he knew of cases where magic spells, aided by the victim's belief, resulted in death. A priestess from the Temple of Isis in Berkeley testified that she was a witch who used occult forces for good, but knew people who had been hurt by evil spells cast by black witches. The testimony seemed to buttress Suzan's claims of a baffling malaise, constipation, and other troubles blamed on Keryn before her murder.

Even a psychic who defected from the Soviet Union to Israel was called to the stand. She confirmed reports in the news media that the Soviets used psychics to make their enemies mysteriously waste away and die, to steal their secrets, or to make their weapons malfunction. It seemed, if the testimony were true, that Suzan could indeed have been in mortal danger from a witch bent on mischief or evil.

But the judge rebelled when the Soviet psychic was asked by a defense attorney to walk to Suzan and touch her psychic Crown of Brahmin at the top of her skull. Suzan, more prosaically, referred to the soft spot as a "head hole." The psychic was instructed there would be no touching of Suzan's head.

During closing arguments, Michael's attorney maintained that Michael believed he was acting in self-defense when he killed Keryn. Michael was convinced he was protecting his wife from a hex that was threatening her life.

District Attorney Tom Norman scoffed at the witchcraft defense. He also pointed out that even if the victim had been a witch—a premise he didn't accept—it is as unlawful in this country to kill witches as it is to kill anyone else.

The jury returned verdicts against the codefendants of guilty of murder in the first degree. During their sentencing hearing a month later, Michael rambled on about witches, homosexuals, and abortionists—all of whom could be justifiably killed, according to his beliefs. And he talked about President Reagan, the Bible, and the Koran.

Suzan was equally loquacious, and more spirited. She accused Keryn of trying to steal her Muslim warrior, accused the judge of being guided by political aspirations, and threatened that the court might someday learn what it was like to be saddled with a witch's curse. Then she started to cry.

Judge Claude Perrasso sentenced each of them to

the maximum term allowable, from twenty-five years to life in prison.

At subsequent trials they were found guilty of the Stephens and Hillyar murders, and given similar sentences of twenty-five years to life.

3 ◆

THE CHICAGO RIPPERS

Robin Gecht, Edward
Spreitzer, Andrew Kokoraleis,
and Thomas Kokoraleis
(1981–1982)

Few crimes can shock or surprise case-hardened
police who deal with the vice, murder, and madness
that infect the festering underbelly of a big city.
Uniform officers and plainclothes detectives quickly
learn that there is little in the way of cruelty and
perversion that the people they are sworn to protect
won't inflict on one another.

However, even city and suburban police in the
greater Chicago metropolitan area, where citizens
lived through the atrocity of merchant seaman Richard Speck's midsummer slaughter of eight student
nurses in the 1960s, and the discovery of thirty-
three victims of homosexual slayer John Wayne
Gacy, Jr., in the 1970s, could hardly have conceived
of the new horror uncovered in the 1980s.

Women were being kidnapped and sexually mutilated in a crazy orgy of devil worship, rape, cannibal-ism, necrophilia, and murder. The hapless victims were snatched from busy downtown city sidewalks, entrances to office buildings where they worked, and suburban highways. They were taken from some of the safest neighborhoods in the city and suburbs, and from some of the worst.

Some were young single women and housewives without the slightest hint of troubles with the police in their background. Others were seasoned prosti-tutes, especially vulnerable to attack and murder because of their trade. With one glaring exception, when two men were shot down on a street corner by someone in a passing vehicle, the victims of the insane spree were always lone women.

The first victim may have been Linda Sutton, a mother of two, with an arrest record for prostitution. The twenty-eight-year-old woman was strolling near Wrigley Field, home of the Chicago Cubs National League baseball team, on a late spring night in 1981 when she was lured into a van.

By the time she realized there were three men inside, it was too late to escape. Ignoring her pleas to be let go, the trio drove her several miles from Chicago's busy North Side to a motel in west sub-urban Villa Park, where she was shoved into a room, stripped, handcuffed to a bed, and gang-raped.

Finally tiring of the sexual assault, the men untied their victim and manhandled her out the door to a brushy area some one hundred feet from the motel. There, one of the gang members began stabbing her with a knife. He was still chopping at her when he growled at a younger companion to return to the van for a length of wire.

The woman was stretched out on the ground when the younger man returned and crouched over the still, bloody form, wrapped the sharp, thin wire about her left breast—and twisted. The wire slashed through the soft tissue, severing the breast neatly from her body. Then, as his silent companions watched, he had sex with the corpse. It was approximately one month before the badly decomposed remains were discovered.

On May 15, 1982, a bright Saturday morning almost exactly a year after the brutal murder in Villa Park, pretty Lorraine Borowski stepped out of her apartment in west suburban Elmhurst for a short stroll to her job as a secretary at the REMAX real-estate office in the nearby Elmhurst Shopping Center. She didn't own a car, and the vivacious twenty-one-year-old beauty looked forward to the brisk morning walks to work in the quiet bedroom community and college town.

At exactly 8:30 A.M., her boss arrived at the office and found the door locked. More disturbing yet, a pair of woman's shoes and several items of cosmetics were scattered on the ground in front of the entrance. Letting himself inside the building, the worried businessman walked straight to his desk and telephoned Elmhurst police, explaining that he had found what appeared to be the contents of a woman's purse on the lawn. Returning outside to keep his eye on the items until police arrived, he noticed that the key chain carried his company name. When he tried the key and it fit the front-door lock, he realized that the scattered possessions belonged to his industrious, blue-eyed, brown-haired secretary. When police officers arrived at his office, he helped them search the shopping plaza for her. After it was determined that she wasn't in any of the other shops or businesses, her parents were notified that their daughter was thought to be missing.

Distressed and baffled, they were unable to provide a single clue to where she may have gone. "We don't think it's a ransom thing," her father, Raymond Borowski, later declared. "She was just at the wrong place at the wrong time. She's not the type to disappear."

Investigators agreed. A middle child among nine brothers and sisters, she seemed to be a well-adjusted young adult, fully capable of taking care of herself. Although she had recently moved from the family home in Elmhurst to be on her own, she remained close to her parents and siblings and had a large circle of friends whom she was fond of. She was the kind of daughter any parent could take pride in.

Checking with neighbors near the young secretary's apartment and with other residents who lived or worked along the route she normally took to her job, investigators determined that she was smartly dressed that morning in green khaki slacks and a white ruffled blouse. And she was carrying a beige purse with wooden handles. After talking with family members and checking her jewelry they also determined that she was probably wearing four gold rings, and an ankle chain that was a gift from her mother.

An alert was broadcast to all Elmhurst officers and to area police departments to be on the lookout for the missing woman. In addition to describing her clothing, purse, and jewelry, it noted that she was five feet, three inches tall, weighed 129 pounds, and had light brown hair and blue eyes.

Reports that she had been followed a few days before her disappearance by a large, husky man who hunched over the steering wheel of his car were checked out but failed to turn up a suspect. Nevertheless, police authorities had little doubt that she had been abducted.

Police Lieutenant Peter Smith stated what seemed to be obvious: "We have no reason to suspect anything else but foul play," he said. "There is nothing in her background to indicate a reason she should be missing."

But the Elmhurst secretary was still missing two weeks later when another slender DuPage County woman dropped suddenly and mysteriously from sight.

Like Lorraine "Lorry" Borowski, Shu Mak was a dream daughter. She was not the type of young woman who would abruptly decide to strike out on her own without notifying friends or family, or to run off with a boyfriend.

The five-foot, two-inch thirty-year-old had arrived in this country from Hong Kong only three years earlier and lived with her parents, a brother, and a sister in Lombard, another western Chicago suburb. Curiously, Elmhurst, Villa Park, and Lombard all lie directly west of Chicago's Loop, or central-city area, in the sprawl of suburbs reaching out from the city and the southwest rim of Lake Michigan. Elmhurst is closest to Chicago, and its westernmost town limits abut on Villa Park, which extends west to Lombard.

As many immigrant families tend to do, the Maks

stuck close together and worked hard. Shui, who was the oldest of the children, worked during the day with her mother at a factory in suburban Downers Grove, and at night joined her parents and siblings in operating a family-owned Chinese restaurant called Ling Ling's, in the town of Streamwood.

She was riding with her twenty-year-old brother, Kent, on her way home from Streamwood when she began to scold him for taking a restaurant table to stand on while he painted the family garage. It was a minor brother-and-sister spat, but Kent eventually pulled the car to the side of the road. He told Shui that she could ride the rest of the way home with the rest of the family, who were following in a second car.

But Shui's younger sister, twenty-two-year-old Ling, who was driving the second car, didn't see the diminutive figure standing on the darkened shoulder of the road and drove on by. It wasn't until both cars arrived at the Mak home in Lombard that they realized Shui had been left behind.

The family's oldest daughter had been left alone, late at night, miles from Lombard in an isolated area of Hanover Park, near the DuPage–Cook County line. She was carrying no money, no identification, and spoke only limited English. Family members piled into one of the cars and raced back to Hanover Park to pick her up. She wasn't there. Distressed and fearing the worst, the Maks notified police of Shui's disappearance.

Chief Robert Sauer, of the Hanover Park Police, and Sergeant James Montesano, of the DuPage County Sheriff's Department, took charge of the search. Appeals were made to the public to watch for a slight, young Asian woman who was last seen by her family wearing a red sweater, black slacks, and sandals.

When Montesano was asked about the search, he confided ominously, "She was not the kind who would go off on her own without notifying anyone. If everything we've been told is true, something's wrong at this point."

Shui, in fact, had already asked for two weeks off from her job at the factory so that she could return to Hong Kong and get married. She had been talking happily with friends about the marriage and about buying a wedding dress in Hong Kong.

The heartbroken Mak family joined law-enforcement authorities and other volunteers in the search. As police set up roadblocks to question motorists, scanned farm fields, vacant lots, country roads, and shopping centers from helicopters, and probed forest preserves, vacant lots, and dumps around Hanover Park with tracking dogs, the Maks distributed handmade posters to area restaurants. The posters carried Shui's photo, a description of her clothes, two telephone numbers, and carried the question: "Has anyone seen this girl?" Petite and pretty, the alabaster-skinned woman looked like an innocent fifteen-year-old in the picture. But no one found either her body or an article of her clothing. And no witnesses were located who could report having seen her either standing alongside the road or getting into a vehicle. Trite as it sounded, Shui Mak seemed simply to have dropped off the face of the earth.

And as the agonized Mak family looked for Shui, the Borowskis were continuing to press an ever more desperate search for their daughter. Mrs. Borowski, also named Lorraine, issued a heartrending public plea:

"All I can say is, whoever's got Lorry, please send her back to us. If she's hurt and can't do for herself, leave her somewhere and contact us," she begged. "If the worst has happened, please let us bury her. Because if you don't, I'll find her anyway—if I have to dig up all the ground in the state. And then I'll go looking for you."

Wally Phillips, one of Chicago's top daytime radio personalities, added his plea, over the air, for help in finding the young woman. But whoever had Lorry Borowski, or knew where she was, either wasn't listening or didn't care.

Several psychics responded to the pleas for help, and one seer who contacted the family told them that their daughter was in a cemetery. They looked in cemeteries all over the area, but they didn't find her.

While the two suburban families searched for their missing daughters, a twenty-three-year-old former St. Louis woman named Angel was picked up on Chicago's North Side by a man in a van, quickly overpowered, handcuffed, and dumped in the back. After a terror ride of several blocks, the van was pulled to a stop, and the young man climbed into the back. Shoving a razor-sharp knife into her hands, he demanded that she cut a hole in one of her breasts. When the terrified captive made a small, tentative incision in one breast, he snarled that the hole wasn't large enough and snatched the knife from her. Then as Angel writhed in pain and terror, he slowly and deliberately carved a deep, gaping bloody hole. When the wound was large enough to satisfy him, he used it to perform a brutal and perverted sex act. Finished with her at last, he hurled her out of the van and drove away. The vicious maiming and rape didn't even rate a notice in the city's newspapers.

Discovery a couple of months later of the mutilated body of a teenage prostitute who was pulled from the north branch of the Chicago River under a bridge on the city's West Side was also all but ignored by the news media. The naked eighteen-year-old, identified as Sandra Delaware, had been strangled, stabbed in the stomach, and her left breast was sliced off. She had also had sexual relations with a man, or men, sometime shortly before or after her death. But streetwalkers who are maimed or murdered are not all that newsworthy in the rough-and-tumble city by the lake. Not even when their deaths are so conspicuously gruesome.

The first brisk breezes of autumn had begun to sweep across Lake Michigan when Chicago police were summoned to the posh Gold Coast, one of the city's safest neighborhoods. A woman's body was lying in a gangway between two apartment buildings. She was lying on her back, had no shoes or purse, and her slacks were disarranged. Her sweater was crumpled nearby.

A garbage collector for a private scavenger company had made the grisly discovery. All it took was a single glance to convince him that she was dead. Her head, which was turned to one side, was a mass of blood and gore. It appeared that she had been clubbed with a heavy piece of wood or a brick.

Although there was no identification near the body, descriptions broadcast by radio soon led to a telephone call to police from a woman who said the victim might be Rose Beck Davis, of Broadview, a small town a few miles southeast of Elmhurst. The caller said that she and her thirty-year-old friend had been nightclubbing in the jumping Rush Street area the evening before.

They met two men at a hotel bar, one whom the caller already knew, the other a handsome European. The woman said that she and her companion left her friend and the man with the Continental accent next to Rose's parked Volkswagen at about 1:30 A.M. The woman told police that she had been unable to reach her friend by telephone later during that day to confirm that she had gotten home safely, and was worried.

Her worst fears were confirmed when her friend's husband was contacted, and identified the victim at the Cook County Morgue as his wife, Rose Beck Davis. An autopsy, and later investigation, disclosed that she had been raped, bludgeoned, chopped with an ax, stabbed with a knife, and strangled with a stocking; her breasts had been mutilated.

Investigators fanned out through the hotel and nightclub area, looking for the handsome European. It wasn't long before they found him. He was a thirty-year-old Swiss businessman, who was in the city to attend a trade show.

He readily admitted being with the marketing executive–housewife, but insisted that he had left her and returned to his hotel after walking with her along the nearby Lake Michigan shore, and sitting on a curb by her car talking for a few minutes. He was released from custody after taking a lie-detector test that indicated he was telling the truth.

With their prime suspect cleared, Chicago police began looking in other directions and soon realized that there was an apparent grisly link between the mutilation of Mrs. Davis's breasts and the grisly sex attacks on other women in and around the city. There was the prostitute, Sandra Delaware; Angel; and others in the city and suburbs whose breasts had been carved with knives—or slashed off with knives or piano wire.

Homicide detectives from Chicago exchanged information about unsolved mutilation murders and unexplained disappearances and suspected slayings of women with their counterparts in Elmhurst, and with investigators for the sheriff's departments in DuPage and Cook counties. The baffling disappearances of Lorraine Borowski and Shui Mak were among the cases studied. There were disturbing indications that a serial killer with a breast fetish was at work and had targeted lone females for sexual attack, mutilation, and murder. The victims were always young women of procreative age.

Then, on September 11, Mrs. Carole Pappas disappeared. Mrs. Pappas and her husband, Milt—who only a few years before had been a pitching star for the Chicago Cubs—were in a festive mood that day. She was planning to fix a big dinner, including a family favorite of yogurt cake, to celebrate the homecoming of their son and his bride from their honeymoon.

It was late morning when the blond housewife and bookkeeper, reminding her husband that she would be home before 2 P.M., stepped out of her front door for the last time. When she hadn't returned to her home in Wheaton, a few miles west of Lombard

Park, her husband sent his daughter to the local
police station to file a missing-person report. Law-
enforcement authorities disseminated a description
of Mrs. Pappas, and of the late-model Buick she was
driving, to all police agencies in DuPage County.
But it wasn't until a few days later that detectives
were assigned to begin actively seeking her.

Reconstructing the Wheaton housewife's movements during her busy Saturday morning, detectives
traced her to a cleaner's, a dress shop, a supermarket,
a jeweler's, a beauty salon, and to the Stratford
Square Shopping Center in the town of Blooming-
dale. A saleswoman at the Marshall Field and Company store there remembered that Mrs. Pappas had
exchanged an item of clothing and had mentioned
that she was relieved to be through with her shopping chores so that she could head for home. It was
about 12:20 P.M. when she turned and walked away
from the clerk. That's when police lost her trail.
The search for the forty-two-year-old homemaker
was no more successful than the searches for Lorraine Borowski or Shui Mak.

But the mystery of Shui Mak's whereabouts,
which had been plaguing her family and law-enforcement agencies since the Memorial Day weekend, was finally solved on the last day of September.
A truck driver found her pitiful remains in a field in
the town of South Barrington, barely a mile from
where she climbed out of the car driven by her
brother. The red sweater, black slacks, pink-and-
white blouse, and thongs she was wearing when she
disappeared, rotting and decayed after four months
in the sun and rain, were identified by her sister.

An autopsy disclosed that Shui's skull had been smashed with a heavy blow.

On a Sunday morning less than two weeks later, the search for Lorraine Borowski ended when a hunter stumbled across her remains in a brushy area in the Clarendon Hills Cemetery near the town of Westmont. Her clothes were scattered nearby. Family members were shocked by the discovery. Acting on the advice of the psychic, they had searched the area earlier in the summer and had apparently been only a few yards away from finding the body.

Medical examiners and other investigators eventually disclosed that she had suffered hideous injuries. She was severely beaten, stabbed six times, and her left breast was cut off.

Between the time the remains of the two missing women were at last recovered, another young woman had been attacked and mutilated in Chicago. The victim was an eighteen-year-old convicted prostitute who was found naked, blood-covered, and near death from hideous wounds alongside Chicago and North Western railroad tracks by a man collecting aluminum cans. Her left breast had been cut off, and her right breast was severely slashed.

The same night, among one of the many seemingly random acts of violence in the city, police recorded the drive-by shootings of twenty-year-old Rafael Tirado, and minutes later of twenty-one-year-old Alberto Rosario. Rosario was treated at a nearby hospital and survived, although seriously injured. Tirado died. Investigators determined that the attacks were unprovoked and seemed to be purely without motive. The two men merely had the bad luck to be in the right place at the wrong time.

In the case of the teenage prostitute, it appeared that she also had been a victim of chance, and had ridden off with the wrong trick. She was rushed unconscious and on the brink of death to the Illinois Masonic Hospital, where the efficient teamwork of doctors and nurses saved her life. When she regained consciousness hours later, she was unable to remember anything about her mutilation. But she remembered a lot about the man who had picked her up the night she was attacked, and about the vehicle he was driving.

She told police that she had been working the streets in an industrial area notorious for prostitution when a good-looking young white man, who appeared to be in his late twenties, drove up and offered her twenty-five dollars for sex. Agreeing to the offer, she climbed inside his red van and was driven to a vacant lot a few blocks away.

Instead of settling for the agreed-upon sex act, however, he suddenly produced a knife and a gun. He handcuffed her hands and feet as she pleaded for her life. Once she was helpless, he looped a thin rubber cord around her breasts, pulled it painfully tight, and raped her. Finally, he shoved some pills into her mouth, and forced her to swallow them with a soft drink from a can he tipped for her. She said she blacked out minutes later, and didn't regain consciousness until she awakened in the hospital with one of her breasts missing and the other terribly mutilated.

Despite the terror and abuse she suffered, the teenager managed to get a close look at the van. And she had a good memory for details. She told detectives that it was a late-model red Dodge with smoked windows and black seat covers. A plywood partition with a hinged plywood door separated the cab from the rear storage area. Wooden shelves, each about a foot long, had been constructed along the sidewalls, and they contained tools and electrical wiring. A roach clip, used to smoke marijuana cigarettes, was attached to a blue-and-white feather and dangled from the carpeted ceiling. A description of the van was broadcast over police radios.

A few nights later Detective Thomas J. Flynn and his partner, Detective Philip Murphy, spotted a 1975 red Dodge van on the North Side. The officers, both veterans of more than twenty years with the Chicago Police Department, were attached to the Area Five Violent Crimes Unit, which covered the area where the attack on the young prostitute occurred. They speeded off in pursuit, turned on their spotlight, and signaled the van to pull over. The vehicle slowed immediately, and the driver nosed it into the curb, pulling to a smooth stop.

Asked for identification, the husky young man at the wheel produced his driver's license and explained that he was Edward Spreitzer, twenty-one years old, and worked for a friend who was an electrical contractor. A sullen youth next to him in the passenger seat identified himself as Andrew Kokoraleis. He was nineteen. Spreitzer said that the van belonged to his boss, Robin Gecht, who operated the R & R Electrical Company.

The driver readily consented when he was asked if it was okay for the officers to look in the back of the van. Swinging open the rear doors, they observed side paneling along the walls of the truck crammed with electrical wiring and tools. The van also had a

plywood partition with a plywood door separating
the driver and passenger compartment from the
cargo area. And up front, a roach clip dangled from
the carpeted ceiling.

The driver and his passenger waited patiently as
the officers looked around. Then the two youths
were told they could continue on a few blocks to an
apartment that Gecht was working on in preparation
for moving inside. The detectives said they would
follow the van. They wanted to talk to Spreitzer's
boss.

Gecht was a good-looking, slender twenty-eight-
year-old, with a unruly tousle of brown hair that
spilled over his forehead and ears and curled in at
the back of his neck. He chatted easily with the
officers and maintained a friendly attitude, even
when they told him how his van so closely matched
the vehicle used in the attack on the prostitute.

He didn't even seem upset when the conversation
was moved to the Area Five police headquarters
several blocks away. Spreitzer, and a relative of
Gecht's who was also at the apartment, went along.

While questioning continued inside the police
headquarters, other officers conducted a closer
search of the red van and began a routine check of
Robin Gecht's background.

A few minutes' work with a police computer
disclosed that Gecht was no stranger to trouble with
the law. He had an intriguing rap sheet that disclosed a history of offenses related to sex and violence. His record showed an arrest when he was
twenty-six, on a charge of contributing to the sexual
delinquency of a fourteen-year-old girl. The girl told
police he raped her at gunpoint, but physicians could

detect no injuries and investigators could not find a gun, so he was not charged with a more serious offense. Gecht was sentenced to two years' probation. More recently he was charged with unlawful use of a gun, and forfeited his bond when he didn't show up in court. That same day he was also charged with aggravated battery in connection with a nonfatal stabbing.

At the time he got into trouble with the fourteen-year-old, he was living in Hanover Park, the same northwestern suburb where Shui Mak disappeared. Investigators learned that he had also once lived near the cemetery where Lorraine Borowski's remains were found.

Police took Gecht, his relative, and Spreitzer to Illinois Masonic Hospital, where the recuperating prostitute could take a look at them in an impromptu lineup. Without hesitation, she pointed to Robin Gecht and told officers: "He's the one who cut me."

Gecht was charged with attempted murder, rape, deviate sexual assault, aggravated battery, and armed robbery. (Some of the teenage hooker's jewelry was reputedly stolen.) The red van and a rifle found in Gecht's home were impounded as evidence. But the investigation had barely begun.

Police were told that Gecht had been banned from the family home when he was sixteen after he was accused of sexually molesting a young female relative.

Equally intriguing, however, was information that he had once worked on a couple of construction jobs for one of the most infamous serial killers in Chicago's history—John Wayne Gacy, Jr. A sadistic homosexual now on death row in the Illinois state prison system, Gacy slaughtered at least thirty-three young men and boys and buried most of them under his house in an unincorporated area of Cook County on the outskirts of Chicago. He ran his own small contracting business and lured several of his victims to their deaths by promising or giving them jobs. But Gecht had obviously been one of the smart ones, or lucky ones. He hadn't ended up in the musty ossuary under Gacy's house.

A friend of Gecht's was later quoted as saying the young electrician had once commented to him, "The only mistake Gacy made was burying the bodies under his home."

Five days after Gecht's arrest, he was released from jail on fifty thousand dollars bail. Somehow the young, self-employed father of three had come up with the five thousand dollars in cash, or 10 percent down.

On the Monday after his release, one of the most bizarre developments in the grisly string of mutilations and murders of Chicago-area women occurred. A slender twenty-five-year-old woman reported to police that she had been picked up by a man in a car and attacked with an ax crudely fashioned from a stick of wood with a large, jagged chunk of broken glass embedded in it. Her arms were horribly slashed.

She said she was on the city's North Side when she climbed into the handsome stranger's car. As soon as she got a good look at him, however, she recognized him as a man who had cut a friend of hers, and she tried to get out. But she couldn't escape, because the latch handle on the passenger door had been removed.

"Relax," she quoted him as reassuring her. "I'll give you $150 if you will tell me the goriest, bloodiest stories you can tell." She said that when she refused, he started flailing at her with the homemade ax.

Raising her arms in an instinctive reaction to protect her face and body, she somehow managed to scramble past him and tumble screaming and bloody out of his side of the vehicle onto the street while he speeded away, she said.

Asked by investigators what her attacker looked like, she provided a detailed description of a man who looked remarkably like Robin Gecht. A new warrant was sworn out for him and he was rearrested at the home of a relative in northwest suburban Carpentersville.

Suddenly, it seemed, almost everybody in Chicago and the suburbs who was involved in homicide investigations was interested in Robin Gecht—and in the slasher assaults on area women. DuPage County sheriff's detectives focused renewed scrutiny on the year-old file dealing with the Linda Sutton murder, and police in Elmhurst and in Villa Park began looking for similarities between the Chicago slashings and the slayings of Lorraine Borowski and Shui Mak.

Newspapers and radio and television journalists were at last aware that a string of rape and mutilation murders had been occurring in and around the city that were apparently connected to the same killer, or killers. News stories about the gruesome assaults began to refer to "the Chicago Ripper" as journalists drew bloody parallels with London's notorious nineteenth-century slasher and disemboweler of prostitutes, Jack the Ripper.

Among the friends, family members, and associates of Gecht whom police had been talking with was one of his former roommates. After the man failed a lie-detector test, he blurted out a ghastly story about bodies buried in area forest preserves and near railroad tracks. Police from the city and suburbs fanned out through the woods and along the tracks, with tracker dogs and special devices that detect and pinpoint methane gas, a by-product of decomposing bodies. But no remains were found.

Others were also talking, however, and one of them was Edward Spreitzer, the van driver stopped by detectives Flynn and Murphy. And it was Spreitzer and his friend Andrew Kokoraleis who were named on murder charges when police announced they had identified and apprehended the killers of Rose Beck Davis and of Sandra Delaware. Spreitzer was charged in both killings, Kokoraleis with only the Davis slaying.

But in announcing the arrests, Chicago Police Superintendent Richard Brzeczek disclosed that Gecht was suspected with Spreitzer and Kokoraleis in up to seventeen homicides in the greater Chicago area. The murders of Shui Mak, Lorraine Borowski, and Linda Sutton were among them.

"The only way I can say it is, it's gruesome, very, very gruesome," Brzeczek declared. "With one exception, these murders followed a common thread: the abduction of a lone female, mutilation, . . . sexual attack, and murder itself."

The exception referred to by the police superintendent was the drive-by shootings of Tirado and Rosario. They were apparently victims of absolutely random acts of violence, committed solely for thrills.

Ironically, the ripper gang had nothing to do with the injuries to the young woman whose complaint to police led to Gecht's rearrest and the stepped-up investigation that culminated in the murder charges against Spreitzer and Kokoraleis. She was simply a clumsy burglar who was trying to climb through a window when she broke the glass and accidently slashed her arms.

Yet, even though her fanciful story to police was a hoax to cover up her injuries, it ultimately landed the trio of friends behind bars. And once they were in custody, they began talking to police and implicating one another in an appalling rampage of murder that was almost too gruesome for even case-hardened homicide detectives to believe. It was a Steven King–esque tale of horror and depravity come to life on the streets of Chicago and its suburbs.

A few days after the arrests of the trio, Thomas Knight, chief of the Criminal Division of the DuPage County State's Attorney's Office, revealed that a relative of one of the suspects was being questioned in the case. Shortly after that, twenty-two-year-old Thomas Kokoraleis, Andrew's older brother, became the final member of the Chicago Ripper Gang to be arrested. He was charged with the abduction and murder of Lorraine Borowski. Thomas was as talkative as his brother and Spreitzer.

It seemed that almost every day there was a new story about murder, intriguing new information about an old story, or a new lead on the unsolved slaying of another woman. Different victims stood out in the recollections of the suspects for different reasons. Shui Mak was remembered because she was the only Asian. Mrs. Davis stood out in the minds of her killers because she was murdered after being abducted from Chicago's brash and bright late-night play area for visiting conventioneers and businessmen. Lorraine Borowski was remembered both because she was snatched from a busy shopping center in broad daylight, and because she was so beautiful. When DuPage County Sheriff's Department officers showed her photo to Andrew Kokoraleis shortly after his arrest, he blurted out: "That's the girl that me and Eddie Spreitzer killed in the cemetery."

Andrew also told police that he was with Gecht and Spreitzer, cruising the Gold Coast in the van, when they spotted Mrs. Davis walking alone at about 1 A.M. When she coldly refused to acknowledge them after they pulled up alongside her and asked if she wanted "to have a good time," Kokoraleis said, he and Spreitzer grabbed her and wrestled her inside the van. She was quickly gagged with a sock, stripped, and handcuffed. Kokoraleis said that Gecht pulled the van to a stop a short distance away, and they forced her into the gangway. There, he claimed, Gecht ordered him to stab her.

"I was hesitant and I did not want to stab the girl, so I poked her, put a couple of puncture wounds in her so that he could not tell I was poking her," Kokoraleis said. "I wanted Robin to believe that I was stabbing her.

"I started getting nauseated. I had blood on my hands and on the knife and spots on my shirt from the punctures," he continued. "I dropped the knife and I backed up against the side of the building."

He told officers that he watched as Gecht raped the woman, beat her with an ax handle, and then used the weapon to chop and slash her.

Thomas Kokoraleis also remembered some of the victims, including a petite young woman whom he said he recalled because of the braces on her teeth. That led police to suspect that she was eighteen-year-old Margaret Stirn, from suburban Woodbridge. The teenager dropped from sight on the morning of September 15, 1978. Her remains were not found until 1986—long after the Chicago Ripper killer team had been broken up—in a shallow grave a few miles from her home.

When detectives showed a photograph of the missing Carole Pappas to Thomas and asked if he had seen her before, he replied that he thought she was one of the cult's victims. He said he remembered that he and two of his codefendents had abducted and murdered a woman who looked like Mrs. Pappas. Although no charges were filed in her death, and authorities could never be certain if she was killed by the Ripper Gang, the mystery of her whereabouts was finally solved in August 1987. That's when workmen draining a small retention pond in Wheaton to prepare for excavation work discovered her car, with her body inside.

In signed, tape-recorded statements, different members of the quartet continued to talk of kidnappings and killings committed while they were high on drugs and alcohol. Only Gecht steadfastly refused to confess to taking any active part in the macabre reign of mutilation and murder.

But it was a former neighbor of Gecht's from Villa Park who provided the first hint that the terrible quartet might be involved in an actual killer cult devoted to torture, mutilation, and violent death. The woman advised investigators and journalists that the strange young man was devoted to reading books about the tortures inflicted on others by members of ancient cultures. He had told her that he was fascinated by the practices of certain ancient people who cut off the breasts of women and saved them for tobacco pouches.

Acting on information developed by their interrogation of the deadly quartet, investigators inspected a tiny attic room in a house that had at one time been occupied by Gecht, and found six crosses painted on the walls. Some of the crosses were black, some red. Thomas Kokoraleis said the room had once contained an altar made from a board and covered with a red cloth. It was there that parts of animals and humans were cut up during grisly satanic sacrificial rituals, he said. Detectives also found literature about devil worship in an apartment that Andrew Kokoraleis had occupied in Villa Park.

The ugly possibility that the mutilation-murder rampage may have extended beyond the Chicago and suburban area was disclosed when police issued a bulletin to law-enforcement agencies throughout the country containing photographs and physical descriptions of the suspected killer cultists. Titled "In Custody for Murder and Mutilation," the bulletin advised:

> The above-pictured subjects are now in custody for several murders wherein breasts of females were crudely removed with a knife and/or piano wire. Sexual gratification was a prime factor in these cases. One or more of

these offenders have taken trips south of Chicago allegedly to Tennessee and southwest of Chicago to Texas. These crimes are known to have occurred during 1981 and 1982, but are not limited to this time span.

When another murder turned up, however, it was in Chicago, and it raised the troubling possibility that additional members of the killer cult might still be at large.

The mangled body of an experienced twenty-two-year-old prostitute, Susan Baker, was found under the Fullerton Avenue Bridge. She had a lengthy record of drug and prostitution arrests under various names in several states. She was sprawled in almost exactly the same spot where the mutilated body of Sandra Delaware had been recovered months earlier.

The mud-covered corpse was naked and bloody. She had been stabbed repeatedly in the chest and stomach, and one breast was horribly slashed. But the fear of a renewed orgy of ritualistic sex slayings was quickly silenced when a truck driver was arrested after a thwarted attack on another prostitute and confessed to the copycat killing.

But even though the slaughter had stopped, grisly new details of the blood cult's demonic rituals continued to surface and circulate for months. At the trial of Thomas Kokoraleis in DuPage County for the slaying of Lorraine Borowski, Assistant State's Attorney Richard Beuke revealed that the severed breasts of some of the gang's victims were removed from a box and placed on the altar. Then the cultists ate the flesh, while Gecht read passages from the Bible. "The ceremonies always took place in the evening, around nine or ten, because Robin's wife worked at night and she wouldn't be home," the prosecutor explained.

Other information about obscene rituals and ghastly human debasement that revolved around devil worship, sex, and cannibalism had already been leaking to the public from various law-enforcement agencies. Stories were told about naked kidnap victims screaming in pain and terror as they were sacrificed at hideous Black Masses where they were first tortured with knives and ice picks, then gang-raped, and finally had one or both breasts slashed from their body with a sharp piano wire. At last they would be killed.

One of the gang members told investigators that at one time more than a dozen breasts were accumulated in a box in Gecht's attic in anticipation of the depraved satanic communion.

Some journalists began referring to the suspected cult killers as "the Cannibal Gang." But while print and electronic-media journalists were busy coining catchy new nicknames for the cultists, law-enforcement authorities and social scientists were puzzling over the complex forces that could turn four young men—three of them with no previous records of violent or sexual criminal offenses—into a crazed gang of blood cultists preying on women.

Gecht, it appeared, was the Svengalilike figure who had led and controlled the actions of the others. He had been married since he and his wife were teenagers, and although the couple became parents of three children, it was a troubled union. At the time of Gecht's arrest, his wife had filed for divorce, citing "inhuman treatment" and "extreme mental cruelty." He was seriously involved with a teenage girlfriend.

The slight youth's entire life was troubled, in fact, and marked by disputes with his parents, siblings, other relatives, and his wife, according to background investigations developed by police and prosecution authorities after his arrest.

Investigators learned that he was a middle child of six brothers and sisters, and was reared by grandparents until they died and he moved in with his family. The new arrangements didn't work all that well, and neighbors talked of frequent quarrels among the siblings that sometimes spilled out onto the sidewalk. Robin didn't get along well with his mother, they said, and by the time he was sixteen he had dropped out of high school, gotten into serious trouble with his family over the alleged sexual molestation of his relative, and moved out. From then on he lived with an uncle and with various acquaintances until he married at nineteen.

His friends were teenagers like himself: slovenly high-school dropouts and tough-talking street kids, often mentally slow, and almost always with no life goals more ambitious than merely to exist. Although undereducated, Gecht himself had a facile, manipulative mind. He was handy at fixing things and at controlling and managing others.

He worked for a while cleaning furnaces, then trained himself as a small contractor and electrician, picking up information and skills by watching others, as well as by trial and error. He developed a reputation among neighbors at the various apartments and houses where he lived with his growing family as a friendly Mr. Fixit. Eventually, he established R & R Electric.

The enterprising street kid was a leader, and the friends he sought out were followers—people like Spreitzer. Like Gecht, Spreitzer was a school dropout. But unlike Gecht, the footloose teenager was impressionable and slow-witted. He looked at the littered, gray streets around him through flat, vacant eyes, he talked in profanity-punctuated monosyllables, and he tended to let his mouth hang open too much. He usually did what he was told to do by those he looked up to. He looked up to Robin Gecht.

The two first met in a doughnut shop, and Spreitzer went to work for the older, brighter, take-charge youth almost immediately. With no permanent home of his own, Spreitzer lived with his friend and employer for a while, both in Hanover Park and in Chicago.

Despite his rootless existence, Spreitzer had previously strayed into serious trouble with the police only twice. Once he was convicted for possession of a stolen car, and about a year later, for theft.

The Kokoraleis brothers were the sons of a Greek immigrant and lived at times with their father, a younger brother, and two sisters in a modest townhouse in Villa Park, and at other times with various friends in Chicago. Their mother died when they were in their early teens. Gecht at one time lived near their home in Villa Park.

The two brothers managed to find only sporadic employment as handymen or housepainters. Thomas was garrulous, and when he wasn't working or listening to country music, he liked to chat with neighbors. Both he and Andrew worked for Gecht doing carpentry and other jobs when work was available.

Gecht, in fact, virtually took care of his three admirers, and during hard times shared his home with one or more of them, fed them, and gave them work. He didn't always pay them, but he saw to it that they had food and shelter.

One of them told police that Gecht was "Mansonlike" in his ability to get others to do what he wanted. (Charles Manson, of course, is the diminutive, hypnotic-eyed former leader of the clan of dopers and dropouts from society who committed a shocking series of ritualistic murders in California twenty years ago.) In a statement to police by Thomas Kokoraleis, he claimed that one time "Robin told us to bring a breast back to the house. He told me to do this to please him." The brothers and their friend, Sprecht, considered it important to please Robin.

Yet, even though police and prosecutors were convinced that Gecht was the undisputed leader of the gang, and his friends accused him not only of masterminding but also of being an active participant in, some of the pitiless killings—he was never charged with murder.

Behavioral experts called in to observe Gecht reported that he showed signs of having multiple personalities. When they were talking with him, he wandered, and his voice would change. Sometimes he spoke like a small child, a teenager, or a businessman. They also reported that the suspect's curious personality changes were very likely the result of a shrewd game he was playing, a hoax that might possibly give him a later courtroom advantage if it was decided he should seek an insanity plea.

The prosecution's strongest case against the reputed leader of the deadly clan was tied to the eighteen-year-old prostitute whose breast was slashed off but who survived the brutal attack. And when he emerged from months of legal maneuvering to become the first member of the accused mutilation-and-murder gang to face trial, it was for that atack. A mistrial was declared after two jurors admitted they had disregarded orders from Cook County Criminal Court Judge Francis Mahon and read newspaper accounts referring to the defendant as the suspected mastermind in a string of Jack the Ripper—type attacks on women.

But a new trial got under way approximately two months later, highlighted by the appearance of the prostitute Gecht was accused of raping and mutilating. Two other women also testified that they had been attacked by Gecht. And his former girlfriend told jurors that he once asked her to cut off her breasts. She said he warned her that if she refused, he would find a prostitute to mutilate.

Assistant State's Attorney Robert Smierciak referred to the girlfriend's testimony in his summation address to the jury. "What he couldn't get from his girlfriend . . . he got from a prostitute. She will live with those scars forever," he declared.

Joel Goldstein, another assistant state's attorney, told the jury: "Robin Gecht thought he had the perfect victim for the perfect crime. In his twisted mind, he thought no one would care because the victim was a prostitute and because she was black.

But we care," he said. "This is a crime that cries out, 'God, what has he done? How could he do that?' "

The arguments were convincing. And the jury returned verdicts of guilty on all counts—rape, aggravated battery, and attempted murder. This time the jury had also paid closer attention to the judge, and there was no mistrial. Gecht was sentenced to a total of 120 years in prison.

During his sentencing statement, Judge Mahon reflected his personal shock at the appalling crime that had been committed. "Only a monster could have done this," he told Gecht. "In all my judicial career, I have never heard a case such as this. It is shocking beyond human imagination. It is atrocious and disgusting. I can't imagine a human being doing this," he said. "The devil must be in you!"

Despite the damning statements from gang members linking Gecht to some of the ritual sex slayings, police had no other significant evidence tieing him to the killings, and he could not be charged. He steadfastly refused to admit he had killed or helped kill anyone.

But Spreitzer, whom prosecutors referred to as "every woman's nightmare," was charged with six murders, including those of Linda Sutton, Lorraine Borowski, Shui Mak, Rose Beck Davis, Sandra Delaware, and Rafael Tirado. After being found guilty of murder and aggravated kidnapping in the Sutton slaying, Spreitzer was sentenced to die by lethal injection. He became the eighty-fourth man on Illinois' death row. Life sentences were ordered in the other slayings. He is currently awaiting termination of the lengthy appeal process.

Andrew Kokoraleis was sentenced to die for the

Borowski slaying. He expressed no emotion when the death sentence, recommended earlier by a jury, was pronounced by DuPage County Judge Edward Kowal. The judge ordered an additional extended term of thirty years in prison on a charge of aggravated kidnapping of the beautiful young secretary.

He was convicted of first-degree murder in a separate trial for the rape slaying of Rose Beck Davis, whom prosecutors described as having been taken on "a roller-coaster ride through hell." But he escaped a second death penalty when the jury reported to the court that they were hopelessly deadlocked seven to five favoring execution. Since the death penalty requires a unanimous vote, the judge had no recourse but to sentence him to life in prison with no chance of parole. Jurors told attorneys for both sides that they were influenced by the defendant's youth at the time of the murder and his lack of prior criminal convictions. He was eighteen. They also pointed out that his confession had portrayed him as a follower, not a leader, in the sex and murder rampage.

Additional sentences in the case were imposed, including sixty years for rape and thirty years for kidnapping. All three terms were ordered to be served concurrently. Murder charges against him in the Sutton case were dismissed, because of the other sentences.

It was during the prosecutor's opening statements at Andrew's trial that it was revealed for the first time that he had confessed the gang may have committed as many as eighteen slayings, one more than the seventeen previously indicated. An assistant state's attorney told the jury that while Kokoraleis was being questioned, he told police: "I know you talked to Robin. Did he tell you about all of them . . . all eighteen murders?"

Detective John Philbin later testified that Andrew had confessed to seventeen or eighteen killings, but pleaded, "There are so many I can't keep them straight." Defense attorney Patrick Driscoll contended that his client made a phony confession to avoid a beating. He pointed out that when Kokoraleis took officers to a nearby forest where he said five or six women had been buried in shallow graves, although the suspect showed them where to dig holes, no bodies were found.

Testimony disclosed, however, that bodies were recovered at two other sites Kokoraleis led investigators to.

The older of the two brothers, Thomas Kokoraleis, was convicted in the Borowski murder, but won a reversal from the Illinois Appellate Court on a technicality. In a plea-bargain agreement before the start of his second trial, he pleaded guilty and was sentenced to seventy years in prison. Also as a part of the plea arrangement, charges in the Sutton case were dismissed.

4 ◆ PINT-SIZED PEEWEE: TERROR OF THE LOW COUNTRY

Donald ("Peewee") Gaskins (1970–1982)

Killing was Donald ("Peewee") Gaskins's business and his joy.

He killed for profit, he killed for sex, and he killed for the pure pleasure of the life-and-death power that murder gave him over others.

During five blood-soaked years Peewee built a reputation for unrepentant evil and sheer savagery, while he littered bodies of men, women, and children through the swamplands, piney woods, and backwater towns of southeastern South Carolina.

Then, after seven years without a kill, the homicidal pipsqueak whose cold-blooded ruthlessness had become a dark legend in his home state carried out one more violent act that captured headlines around the world.

Peewee grew up small and mean, and by the time

he reached adulthood, he had put a lean and scrappy 126 pounds on a five-foot, two-inch frame. Although he had a facile mind, a fast tongue, and could be charming when he wanted to be, he had a reputation in rural Florence County as a man it didn't pay to cross. He had no trouble finding jobs as a roofer and sheet-metal worker, but the work was too hard and too hot, even for Peewee. He preferred to busy himself in the more profitable activities of South Carolina's thriving underworld, a parasitic society of low-country Al Capones who fed off the weaknesses and mistakes of others.

Peewee's specialties were stolen cars, prison escape, teenage girls, and contract murder.

But the world of the backwoods hit man and peckerwood terror didn't begin caving in for good until he was named on the seemingly relatively tame charge of contributing to the delinquency of a minor. Peewee became involved with a naive, slow-witted thirteen-year-old neighbor girl.

He was accused of spiriting away Kim Ghelkin from her home in North Charleston. She was reported missing shortly after the beginning of the fall school term in 1975.

Unlike officers with some big-city law-enforcement agencies who tend to mark up most reports of missing children as runaways, Detectives Rufus Stoney and Roy C. Green, of the North Charleston Police Department's Juvenile Bureau, took the report of her disappearance seriously and began an immediate search.

While interviewing family members, they learned that Kim's father had received a letter reputedly from her, claiming that she was staying with a

preacher. There was also a story that she was staying
in the small town of Lake City in nearby Florence
County with a man named Peewee. Kim's family
knew Peewee as a tough but friendly neighbor who
lived just across the street. His real name was Donald Henry Gaskins, and Kim had taken trips with
him and his wife.

The letter was quickly ruled out as a hoax. And
when Kim's family went to Lake City to look for
her they were told that a relative of Peewee's had
taken her to New York. The detectives didn't believe
that story any more than they believed that the
letter Kim purportedly wrote was the real thing. A
warrant was sworn out for Peewee's arrest for contributing to the delinquency of a minor.

But when the sleuths tried to question residents
along the North Charleston street where he had
lived, they quickly realized that everyone was afraid
to talk about the bandy-legged little roofer.

Some people insisted they knew nothing about
him. Others refused to come to the door when they
saw the officers outside. And when Green stopped a
woman in the middle of the street to identify himself as a detective, the color drained from her face
and she tried to pull away. She pleaded that she was
afraid to be seen with him because talking could get
her killed.

But Green and Stoney persisted, and eventually
people did begin to talk about the menacing little
man some knew as Junior and others guardedly
referred to as Peewee. And the stories they had to
tell quickly convinced the two detectives that they
were pursuing an investigation with overtones much

more ominous than the mere tracking down of a runaway.

They learned that a pair of half brothers had also dropped from sight. Twenty-nine-year-old Dennis "Beegee" Bellamy and fifteen-year-old John Henry Knight hadn't been heard from since a few days after Kim was last seen by her family. Then family members told Stoney and Green that not only were the brothers missing, but their twenty-nine-year-old sister, Diane Bellamy Neeley, had also dropped from sight the previous April.

As the detectives were talking with the family, another woman drove up and joined the conversation. She added the name of her son, Johnny Sellers, to the missing list. She said she hadn't seen him since June 1975.

The juvenile officers suddenly had a list of five missing people on their hands—seven if Peewee and his wife were counted. Curiously, every one of them had some connection to the diminutive roofer. Peewee was obviously the key to solving the growing riddle of missing people.

A records check revealed that Peewee wasn't a stranger to police. He was a petty thief and womanizer who had been involved in run-ins with the law off and on for much of his thirty-eight years. His first serious brush with police occurred when he was thirteen, and landed him in reform school for an assault on a fourteen-year-old girl.

He wasn't free long before he got in trouble again with a juvenile girl, and was on trial for statutory rape when he leaped from a second-floor window of the old Florence County Courthouse in Florence. He hid out in the swamps for weeks, and when police

trackers used bloodhounds to run him down he
caught the dogs and tied them to trees. Then he
sneaked out of the swamps and brazenly scribbled
his name in the condensation on the rear windows
of the police cars—some say, while lawmen were
sitting inside. But he was eventually recaptured and
sent to prison. And his daring leap to freedom had
left him with a limp that he would carry the rest of
his life.

Another time, in 1966, when he was doing time
at South Carolina's high-security Central Corrections Institution (CCI) in Columbia, the state capital, he commandeered a prison truck to carry out a
daring escape from a work detail. He was back behind bars within twenty-four hours. The slippery
little career criminal did time in state and federal
penitentiaries for a house burglary, auto theft, assault and battery, and accessory after the fact to
murder, in addition to the various sex offenses.

There had been talk more recently, guarded
though it was, of Peewee's interest in a hot-car ring
that was giving police fits in the southeast corner of
the state.

Bits and pieces of information continued to trickle
in, and the investigators learned that Peewee had
always been a little threatening and strange even
when he wasn't stealing or sexually assaulting
young women. It was downright creepy, some
thought, the way he used to cruise around Prospect,
a town near his rural boyhood home, in a black
hearse, a white toy skeleton dangling from the rear-
view mirror.

One time a few years back when he pulled up in
front of the gas pumps at a grocery store in the

crossroads community of Prospect, a woman asked him why in the world he drove an old hearse. "This way I can carry 'em dead or alive," he chuckled. Despite Peewee's chortle, there was something about his remark that was more discomforting than funny.

Then people started whispering about a makeshift graveyard near Prospect where bodies were surreptitiously dumped in the ground without coffins, funerals, or other ceremony. It was Peewee's private ossuary, they hinted.

When a couple of deer hunters stumbled on a stolen late-model Ford in a field a few miles from Lake City, police began talking to Walter Leroy Neeley about hot cars. Then they started talking about dead bodies and hidden graveyards. Neeley was an old prison friend of Peewee's and the husband of one of the missing women—Diane Bellamy Neeley. After a certain amount of prodding, he agreed to show police the graveyard.

Joined by sheriff's deputies from Florence and Williamsburg counties, Green and Stoney crisscrossed the swamplands and piney woods, digging more than forty holes at dozens of sites pointed out by the nervous man. One of the locations was on property where Peewee lived for a while in a house trailer near Roper's Crossing, but most of the digging was around Prospect.

Finally, after more than two weeks of disappointment, and while the frustrated lawmen were grumbling about "wild goose chases" and were about to give up in exasperation, their efforts were rewarded. Neeley led Williamsburg County Deputy Glen Ard to a remote patch of woods at the edge of a cornfield

in an area of Big Lake Swamp, just east of Prospect.
Ard recognized a possible grave. A short while later
lawmen started turning up bodies. It was about two
o'clock on a dark and chilly early-December afternoon.

A badly decomposed body under about eighteen
inches of dirt was the first to be recovered. Then,
about twenty-five feet away, the remains of a woman
were uncovered. She was lying faceup under a thin
layer of earth. A man's foot was sticking through the
dirt beside her, and after a few more minutes of
careful digging, a male body was uncovered beneath
the woman. The man was Johnny Sellers. He had
lived in North Charleston but grew up around Prospect. Like the first body, the female couldn't be
immediately identified, but she was too old to be
Kim Ghelkins. Area residents speculated that she
might be a woman who was known as the Gypsy
Girl, who had shown up in the neighborhood a few
years earlier, then vanished as mysteriously as she
had appeared.

Investigators from the South Carolina State Law
Enforcement Division and the Florence County
Medical Examiner's Office joined the officers already
at the site to help with exhumation and identification. Long before nightfall, dozens of officers from
state, county, and other local jurisdictions had
crowded into Prospect and the little clearing in the
woods. Then two forensic pathologists from the
Medical University of South Carolina in Charleston
were flown in to the search site by helicopter. A day
later a device used to help locate bodies by detecting
gases released by decomposing flesh was flown in,

on loan from the Florida State Criminal Investigation Bureau in Tallahassee.

With that much activity and so many policemen around, it didn't take long for word to get out that Peewee was suspected of having something to do with planting the ghastly garden of corpses. Some five hundred people lived in and around Prospect, and most of them found their way to the site to watch the goings-on. Some perched on the backs of pickup trucks or on the hoods of cars, chatting animatedly with neighbors and watching the activity intently. Some of the onlookers used binoculars. It was like a church picnic, without the preacher but with the prayers, recited audibly or muttered nearly silently. Most of those present knew Peewee, and most also found it hard to believe that he could be a killer. Many of the neighbors knew him as Junior Parrott (Parrott was his mother's family name), and despite his strangeness, his frequent brushes with the law, and his reputation for occasional meanness, he was well liked. He was considered a friendly person, and he was known for being quick to lend a hand when someone needed help with a hard job or a fix-up project around the house.

When talk turned to a car-theft ring, some of Peewee's friends and former neighbors reluctantly conceded that it wouldn't surprise them if he were somehow involved. But murder? There was just no way that could be true!

Yet they couldn't deny that Peewee could be a hard character when he wanted to be. And he knew the area like the back of his hand. The ruins of the modest farmhouse where he lived as a boy were still present in a small grove of trees barely a half mile

up a winding dirt road from the wooded burial
ground.

And he still kept a mobile home at nearby Roper's
Crossing, which he occupied off and on when he
wasn't in North Charleston. His daughter, Shirley
Ann Evans, lived in another house trailer a few feet
away with her brood of four little ones.

Over the next couple of days, before a chill prewin-
ter drizzle washed away most of the fetid smell of
death that clung to the little clearing in the woods,
three more bodies were pulled from the earth. All
six bodies had been buried two to a grave. They were
spotted in a half-circle, each about twenty-five yards
from the other. Some of the remains were badly
decomposed. Other bodies appeared to have been
buried only a few days or weeks and were in better
condition.

None of the bodies was that of the trusting teenage
girl whose disappearance ultimately led investigators to the burial ground. All along, police had been
hoping to find her alive, but discovery of the six
cadavers stirred up fears that she, too, had become a
victim.

Although she had already entered her teens, the
budding young woman was only in the fifth grade at
the Chicora Elementary School in North Charleston. She had never been a discipline problem and she
tried hard at her studies, but it was difficult for her
to learn. She was a little slow.

Her fifth-grade teacher, Mrs. Mary Ann Griffin,
described her to a journalist as "an immature thirteen."

It was apparently Mrs. Griffin who filed the first
missing report on Kim with authorities. Kim had

been in class only four days at the start of the new school year when a family member reported that the girl had run away. Mrs. Griffin was told that a missing report had been filed with police, but when she heard nothing more about Kim after a few days she notified authorities herself. They said they knew nothing about the disappearance.

But three months later, when the bodies were discovered in the Prospect burial ground, Kim still hadn't been found. Peewee had been located weeks before that, however. He was riding in the back seat of a taxi near Sumpter on his way to the Greyhound bus station when a posse of lawmen led by the Sumpter County sheriff swooped down and took him into custody on the delinquency warrant and on a charge of auto theft. They also confiscated a cardboard box they found next to him on the cab seat, and when it was searched they found a .32-caliber semiautomatic Beretta pistol and a .30-30 Model 94 Winchester live-action rifle as well as ammunition for both weapons. Peewee was carrying a change of clothes and a one-way bus ticket to Mississippi, as well.

After a brief stay in local lockups, he launched a hunger strike and two days later was transferred to the CCI in Columbia. He was being described by law-enforcement authorities and in news accounts as the prime suspect in the grisly multiple murders uncovered at Prospect. Neeley was being held in Florence, the seat of Florence County, as a material witness in the murder case.

Detectives Stoney and Green had done the initial spadework in what had now blown into a large-scale probe that was being spearheaded by skilled officers with the South Carolina State Law Enforcement Division (SLED) who were specially trained in homicide investigations.

As the search for Kim continued, SLED disclosed that it was believed some of the victims of the killings were forced to stand in their own graves before they were slain. "We don't know if they were forced to dig their own graves or what," added a spokesman. Four of the victims appeared to have been shot. The other two showed indications that their throats had been cut. But confirmation was withheld pending completion of autopsies still to be performed at the Medical University of South Carolina's forensic-pathology department.

The Charleston County Medical Examiner, however, identified two of the bodies as those of the missing half brothers from North Charleston, Dennis Bellamy and John Knight. The identification of two women and a man were still unknown, but investigators privately speculated that one of the victims was Diane Bellamy Neeley. They weren't alone in their suspicions. Grief-stricken members of the Bellamy family began planning three funerals.

After the new identifications, Florence County Sheriff William C. Barnes announced that Gaskins and Neeley had been charged with murder in the slayings of the three known victims. Among other evidence, ballistics tests had linked the .30-30 rifle found in the box to the slaying of the unidentified man.

Murder charges were also filed against a third man, twenty-three-year-old James Kony Judy, who was arrested at his mother's home in Charleston. He was accused only in the Sellers slaying. Police said they had an eyewitness to the killing.

Investigators still didn't have all the answers or motives for the slaughter, but they were beginning to sort it out. The suspects and the victims, it appeared, had been involved in a confusing jumble of familial, marital, and professional relationships. And they were caught up in a twisted mélange of love triangles, thievery, and merciless executions. Everyone seemed to be related, or otherwise closely tied, to everyone else.

Peewee and Neeley were thought to have met in prison, and continued their relationship in North Charleston. Neeley was a dim-witted thirty-year-old man who openly admired the wiry, more experienced ex-con and was often seen visiting the Gaskins home.

Judy, the third suspect arrested in the serial-murder probe, was brought into the cloudy mix of relationships through his wife, Jessie Ruth. Sellers and Mrs. Judy dropped from sight on June 22 after they told acquaintances they were going to the Gaskins home. The thirty-six-year-old man and the twenty-two-year-old married woman were lovers.

A few days after the Prospect graveyard was uncovered, the skeletal remains of another body were discovered by a hunter just down a dirt road leading to a swimming hole about a mile east of where the other six were dug up. Lawmen converged on the site near Alligator Landing on Lynche's River, looking for still more bodies and sifting the soft dirt for additional clues. But their efforts were hampered by a steady drizzle of cold rain that turned the earth into a gluey mess. An aging tobacco shed was taken over for temporary shelter, and a police major busied himself there cooking a steaming-hot iron pot of chicken bog to feed the bedraggled men during rest periods.

Despite the terrible weather that continued on through the next day, the search team, using probes and metal detectors, located an eighth body. This time, the remains of a child about two or three years old was pulled from the thick soggy mud of a shallow grave about ten feet from the seventh body. The skeleton recovered earlier had been identified as that of an adult female, about twenty years old, and investigators speculated that it was the mother of the baby. The remains of the suspected mother and child were the last that would be found at the Prospect burial grounds, but not the last murder victim that Peewee would be linked to. And there was still no trace of Kim.

Positive identification was made on the body of Diane Bellamy Neeley, and a few days later she and her brothers were reburied after a triple funeral. Florence County Medical Examiner William T. Eaddy revealed that Mrs. Neeley had been shot under the chin and stabbed in the chest.

Eaddy said that a knife, a rifle, and a .32-caliber pistol were used in at least five of the slayings. Bellamy and his brother, John Knight, were shot with a .32, and Sellers was shot with a rifle.

Dental records were used to make the next identification of a victim as thirty-five-year-old Avery Howard, Jr. He and Mrs. Neeley were sweethearts, and their bodies were found in the same grave.

In mid-January 1976, the woman and child unearthed from the second burial site were named as twenty-year-old Doreen Hope Dempsey Geddings and her two-year-old daughter, Robin Michelle Dempsey. Mrs. Geddings and the child had lived with Peewee for a while in Sumpter before dropping from sight in 1973. Both had apparently been clubbed to death. Several weeks later the last remaining unidentified body, found buried with Sellers, was officially listed as Mrs. Judy.

Investigators had called off the search in Big Lake Swamp when Neeley led them to a landfill and car graveyard near the city limits of North Charleston. Nothing more exciting than decaying garbage and rusting auto parts was turned up. The sophisticated gas-detecting device borrowed from Florida was useless in the landfill because of the confusing vapors emitted by decaying vegetable matter.

Two weeks later searchers following up another tip were led not to more bodies, but to a buried liquor still.

Peewee's wife led authorities to yet another search area in a section of upper Williamsburg County known as Black Mingo. But no additional bodies or evidence was found there.

Law-enforcement authorities had practically given up hopes of finding Kim Ghelkins alive. No one had been found who would admit to having seen her alive since the previous November at Peewee's trailer home at Roper's Crossroads.

Named on eight murder charges, Peewee was first tried in Florence General Sessions Court for the shooting death of Beegee Bellamy. He tried to shift the blame to his codefendant and onetime admirer, Neeley, who was scheduled for a separate trial.

Testifying in his own defense, Peewee claimed that

Neeley had shown up at the house trailer in Roper's Crossroads and asked to borrow his pickup to dispose of some things. Peewee said his .32-caliber Beretta semiautomatic, a 12-gauge shotgun, and a .30-30 rifle were in the truck when he loaned it to his friend.

Although he didn't see them, Peewee added, Neeley told him that John Henry Knight and another man were with him and waiting outside. Neeley returned the truck about five the next morning, Peewee testified. But when he checked his pistol, he found that it was fully loaded, although it had had only four cartridges in it when the truck was borrowed.

Talking as casually as if he were tipping a beer with a couple of friends, Peewee also hit back hard at previous testimony by his daughter, Mrs. Shirley Ann Evans, and by a former neighbor in North Charleston. He said his daughter was forced to take the stand against him by threats to take her children away. Although he didn't name the mysterious individuals or authorities who had made the reputed threats, he said she had to give in because "she loves those children more than anything in the world."

Mrs. Evans testified that her father and Neeley arrived at her house trailer, a few feet from Peewee's, at about 9 P.M. on October 10, 1975. She said that two young men, whom she later learned were Bellamy and Knight, pulled up to the trailer in another car. "I heard Daddy call one man Denny, Dennis, or something like that," she told the jury.

A few minutes later all four men got into her father's car and he drove away. "I never saw the two boys again," she said.

Thomas Wright, Sr., testified that he lived next door to Peewee in North Charleston for about two years, and that his wiry little neighbor had talked to him about "private graveyards" in Florence County. Peewee also said he kept a pick and shovel in his truck to get rid of bodies, Wright told the jury.

Peewee insisted to the jury that he had merely been talking about a family graveyard near the Williamsburg–Florence County line in the area where he grew up.

He also testified that on the day he was arrested, he was headed to Sherman, Mississippi, to look for Kim. He said he knew that he was being accused of contributing to her delinquency and wanted to find her so that he could prove his innocence.

Twelfth Judicial Circuit Solicitor T. Kenneth Summerford, who headed the prosecution, used his opportunity at cross-examining the defendant to ask, "Do you deny that you took Johnny Knight and Dennis Bellamy to the woods behind your old homeplace and that you told Dennis Bellamy to look at a tree, and shot him in the head?"

Seemingly unruffled, Peewee responded: "I deny that, yes sir, I deny that."

Summerford scoffed at the idea that it wasn't Peewee who planned and carried out the double murder, but that it was instead the slow-witted Neeley. "Walter Neeley didn't have sense enough to come in out of the rain unless this man told him to," the prosecutor fumed during his summation to the jury.

At the conclusion of the weeklong trial, the panel of seven women and five men took less than two hours to find Peewee guilty of premeditated murder. He was sentenced to death in the electric chair.

Neeley was tried for Bellamy's death soon after, and was also found guilty of a single count of murder. At his trial, however, Summerford pointed out to the jury that the defendant, who had been described by a psychiatrist as moderately retarded, with an I.Q. of about sixty, could pull the trigger of a gun "just as well as a smart man." Neeley did not testify, but like Peewee, he was sentenced to death in the electric chair.

In a plea-bargaining arrangement, Judy pleaded guilty to a reduced charge of accessory after the fact of murder in Sellers's death. He was sentenced to a ten-year prison term.

Appeals were automatic in both death sentences. But equally important and disturbing to law-enforcement authorities, the question of capital punishment in the nation had been in a legal limbo since 1972, when the U.S. Supreme Court struck down the death penalty as then administered by the various states as being "arbitrary and capricious."

Most individual states that had previously provided for the death penalty passed new laws that were being tested in state and federal courts on the way to a new U.S. Supreme Court ruling.

As authorities awaited decisions in the higher courts on the two death sentences returned in the dreadful serial slayings, police continued to investigate new stories about buried bodies. Acting on a tip from a relative by marriage of Peewee's, police from Charleston and North Charleston moved the search to nearby John's Island. The woman said that Peewee and Neeley had told her they buried three bodies there, including that of a black man and a fifteen-year-old girl, Janice Faye Kirby.

Police took the tip seriously, because they knew that the Kirby girl and a seventeen-year-old companion, Patricia Ann Alsbrook, had left their Sumter homes together in 1970 and were never seen again. And Patricia was Peewee's niece. Nevertheless, the search team was unable to turn up any trace either of the girls or of the black man.

Although barely a month after Peewee's sentencing the U.S. Supreme Court ruled that the death penalty could, indeed, be constitutional punishment for convicted killers, the death-penalty statute in South Carolina failed to survive the legal challenges in its then-present form. Consequently, Peewee and Neeley were eventually resentenced to life terms. But Peewee wasn't yet safe from death row.

More bodies had been found buried in the coastal-plain counties he roamed and terrorized as a free man.

In fact, shortly after his conviction in the Bellamy case, Peewee led investigators to a secluded patch of woods near Roper's Crossroads. There, the search for Kim Ghelkins at last ended when her skeletal remains were unearthed from under a few inches of dirt. But even though he led searchers to the teenager's grave, he continued to stoutly deny that he had anything to do with her murder.

Another body, that of a young woman, was pulled from a septic tank near Roper's Crossroads. It was eventually identified as Patricia Ann Alsbrook. There was no trace of her companion.

But another body, found near Roper's Crossroads, was quickly identified as Silas Barnwell Yates, a forty-five-year-old farmer from the tiny agricultural community of Turbeville in Florence County. He had left his wife several years earlier to move into a mobile home in Lake City. And he had broken up with a young girlfriend shortly before he vanished in February 1975. Investigators learned that he had known Peewee.

Within hours of discovery of the well-to-do landowner's skeletal remains, new murder charges were filed against Peewee, as well as two other men and a woman who were quickly rounded up. The woman was Yates's former girlfriend, twenty-nine-year-old Suzanne M. Kipper Owens; her husband, twenty-two-year-old John Philip Owens, Jr.; and a former resident of lower Florence County, thirty-year-old John William Powell, Jr. Powell was arrested in DeLand, Florida. The Owens couple were taken into custody at their home near Lake City.

The farmer's remains were found in swampy woodlands near the old Roper plantation, where almost exactly a year earlier Detectives Stoney and Green along with fellow lawmen had dug dozens of holes without success. An autopsy disclosed that Yates was stabbed twice just below the heart.

Discovery of Yates's body occurred at an especially bad time for Peewee, because when North Charleston police picked him up at the CCI for questioning in the case, a filed-down handcuff key was found taped to the label of his sweatshirt. Guards tried the key and determined that it worked on his handcuffs, despite the alteration. Filing the key down allowed it to be concealed more easily.

After an investigation, a prison spokesman disclosed that Peewee had apparently been working on a scheme for about nine months to stage his second escape from the high-security institution and had confided his plan to other prisoners. He reportedly obtained the key from a guard in return for a thirty-five-dollar bribe. The guard was permitted to resign, and prison authorities explained that he was not prosecuted because there would have been no chance of proving the case in court.

Events outside the CCI were going no better for Peewee. John Philip Owens, Jr., was talking to police, and he confessed that he and his wife were present when Peewee and Powell took Yates from his mobile home and killed him.

Owens told agent Tom Henderson, of the State Law Enforcement Division, that the farmer had begun legal action to repossess a car that he had given to Suzanne, along with money, when the two were dating before their falling-out and her marriage. He said his wife swore that she would get even with her old sweetheart, and told him that she had arranged with Peewee and Powell "to do a job on Barnwell Yates" for one thousand dollars.

Continuing the confession, Owens said that the quartet went to Yates's mobile home near Turbeville and parked about a quarter of a mile away. Gaskins and Powell walked to the trailer, and when they returned with the farmer, they shoved him into the car trunk. Then the hired killers drove to Roper's Crossroads, where they removed Yates from the trunk and marched him into the woods. Owens and his wife waited in the car for a while before walking into the woods themselves. There, Owens claimed, they found Yates lying on the ground with his hands cuffed behind him and his throat cut.

When the killers demanded more money a short while later, Owens said, he gave his wife an additional five hundred dollars, which she handed over to them.

The young husband was permitted to plead guilty to accessory after the fact of murder and received a light sentence, in return for agreeing to testify against other suspects in the case.

Acting on a defense motion for change of venue because of excessive publicity, a judge moved the trial from the originally scheduled site at Kingstree, in Williamsburg County, west across the state to Newberry, in Newberry County—a hundred miles or so from Peewee's home grounds. It apparently made little difference in the outcome, because the diminutive backwoods hit man was again found guilty of murder and sentenced to life in prison. The sentence was ordered to be served consecutively, after serving his time for the Dennis Bellamy killing. Mrs. Owens was given a life term in prison.

During Peewee's trial testimony, he startled the prosecution and other court authorities by confessing to the slaying of two more female victims.

One was thirteen-year-old Margaret Cuttino. The Sumter girl was abducted a week before Christmas in 1970, after leaving her house to meet her sister at a nearby school. Her body was found twelve days later in the nearby Manchester State Forest.

Peewee was as notorious for his ability to lie without blinking an eye as he was for carrying out killings without a trace of either mercy or regret. And his story of the Cuttino slaying was especially suspicious, because another man had already been convicted of the vicious kidnap-murder.

William ("Junior") Pierce, who was serving multiple life sentences in a Georgia prison for murder, nevertheless won a postconviction relief hearing in the Cuttino case on the basis of Peewee's yarn. But a judge ruled against his move for a new trial based on Peewee's confession.

Much later Peewee reversed his confession, denied that he had anything to do with the girl's killing, and conceded that he was simply trying to "take some pressure off Pierce."

Even though Peewee recanted his confession to the murder of the other victim as well, it seemed more likely that he was really involved. He identified that victim as a young black woman in her late teens that he knew only as Clyde. Police believed that Clyde was Martha Ann Dicks, who was known by that nickname and who disappeared from her South Sumter home in the early 1970s. Following Peewee's directions, a search party drained a ditch shortly after the trial and found the skeletal remains of a young woman buried under one of the banks. A medical examiner confirmed that the bones were those of a black woman, and detectives suspected that they had found Clyde. Peewee claimed on the witness stand that a Sumter lawman had ordered her death, and that he also killed three men in Charleston in the early 1970s at the direction of three men with badges. It was difficult to figure out whether Peewee was telling the truth or merely running off at the mouth to settle old grievances.

But authorities listened closely when he pulled another, bigger surprise shortly before the scheduled beginning of testimony in his trial for the John Knight murder. A jury had already been selected, and prosecutors stated they were seeking the death penalty.

After extensive plea negotiations, Peewee agreed to plead guilty to seven charges of murder, in addition to the two he was already serving time for. In return, he was promised that no solicitor in South Carolina would seek the death penalty against him for slayings he had already carried out.

It wasn't a deal that prosecutors found easy to swallow, but there were still embarrassing murder cases to be cleared and bodies to be recovered so that long-grieving families could at last put their loved ones to rest in hallowed ground after proper funerals. Importantly, it appeared, as well, that the slayings occurred prior to 1976, when the state's former capital-punishment law was declared unconstitutional by the U.S. Supreme Court—and before the new capital-punishment law was adopted by the legislators in 1977. Significantly, the validity of the new law could still be expected to face serious challenges and tests in the higher courts as well.

Peewee also offered to lead police to the missing remains of his victims, to name everyone else involved in the slayings, and to testify against his accomplices. The master criminal and hit man who had been branded in court as a pathological liar even agreed to submit to questioning while under the influence of truth serum to confirm his far-reaching confession to serial murder.

The truth serum, sodium amytal, was administered by a psychiatrist at a Florence hospital, and Peewee was questioned by Summerford, Florence County Sheriff William Barnes, and SLED agents. During the interrogation, which was closely monitored by his attorneys, he described the murders of thirteen victims, including four adult men, three adult women, four teenage girls, one teenage boy, and a baby. In a brief sixty minutes, Peewee confirmed facts that made it possible for detectives to sort out information they had labored three years to collect.

Among new information produced during the truth-serum session and other talks since plea bargaining had begun, police learned that Doreen Hope Dempsey Geddings and her daughter, Michelle, were not clubbed to death as previously believed. Peewee had marched the terrified woman to a pond in back of an old store where she was living, and pushed her in, drowning her. She was pregnant. Then he went back to the store and got the little girl, took her to the pond, and drowned her. He used his hearse to transport the bodies to the burial sites.

During a press conference in the same room that only a few minutes before had been darkened for Peewee's whispered, drug-induced recapitulation of a half-decade of murder, the law-enforcement officers told journalists that they believed they had at last extracted the full truth from the diminutive killer.

They said that Peewee had implicated yet another accomplice, and had admitted falsely accusing others of involvement in the Knight murder because he had a grudge against them. The questioning had also definitely cleared him in the Cuttino case, and ruled out any law-enforcement-ordered slayings.

A forty-six-year-old distributor of auto stereo equipment, Belton Eaddy, was arrested. The former operator of a general store near Prospect, Eaddy, after

being carried into General Sessions Court in Florence on a stretcher with a physician in attendance,
pleaded guilty to accessory to murder before and
after the fact, and was sentenced to a ten-year prison
term.

Eaddy, who suffered from hypertension, was accused of standing guard at an isolated Florence
County road while Peewee shot Sellers through the
spine with a rifle, then buried him.

Finally, the skeleton of Peewee's long-missing
niece, Janice Faye Kirby, was pulled from a shallow
pit in woods near an old graveyard in Prospect where
it had lain for more than seven years. It seemed that
Peewee had given up the last body of his victims,
and that law-enforcement authorities were finally
about to lock prison-cell doors for good on the most
prolific serial killer in modern South Carolina history.

Free of handcuffs, but closely guarded by a cautious posse of somber SLED agents, Peewee stood
before Judge David W. Harwell in Florence County
General Sessions Court and pleaded guilty to seven
counts of murder, and a single charge of burglary for
the 1975 break-in of a private home and theft of a
TV set and video recorder. He was given eight consecutive life sentences, to be piled on top of the two
previous terms he was already serving.

Judge Harwell noted that Peewee had been saved
from the electric chair by the U.S. Supreme Court
ruling that struck down South Carolina's previous
death-penalty statute. "I'll be honest with you," the
judge declared. "I can't think of a man who would
be more deserving of the punishment."

Once more the slippery little hit man had wiggled

free of the death penalty. But even though Peewee could expect to spend the rest of his life behind bars, that didn't mean he was through killing. Seemingly unrelated developments along the Atlantic Coast near Myrtle Beach just outside tiny Murrell's Inlet a few weeks before Peewee's surprise deal with prosecutors would ensure that he still had some shock headlines left in him.

Bill and Myrtle Moon were about to close up their mom-and-pop grocery store and gas station, Moon's Exxon, for the night when a skinny, wild-eyed youth suddenly barged through the front door, waving a mean-looking 12-gauge pump-action shotgun. Mrs. Moon had just begun counting the day's receipts, and she was holding a handful of currency.

Her husband was a rugged-looking fifty-year-old who had retired from the Air Force as a military policeman a few years back. He looked like he could handle himself. So the intruder squeezed off a blast from the shotgun—just to scare the burly storekeeper, he said later. Moon was slammed backward, and dropped to the floor with a hole in his chest the size of a fist. Mrs. Moon screamed in agony and fear. The intruder squeezed the trigger again, but nothing happened. The gun had jammed. So he pumped another round into the chamber and squeezed the trigger a third time. The blast of birdshot ripped a gaping hole in her chest and nearly tore off her left arm. Quickly, the intruder scooped up a handful of bills, some of them bloodstained, and fled outside, where a seventeen-year-old accomplice was acting as lookout.

The murdered couple were found by a couple of teenage girls from the neighborhood when they

dropped into the store to pick up soft drinks and
candy. The mutilated bodies of the Moons were
awash in blood and chunks of flesh. The girls fled
from the charnel house, screaming in terror. Their
shrieks were heard by Tony Cimo.

Cimo, whose mother had married Moon when he
was two, was lying on a couch in his trailer across
the road watching John Wayne in *Rio Lobo*, on television. Rushing to the store, Cimo was confronted
with the same ghastly scene the girls had walked in
on. The terrible injuries left little doubt that his
parents were both dead, yet he knelt beside his
mother and desperately felt for a pulse. There was
none. Then he did the same for the retired Air Force
man who had been such a loving father to him for
more than thirty years. Again, there was no pulse.
On the counter, the cash-register drawer was open.
A spent shotgun shell was on the floor. Tony Cimo's
parents had been brutally executed for a measly
handful of small bills.

Outside, eighteen-year-old Rudolph Tyner min-
gled in the crowd that had gathered, and watched as
the bodies were carried away. Cimo jumped into his
truck and headed for the back roads, aiming his
flashlight into the brush and trees. He wanted the
killer. But it was police who made the arrest.

Acting later that night on a tip that a brash kid
from Harlem had been in the area making trouble,
officers picked up Tyner at the home of friends
barely two hours after the shootings. The New York
youth was arrogant and defiant, until officers caught
him trying to hide a spent shotgun shell. They found
a pump-action shotgun in a closet at the home
where he was staying. It was the weapon used in the

double murder. He was carrying more than one hundred dollars in one of his pockets. Tyner confessed. "Yeah, man, I shot them," he said.

As his trial, he attempted to retract the confession, claiming that he had felt threatened by police. His attorney pointed to the junior high school dropout's low IQ, and argued that he was a poor ghetto kid from a broken home who was so mentally deficient that he couldn't fully understand his constitutional rights when they were read to him. Police read the so-called Miranda warning, which advised him of his right to remain silent when questioned, five times.

Tyner was bright enough, however, to stand before the jury minutes before they began deliberations and plead: "Ladies and gentlemen, I know I made a mistake. For God's sake, please have mercy on me."

The racially mixed jury had heard a tape recording of the confession, and they knew in horrifying detail about the savagely brutal manner in which the well-liked mom-and-pop grocers had died. They returned a guilty verdict on two counts of murder, and recommended the death penalty. Tyner was sentenced to die in the electric chair. His teenage lookout was given a life sentence.

Surviving members of the Cimo and the Moon families returned to their homes, to try to pick up their lives and to put the devastating tragedy behind them. Justice, it appeared, had been done.

As the lengthy appeals process that is automatic in capital-punishment cases began, Tyner was transported to the CCI and locked in a cell on death row. It was there that the savage young black kid from Harlem met Peewee, the grizzled serial killer whose reputation for bloody exploits had followed him to the formidable fortresslike graystone maximum security prison. Their cells were located back to back.

Although Peewee's deal had ruled out the electric chair for the thirteen homicides he was known to have committed, he was recognized for the dangerous and savage killer he was. And he had also proven himself as an escape artist, so he was confined in the same high-security area as Tyner and other killers.

Peewee thrived in Cell Block Two, which included death row. He was not only the institution's most infamous inmate but also one of the most cold-blooded killers ever brought to justice in the long and bloody history of the Palmetto State. All this, coupled with the respect from other cons that went with his reputation for escapes, immediately moved Peewee to the top of the prison hierarchy.

Even guards were apparently impressed, and Peewee quickly won a coveted position as building man in the cell block, a position that permitted him to keep tools and other equipment in his cell to make minor plumbing and electrical repairs. But he also controlled delivery of meals to inmates, could obtain privileged jobs for those he favored, and could move freely among them day and night. Peewee began making extra money running errands and fixing appliances, loaning cigarettes and other items used for prison barter, dealing dope, and selling coffee. He quickly developed a reputation as the convict who ran death row. Whatever other inmates might desire, if it was available in prison, they realized that Peewee was the man to see. He was the acknowledged King of Cell Block Two.

was the man to see. He was the acknowledged King of Cell Block Two.

Outside, the Cimos and the Moons were beginning to wonder what had happened to the speedy justice they had heard so much about. It seemed that Tyner's appeals were dragging on endlessly. The state supreme court ordered a new trial, ruling that the prosecution had biased jurors and lessened their burden by reminding them that any death sentence would be automatically reviewed. Four days into jury selection for the second trial, the judge ordered a change of venue to another county in order to seat an unbiased panel. Once more, authorities began gearing up for still another new trial. Tony Cimo was devastated at the frustrating twists and turns Tyner's road to justice was taking. And he was very much aware that the last legal execution in South Carolina had occurred in 1962, and it was likely to be years before another was carried out. Perhaps never.

"I got to realize that the death penalty is just a farce, that there is nobody getting executed unless they want to," he would later say. "It's sort of a volunteer death penalty."

He heard that Tyner had been bragging in his cell about how Mrs. Moon had begged on her knees for mercy. Cimo lay awake nights thinking about that. At other times he sat for hours at the graves of his mother and stepfather, morosely brooding. Finally, he began showing up in some seedy bars along a section of State Road 501 leading into Myrtle Beach, and in other sleazy taprooms and hangouts. Previously a gentle and loving man who preferred to spend his time picnicking with his family or bass

fishing, he began turning to new acquaintances selected from among the worst kind of street-corner
toughs, bikers, and ex-convicts.

Eventually he met someone who knew an experienced burglar and thief who was locked up at the
CCI. The burglar knew Peewee. Soon, Cimo began
talking at a friend's house with Peewee in a series of
Sunday-morning telephone calls. The first time Peewee telephoned him, Cimo would remember, the
little man's high-pitched drawl "sounded just like a
good ol' country hick."

It didn't bother Cimo that Peewee was one of the
most hated and feared killers in South Carolina
history. "You don't hire a librarian to clean out your
septic tank," the revenge-seeking vigilante observed.

Peewee agreed to do the job for a few hundred
dollars. He didn't like blacks anyway. Little Michelle Dempsey was black, and the fetus her mother
was carrying when they were murdered by Peewee
had a black father.

Peewee began going out of his way to make friends
with Tyner. He started sneaking his new chum gifts
of food, cigarettes, and drugs. Then the little serial
killer asked Cimo to get him some poison. Cimo
was no expert on such subjects, but he searched
through an Encyclopaedia Britannica, and telephoned the South Carolina State Poison Control
Center for advice. He was advised that oleanders
were deadly. The toxic bush grew all over South
Carolina, including his own backyard. So he harvested some oleander leaves, boiled them down, and
smuggled the residue to Peewee inside the heel of a
boot. The grieving bricklayer had been told that just
one leaf was enough to kill a child.

Peewee sprinkled the home-brewed poison on some of Tyner's food. Sure enough, the killer from Harlem got sick to his stomach and turned pale and weak. But he didn't die. It wasn't long, in fact, before he was feeling so good that he was pestering Peewee for soda pop, cigarettes, and a can of Vienna sausages.

An effort to poison his food with an overdose of Thorazine also failed to produce a kill. So some cyanide and strychnine were smuggled into the prison for Peewee. But the death-row hit man was disgusted with poison, and changed his plans. Poison was traditionally a weapon used by women who wished to kill, anyway, and Peewee decided to use a more manly technique to dispose of his latest targeted victim: dynamite!

Peewee passed his order in a profanity-punctuated message to the vengeance-seeking survivor. "I come up with something . . . it can't be no making sick on it. I need one electric cap and as much of a stick of damn dynamite as you can get. I'll take a damn radio and rig it into a bomb to where he plugs it up, that son of a bitch'll go off and it won't be no damn coming back on that."

Cimo was still trying to round up the material and figure out a way to get it into the CCI when Peewee came up with the ingredients himself.

Unknown to Cimo, Peewee had been collecting some other materials as well. He had recorded his telephone conversations with the Murrell's Inlet family man, and planned to use the recordings to blackmail Cimo into turning over much more than the previously agreed murder-for-hire payoff.

Meanwhile, Peewee continued to work on his

murder scheme. He confided to Tyner that he was
going to put together a makeshift intercom they
could use to talk back and forth. That sounded good
to Tyner, and he told Peewee to go ahead.

Soon after that, Peewee passed a blue plastic cup
similar to those used in the cafeteria to the death-
row "tier man" and asked him to give it to Tyner.
The tier man, whose job it was to deliver food,
cleaning implements, and other items to inmates
who were locked in their cells, apparently wasn't
aware that the cup was packed with explosives, but
he did notice a small speaker inside. He passed the
cup to Tyner. Then Peewee busied himself running
a wire from a vent in his cell across a passageway
and through a vent in Tyner's cell.

Desperate to find any respite from the corrosive
idleness of his caged world, Tyner could hardly wait
to try out the ingeniously rigged speaker. As soon as
it was ready, he picked it up, cupped it to his ear,
and, anxious to hear his first message from Peewee,
pushed the plug into the electrical outlet.

The explosion blew away most of his head, as well
as the hand holding the cup.

Cimo heard the welcome news on the radio. He
was pleased, but astonished. He couldn't figure
where Peewee had gotten the explosives and other
materials for the job.

Prison authorities had a pretty good idea who was
behind the dreadful incident that had blown away
the condemned killer before the state could do the
job legally several years, or decades, down the road.
They searched Peewee's cell and found the damning
tape recordings of his talks with Cimo. The poison-

ing attempts were outlined on the tapes, as well as plans for murder by explosion.

In rapid order embarrassed prison authorities began trying to figure out how the deadly explosives and triggering devices were smuggled into the prison; explaining to the press and public why such a bloodthirsty killer as Peewee had the run of death row; rounding up accused conspirators; and preparing for new murder trials.

State Corrections Director William D. Leeke asked SLED to investigate the privileges extended to Peewee by CCI personnel, and disclosed that a new rotation plan had been initiated to move guards around different cell blocks or areas of the prison more often. He conceded that guards had permitted Peewee to obtain an excessive amount of control in Cell Block Two. "We're convinced that there was too much familiarity between Gaskins and prison guards," Leeke said. "They let him do a little more than they should have."

Addressing the presence in the CCI of plastics explosives, prison spokesman Sam McCuen declared that a piece no bigger than a stick of chewing gum would be plenty to carry out the murder scheme. "You could walk through La Guardia Airport with a piece of it stuck to your nose and no one would notice it," he said.

And Leeke pointed out that it will always be difficult to keep contraband from convicts. "It's thrown over the fence to them inside rubber balls in the exercise area," he said. "And it's passed with kisses during visitation and smuggled in inside people's bodies."

Finally, Cimo and a carpenter friend were arrested.

Along with Peewee and McCormick, two other convicts were accused of being linked to the ingenious murder scheme as well.

This time, even other convicts on death row had enough of the murderous little criminal mastermind. They were scared to death of Peewee, and didn't want him around them anymore. Corrections officials also became concerned over his safety after word of the killing spread through the prison grapevine. For his own protection, they transferred him to another maximum-security unit for safekeeping until he could be tried again for murder.

This time Peewee's conviction on charges of murder and of accessory to murder before the fact was swift and sure. The tapes weren't all the evidence the jury heard or inspected, but they were the most damning. On one of the tapes Peewee was heard boasting, "I'm little, but hell, I tote a hell of a knife. I got three of 'em and all kinds of screwdrivers and stuff. I got them needle-nose pliers and I got a big old pair of scissors. . . . I keep plenty of ammunition to fight with now." There seemed to be no question. Peewee had all the tools he needed, as well as freedom of movement, to carry out the contract killing.

The tier man who had passed on the explosives-packed cup to Tyner also testified that after hearing the blast he stepped into Peewee's cell and found him pulling wiring out the bottom of the vent. He said Peewee ordered him to keep his mouth shut, and promised him two hundred dollars for his silence.

When he was asked how well he knew Peewee, the tier man replied: "I guess you'd say we had a onetime relationship."

"What kind of relationship?" he was asked.

"Homosexual," the tier man replied. It was after he had sex with Peewee that he got his privileged job delivering food to other inmates.

The Richland County jury was given an intriguing glimpse into the twisted resourcefulness of Peewee's mind when Solicitor James Anders pointed to a letter the defendant had written asking another inmate to confess the murder to a prison priest. Then the priest could testify at the trial that someone else had confessed, but would be bound by his religious vows not to reveal the identity of the professed killer, Peewee had reasoned.

"Would an innocent man go to that trouble?" Anders asked.

Peewee's defense attorney attempted to paint one of the other prisoners implicated in the plot as the man who masterminded the scheme, then worked with another convict to falsely pin the blame on his client.

Family members, including Peewee's wife, his daughter, and his ten-year-old son, were in court and visited with him during recesses. One time Peewee produced a picture album and smiled and chuckled with them over the family photos.

During summations at the conclusion of the dramatic monthlong trial in Columbia, Deputy Solicitor Richard Harpootlian declared, "The SPCA that puts dogs to sleep—stray dogs are treated better than Gaskins treated Mr. Tyner. I submit to you," he said, "that this defendant is inhuman."

After deliberating only forty-one minutes, the jury of eight women and four men returned a verdict of guilty of first-degree murder, and—after a separate hearing—recommended execution in the electric chair.

Asked if he had anything to say to the court before sentencing, Peewee declined comment. Judge Dan F. Laney then passed sentence, ordering him to be put to death in the electric chair.

Cimo appeared in court for his date with justice, amid an international outpouring of sympathy. But he spared himself and his family the anguish of a showcase trial by entering a guilty plea to a charge of misprision of a felony (not reporting a crime of which he was aware); threatening the use of explosive devices; and conspiracy to commit murder. Even Circuit Judge James M. Morris remarked during sentencing that he didn't consider Cimo to be a hardened criminal who should be imprisoned for a long time. "I do not sympathize or condone what you did, but I understand it. The wheels of justice do turn slowly. There are others such as yourself who would like to see them move more swiftly," the judge said. "But, in order to deter others, I am going to incarcerate you."

Cimo was given a total of twenty-one years in prison, two eight-year sentences and one of five. But it was stipulated that they would be served concurrently, with the consequence that he would become eligible for parole after a little less than three years. Charges against one of the accused coconspirators were dismissed, and short or lenient sentences were ordered for others.

After six months behind bars, Cimo entered a work-release program. In less than three years he was paroled, and he returned home to his family in time to attend a daughter's wedding. He was greeted by his wife and two teenage daughters, other family members, and beaming neighbors. His wife and his girls were holding up a big "Welcome Home" sign.

In 1985, Peewee made news again when he asked a Charleston legislator for help with a plan that would allow him to live out his life on a desert island, or in a jungle.

"You'll volunteer for the North Pole if you think you're going to the electric chair," the legislator replied. But he offered no help with Peewee's latest scheme, and the pint-sized hit man remained locked up in a maximum-security center at the CCI with about one hundred other men considered to be South Carolina's most dangerous criminals.

5 ◆

THE BARFLY KILLER

Carroll Edward Cole
(1946–1980)

Carroll Edward Cole said he hated female barflies who picked up men in taverns and slept with them, because they reminded him of his mother. So he roamed a half-dozen states in the far West and Southwest, looking for pathetic drunks and easy pickups—and murdered them.

The hard-drinking, handsome killer who would later be described by a law-enforcement official as looking like "a squat Clark Gable" smothered or strangled most of his victims. Most were killed after bouts of drunken sex, then sexually assaulted again after they were dead in disgusting acts of necrophilia that sometimes continued for days.

And one time he confessed to a shocked judge and jury that he emerged from the confused shadow land of a lengthy drinking binge to find bits and pieces of a barfly lover he had slaughtered, dissected, and cannibalized. Eventually, Cole was so disturbed and revolted at his own vile crimes that he decided he didn't deserve to live and should be executed.

By his own admission, he had been a killer since he was old enough to read and write.

Cole claimed that his first victim was a playmate named Duane whom he drowned in a pool in Richmond, California, near San Francisco. He was eight years old. The other boy had been teasing him, so he held him underwater until he died. Authorities ruled the drowning an accident.

Even before the drowning, Cole was obsessed with violence, sex, and power. He experimented with his early powers over life and death by periodically choking the family dog into near unconsciousness. He was only seven when he had his first sexual experience with a six-year-old neighborhood girl. And when he was in junior high school he maimed the hand of another boy, who had beaten him in a yo-yo tournament, so badly that it had to be amputated.

By the time he was a teenager he was already an embittered reject who had developed a taste for alcohol and violent sex, and who seemed to have no ambition in life. He dropped out of high school when he was in the eleventh grade and by early 1957 had built up a juvenile record of arrests and other troubles with authorities for curfew violations, truancy, and burglary.

So he enlisted in the Navy, where he would have a chance to develop job skills and perhaps find a career while straightening out his life. It didn't work that way, however. Instead, his perverse behavior continued and in less than two years he was released with a bad-conduct discharge after stealing two .45-caliber pistols from an armory.

Although he claimed that he took the weapons so that he could kill a woman he thought had given him a venereal disease, he sold them to a cab driver. And there was apparently no attempt to get revenge on the woman he blamed for his troubles.

But it was only a short time before he was in trouble again for attempting to kill his first wife by setting fire to a Dallas motel room she was staying in. The murder scheme didn't work, but Cole spent two years in a Texas prison for his efforts.

He wasn't free long before he drifted to Tuscumbia, Missouri, where he got into trouble once more. He tried to strangle an eleven-year-old girl who was an acquaintance, and served part of a five-year-term in a Missouri prison.

The miserable pattern of the movie-star look-alike ex-convict's life had been well established. He was a confirmed drifter and drinker by the time his murderous assaults on females led to another death. The victim was thirty-nine-year-old Essie Louise Buck, and she was just the woman he had been looking for.

He picked her up in a San Diego bar in 1971, and strangled her in his car. He dumped her naked body in a field near the small town of Poway. San Diego County Sheriff's investigators quickly identified the woman and learned that she had left the bar with Cole. By the time they tracked him down, he was in jail in San Diego on a bad-check charge. He was questioned, but no charges were filed against him in the death. Medical examiners had confirmed a high level of alcohol in the woman's blood, and a coroner's report failed to pinpoint a cause of death.

The barfly killer had tasted blood for the first time since childhood, and he liked it.

Cole got married again, this time to a Texas woman. But that didn't stop his wandering ways, his casual boozy affairs, or his alcoholic downward spiral into absolute depravity. Leaving his wife in San Diego, he drifted to Texas, then back to California, and east again to Oklahoma, working occasionally at construction, as an auto mechanic, handyman—and burglar.

In May 1977 Cole was doing part-time construction work in Las Vegas during the day and blowing his money in bars at night when he met a pretty twenty-six-year-old redhead named Kathlyn Jo Blum. They drank at a tavern a short distance from the brightly lighted Las Vegas Strip until nearly midnight, and she readily agreed when he suggested they catch a cab to his apartment, where they could spend the night together.

They were in the parking lot of the apartment complex when Cole turned on his startled companion and clasped his strong hands around her throat in a death lock. He squeezed until her eyes bulged from their sockets, and her body collapsed. He dragged the limp body through the grass and dumped it under a large oleander bush next to an alley. Hungrily, he ripped off her clothing and threw himself on the corpse.

The nude body was found the next morning by a woman walking her dog, and police were called. The victim's neck was so badly mangled that initial news reports indicated her throat had been cut. She had been choked with such force that blood vessels in her throat were ruptured, causing blood to gush outside her mouth onto her neck and breasts, giving the appearance she had been slashed with a knife. But medical examiners concluded after an autopsy that the cause of death was strangulation.

Investigation indicated classic signs of the rape murder of a woman who may have unwittingly marked herself for violent death by heavy drinking and a careless choice of companions. Drag marks were still visible where she had been pulled across the grass, and bruises indicated that she had been grasped by her wrists. Her clothes and few personal possessions—including a pair of cowboy boots, rose-colored wire-rim eyeglasses, and a crucifix—were scattered nearby.

No identification was found among her possessions, and investigators considered the possibility that she might have been a streetwalker who hung around the bars and avenues just off the nearby Las Vegas Strip. She was a long-legged, five-foot, four-inch, 115-pound freckle-faced beauty whose soft auburn hair hung well below her shoulders, and it seemed plausible that she could have been killed by a brutal trick or a pimp.

A fingerprint check revealed, however, that she was Kathlyn Blum, a part-time waitress; she had had her prints taken when she applied to join a restaurant employee's union. And a bartender was eventually found who recognized a photograph shown to him by police as that of a young woman who had been a regular customer for several months. He recalled that she was drinking at the bar before her body was discovered, but although she frequently left with men she met there, he said he couldn't remember if she had found a date that night.

Months later police were confronted with the disquieting possibility that the infamous Hillside Strangler might have moved his operations to Las Vegas from Los Angeles, where he had been littering bodies of young women around suburban streets and hillsides. Homicide detectives contacted officers with a task force formed in Los Angeles to find the Strangler and pointed out that the Kathlyn Blum slaying appeared to be similar to some of those involved in the California investigation. Most of the victims there were found naked, raped, and strangled. The Las Vegas case was similar, but after several grueling weeks of exchanging information and further investigation, the possibility that Miss Blum had been one of the Strangler's victims was ruled out. (Two killing cousins, Kenneth Bianchi and Angelo Buono, were eventually arrested and convicted in the Los Angeles–area sex slayings.)

Meanwhile, as the Blum case file began to gather dust in Las Vegas, Cole had wandered back to San Diego, where he picked up thirty-nine-year-old Bonnie O'Neil at a bar on a late summer night in 1979. They walked a few blocks before he turned and strangled her, just as he had done with Kathlyn Blum. Continuing to mimic the earlier killing, he dragged her a few feet to a more secluded spot in an alley, ripped off her clothes, and raped the corpse.

The next known victim of the barfly killer was his second wife, Diana Faye Cole. The thirty-five-year-old woman's naked body was found propped against a closet wall in her one-bedroom San Diego apartment about a month after Bonnie O'Neil's death. A coroner's report indicated that she had been dead about two weeks when her corpse was discovered and that she had died of a combination of ethyl alcohol poisoning and a liver disorder.

The handsome killer wandered back to Las Vegas, and fifty-one-year-old Marie Cushman died. Cole met the lonely woman at a little neighborhood bar just off the Strip, and after sharing a few drinks they walked to his modest room at the Casbah Hotel. They took a bath together, and made love in the bathtub. They they made love on the bed, before Cole climaxed the erotic encounter by strangling the woman with his hands. He looped a strong cord around her neck and tightened it to make sure she was dead.

The killer had been out of town for hours when a maid found the naked body sprawled on the rumpled bed the next morning.

Cole got caught in a mail-fraud scheme and did a brief stretch in a federal prison in Missouri before he moved into a halfway house for ex-convicts in Dallas late in 1980. While in prison he had been diagnosed as someone who, though capable of distinguishing between right and wrong, chose to break the law; he was not considered to be mentally ill. Nevertheless, by the time he left federal prison, his hard-drinking life on the road as well as his time behind bars and in nearly a dozen mental hospitals had taken a devastating toll. He had lived too long in an alcoholic haze where it was difficult to separate his boozy mirages from the real world. His darkly handsome features had long ago begun to betray the haggard, unshaved look of an alcoholic, and his poor diet and nearly nonstop drinking had turned his five-foot, six-inch frame from lean to scrawny. He was so weak and shaky that any healthy, sober woman his own size would have a good chance of beating him in a fair fight.

But Cole didn't prey on healthy, sober women who could wage a fair fight. He was a scavenger who looked for lonely alcoholics and barflies who were so weakened as a result of their dissolute living that they had no chance of defending themselves. Consciously, or subconsciously, he trolled for victims who were so vulnerable and ill that their deaths might easily be mistakenly attributed to natural causes. They were broken, bruised, and defeated. And most either had lost contact with their families or had no close friends who would create a fuss over their deaths.

As Cole's own health and mental acuity deteriorated in the constant reek of alcohol, the periods between violence grew increasingly shorter. On November 11, 1980, three days after moving out of the halfway house, he choked the life from fifty-two-year-old Dorothy King. Typically, he met the woman in a Dallas bar, and after sharing a few drinks they left together for her home. She changed into pajamas and they went to bed before he killed her.

The next night he picked up thirty-two-year-old Wanda Faye Roberts in a bar and killed her in the parking lot of an apartment complex. They had both been drinking heavily and were thinking romance when the pretty brunette's mood suddenly changed and she began screaming, he later confessed. Frightened and frustrated, he grabbed her by the neck and squeezed until the screaming stopped.

An area resident discovered the body the next

morning when she walked out of her apartment building. The dead woman was lying faceup on the asphalt, wearing only a bra and a blouse unbuttoned down the front. Her slacks were crumpled in a heap under a tree several feet away. They were ripped in front, as if they had been forcibly torn from her body. Her shoes were found in a nearby vacant lot.

In classically unemotional police jargon, investigating officers wrote on the offense report: "It appeared that comp had been dragged to where officers found her. Unknown at this time how comp died. It appeared to be a homicide and possibly a rape."

After a deputy medical examiner found ugly purple marks on her neck, there wasn't much doubt that she was murdered. Someone had strangled her with such force that the outline of the fingers that had curled around her neck could still be made out. Flecks of blood were crusted on her mouth.

Identification found in the slacks revealed the victim's name, and Detective Gerald Robinson began tracing her movements during her final hours of life. Following up information from the medical examination indicating she had been drinking heavily shortly before her death, Robinson armed himself with morgue photos of the victim and began making the rounds of the darkened bars and honky-tonks in the area.

A bartender at a tavern about a block from the parking lot recognized the woman as a regular patron and recalled that she had been drinking there the previous night. He said she may have left with another regular customer named Carroll Cole, who fancied himself as a ladies' man and regularly chatted up the women. Several bewildered survivors of his personally waged holocaust interviewed at the bar and at other dimly lighted watering holes later confirmed Cole's self-image as a ladies' man. He was a charmer. They liked his good looks, gentlemanly manners, and easy sense of humor.

A computerized-records check quickly disclosed that Cole was a well-known police character who had done time in prisons and mental institutions in both Texas and other states. His Texas record, which extended back to 1963, included arrests for auto theft, vagrancy, procuring or pimping, and assault with intent to kill for setting fire to the motel room of his former wife. He had also been in a Dallas hospital a few years earlier following an unsuccessful suicide attempt.

And there were statements by psychiatrists that were truly alarming. One doctor had described Cole as acutely disturbed. His mental examination had indicated that he was a menace to society.

Another psychiatrist observed that Cole felt threatened by females. "He dare not rape the woman of his obsessions. He must kill her first, then rape her," the doctor wrote ominously.

Investigators traced Cole to the halfway house, but learned that he had dropped out of the program only a few days before and apparently vanished. An all-points bulletin was issued for his apprehension.

Cole knew he was out of control, but he didn't know how to stop his kill-crazy descent into madness. Shaken by the latest murder, yet certain that he would kill again, he returned to Miss King's apartment and slept with her corpse.

The woman had been dead for four days when her body was discovered and police were notified. Investigators found her lying faceup on the bed, wearing only her pajama top. Her purse had been rifled and cosmetics and other contents discarded on the floor. There was no money.

An autopsy disclosed that she had such a high alcohol content in her blood that it was possible she died of alcohol poisoning, but suspicious bruises on her throat also pointed to the possibility of strangulation. The cause of death could not immediately be determined.

It was nearly three weeks after the back-to-back murders of Dorothy King and Wanda Faye Roberts that Cole strangled forty-three-year-old Sally Thompson. He met her in an East Dallas tavern, and they returned to her apartment for more drinking and lovemaking at about 4:30 on a warm late-November afternoon. But she rebelled when he suggested that they do some Saturday-night celebrating at a sleazy neighborhood honky-tonk popular with prostitutes. There were angry shouts, and she screamed for him to get out.

"I remembered thinking, Why can't you . . . leave me alone?" he later recalled. "I turned around and grabbed her by the neck and started choking her."

Neighbors were alarmed by the noisy ruckus and began pounding on the apartment door. After a minute or two, an unshaven stranger opened the door. His hair and clothes were mussed and dirty. He was reeking of booze, and his dull eyes stared in bewilderment from the haunted hollows of his sunken cheekbones. The neighbors demanded they be allowed to talk to Sally. Unsteadily, he moved aside, allowing them to walk in.

Sally was stretched facedown on the floor. Her

blue jeans were unzipped and her blouse was pulled up, exposing her stomach and breasts. There was no sign of breathing. One of the neighbors slapped the disheveled stranger. He merely moved over to a couch and slumped down on it, while another of the neighbors left to telephone for police and paramedics.

The man on the couch identified himself to police as Carroll Cole, and he agreed to accompany an officer to the police station for questioning. At the station, he said that he and the woman were preparing to make love and he was helping her take her blue jeans off when she suddenly dropped dead. He claimed he was just about to call for help when the neighbors began pounding at the door. It was not an easy story to accept, but police had to free him after they were advised that the initial medical examiner's report failed to show any evidence the woman had been strangled or poisoned. She was a heavy drinker, and there was a high concentration of alcohol in her blood, giving some credence to the possibility that it was an alcohol-related death.

Robinson didn't learn until late in the day that the lethal ladies' man he had been seeking for three weeks had been in police custody and released. Investigators were aware that his wandering ways could have led him out of Dallas at any time and back on the road, where he might continue his murderous cross-country crusade against barflies for years before running afoul of the law.

But even Cole had finally had enough. He was sickened when, during more lucid moments, he recalled his own squalid atrocities. And he had never made much of an effort to cover up his crimes or his trail. In fact, when he was picked up and questioned after strangling Sally Thompson, he gave police the real address of his room in Dallas.

When police knocked on his door on December 1, he made no effort to get away. He was ready to talk. "I've got something on my mind. I need some help," he told startled investigators.

But even case-hardened homicide detectives who have seen just about everything nasty one human being can do to another, from burning alive to dismemberment, were hardly ready for the talkative suspect's ghoulish recitation of serial murder and necrophilia.

Speaking as easily as if he were having a barroom chat, Cole admitted that he had strangled Sally Thompson, as well as two other women he picked up in city bars in the previous few weeks. And he confessed that he killed several more in other states. His nine-year murder binge had ended at last.

"I need some help. I am tired of killing," he pleaded. "I have been in mental institutions for twenty years, and all I do is get worse. I see a woman with a drink in her hand and I have to kill her."

Cole admitted that details of his murderous wanderings were hazy, and he didn't really know how many homicides he may have committed. "I wouldn't be surprised if I killed thirty-five women," he suggested. "There were a bunch, and I was so drunk much of the time I can't really remember."

The story tumbled out in a dreadful somersault of horror, perversion, and death as he told about murders in San Diego and Las Vegas. And he claimed others, in Casper, Wyoming, and in Oklahoma City, Oklahoma.

He said that in 1975 he met an Indian woman nicknamed Teepee in a tavern in Casper. He bought her a few drinks, and she didn't object when he suggested that they move outside to the privacy of his car. But she objected when he tried to make love to her, so he strangled her. Then he had sex with the corpse.

Experienced law-enforcement officers know that not everyone who confesses murders or other crimes is telling the truth. People falsely confess to even the most dreadful crimes for a bewildering number of reasons. Some are just plain insane, others want publicity at any price, and false confessions are even made in efforts to protect friends, lovers, and family members.

Police are naturally anxious to clear up investigations of serious crimes, especially murder. But they know that it takes more than a confession to prove a case in court. And no police officer welcomes the wasted man-hours and embarrassment that can result from giving too much credence to a false confession.

However, detectives quickly confirmed the Dallas homicides, and murder charges were filed against the confessed killer. Las Vegas police also gave serious consideration to Cole's claims, and arranged to fly a detective to Dallas to question the prisoner.

Authorities in San Diego indicated they would take another, closer look at the deaths of the three women Cole claimed to have killed there as well. But police in Casper and in Oklahoma City were more skeptical, although they dug into their files to reexamine some of their unsolved homicides and deaths from unexplained natural causes.

Dallas had first crack at the confessed serial killer,

however, and in early April he went on trial before State District Court Judge John Mead for the three Texas slayings. Cole pleaded innocent by reason of insanity.

He conceded that he was a man who lived out his sexual fantasies by strangling females he considered to be "loose women." He told the jury that during the previous nine years he murdered women he referred to as "barflies" in Dallas, San Diego, Oklahoma City, Las Vegas, and Casper. He killed them all, he insisted, because he was repulsed by their loose morals and because they reminded him of his mother. "I think I kill her through them," he said.

Cole claimed that he had fantasized about strangling women and having sex with their dead bodies since he was about twenty years old, when he learned that his mother was in the habit of picking up men in a San Diego bar. Earlier he had told police investigators and mental-health experts that his mother beat him when he was a child. "I developed a hatred for prostitutes and women who hung out in bars," he said. "I wanted to strangle them and have sex with their corpses."

Although he formally confessed to killing twelve women in his madcap cross-country murder spree, Cole told the jury during a grueling four hours on the witness stand that he also attacked several other barflies and prostitutes but stopped short of murdering them for a variety of reasons. One woman in San Diego was saved when a police officer showed up unexpectedly, he said. A Dallas woman lived through a choking attack in 1963. And he stopped choking another when he suddenly realized that "something about this ain't right."

Despite the numerous assaults and murders, before confessing to Dallas police he had been questioned by police in only one case: the strangulation of Essie Buck in San Diego.

Turning to the Dallas murders, Cole said that each of his victims there had "come on" to him in bars before he picked them up and killed them.

But the most appalling testimony from the handsome drifter with the salt-and-pepper hair occurred when he confessed on the stand that he murdered and apparently cannibalized a woman in Oklahoma City. He couldn't remember her name, but said he recalled that she was about thirty or thirty-five years old, pretty, and a bit plump. He said he picked her up in a bar on a chilly night in November 1976 and took her back to his cramped one-room apartment for drinking and sex.

"She was like the others. You know, the barfly type—you buy them a couple of drinks and then they go to your place and climb in bed with you," he recited.

Cole testified that when he woke up a day or two later, he was hung over, and lit a cigarette before staggering into the kitchen to make coffee. "Evidently I had done some cooking the night before. There was still a chunk of meat in the frying pan and part that I hadn't eaten on a plate on the table. It looked like it might have been round steak."

Continuing his stomach-churning testimony, he said he went into the bathroom and found the woman's body in the bathtub. A slab of her buttocks had been sliced off, and her feet, hands, and arms were missing.

He said he realized that he must have been responsible, but his memory was vague. Then he returned to the kitchen and peered into the refrigerator. The missing body parts, except for the chunk of flesh sliced from her buttocks, were inside. "I tried to remember cooking and eating her meat, but it was still pretty vague," he said.

Jury members were left squirming in their seats by the gross litany of depravity and evil that spilled so casually from Cole's lips. Some turned pale. Others unconsciously lifted their hands to their mouths, or simply stared at the defendant as if they were wondering if he was indeed human. Cole appeared to be oblivious to the shock and disgust.

Struggling to dredge his memory for facts he could separate from alcoholic hallucinations, he said he vaguely recalled purchasing a hacksaw and several packages of plastic garbage bags from a nearby hardware store. Then he returned to the apartment and spent most of the morning and part of the afternoon cutting the body into small pieces. He said he knocked out her teeth and burned the fingertips of her hands by holding them in a hot frying pan.

Finally, he stuffed the bloody chunks of flesh into the garbage bags and tossed them into dumpsters in the neighborhood. "I don't think they ever found any of the parts, and I never heard anyone say she was missing," he said. "I guess nobody will ever know who she was."

Cole said that although he didn't believe he ever consumed human flesh at any other time, sometimes while having sex with women he had killed he bit them. He remembered the sweet taste of blood in his mouth.

Cannibalism had now been added to the nauseat-

Suzan and James C. Carson, who considered
themselves hitmen for God, being questioned shortly
after their arrest in California in 1983. Convinced that
it was their mission to exterminate witches,
homosexuals, and abortionists, they carried out a
three-year blood spree along the West Coast before
they were stopped. None of their victims were
witches, homosexuals, or abortionists. *San Francisco
Chronicle photo.*

Barfly killer Carroll Edward Cole, 47, shortly before his execution at the Nevada State Prison in Carson City. Cole was convicted of murdering five women, and confessed to thirteen other slayings. *AP/Wide World Photos.*

Conrail Killer Rudy Bladel being escorted by police officers into a Michigan courtroom during his trial for the murder of three railroad employees. *Photo courtesy of Louis Mumford, South Bend Tribune.*

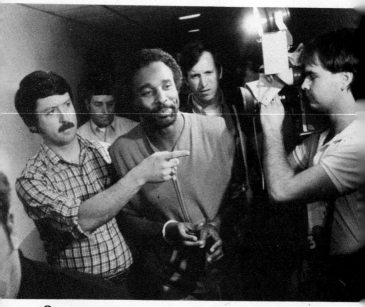

Stocking Strangler Carlton Gary being escorted by police detectives into the Columbus, Georgia, Police Department Headquarters shortly after his arrest. *Ledger-Enquirer Newspapers.*

Army Specialist Fourth Class William Henry Hance being escorted from the Muscogee County Jail in Columbus, Georgia, after his arrest as a suspect in the Forces of Evil slayings. *Ledger-Enquirer Newspapers.*

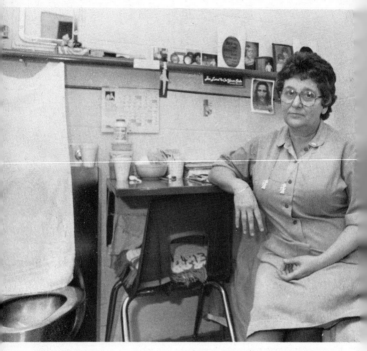

Margie Velma Barfield, in her death-row cell in Raleigh, North Carolina. During six exhausting years on death row her case was reviewed by eight courts and twenty-one judges before she was executed by lethal injection. *Photo by Robbin Hyde, News and Observer Publishing Co.*

Elmer Wayner Henley, Jr., showing police officers the location of bodies of young men buried along a stretch of deserted beach along the Texas Gulf Coast. Henley teamed up with David Brooks (*below*) and Dean Corll in a series of homosexual torture slayings of young boys. *Houston Chronicle photo.*

David Brooks helps police recover bodies. Brooks and his companions in the murder ring were responsible for at least twenty-seven deaths of youths from the Houston area. *Houston Chronicle photo.*

Wayne Clifford Boden, at court in Montreal, Quebec, where he entered guilty pleas to the strangulation sex slayings of three young women during a series of murders by a shadowy man-about-town dubbed the Vampire Rapist by the press. Earlier, Boden was convicted of another slaying in Calgary, Alberta. *Photo by the Gazette.*

ing account of mother hatred, alcoholism, madness, murder, and necrophilia. It seemed there was nothing left to jar the jury with.

The witness did, however, manage one more devilish touch when he told Assistant District Attorney Mary Ludwick that he would like to strangle her, but was controlling the impulse.

Ludwick later referred to those comments when she argued during summations that Cole was not insane at all, but was using insanity as an excuse to avoid prison. Testimony had clearly shown that he carefully planned his killings, and his threat against her from the witness stand demonstrated his true nature, she declared. "He's not insane. He knows exactly what he's doing. He knew exactly what he was doing every time he picked up a victim," she insisted. Cole, she pointed out, had a tendency to exaggerate.

Pointing to medical records introduced at the trial revealing that Cole had told psychiatrists in at least ten mental hospitals in California and Missouri about his compulsion to strangle women and rape the corpses, the prosecution insisted it was all part of a carefully thought-out scheme to escape imprisonment. The talks with psychiatrists had all occurred, the prosecutors noted, after Cole's convictions for assault with intent to kill, arson, mail theft, and car theft.

After two decades of drifting in and out of mental hospitals and prisons, Cole was well versed in psychiatric mumbo-jumbo and game playing. He knew exactly what his therapists wanted to hear.

Defense Attorney Doug Parks read different motivations into Cole's behavior and into his testimony, however. He argued that Cole had repeatedly sought help for his uncontrollable homicidal impulses, but had been let down by a psychiatric system that was found wanting. "The evidence screams out: That is a sick man," Parks declared. He said Cole had been seeking help for twenty years without success.

Parks's fellow court-appointed defense·attorney, Ed Mason, was equally determined to convince the jury that Cole was insane. "Can you call all of this antisocial conduct?" he asked of Cole's loathesome accounts of his murders. "Can you buy that? Murder? Necrophilia? Cannibalism?"

The jury deliberated for twenty-five minutes before rejecting the insanity defense and returning verdicts finding Cole guilty of three counts of first-degree murder. But the panel of ten women and two men recommended against the death penalty. Having found Cole to be a habitual criminal because of two prior felony convictions, Judge Mead subsequently sentenced him to three life terms in prison, with two of the terms to run consecutively. The unusual sentencing schedule meant that the confessed killer would probably have to serve at least twenty-five years behind bars before becoming eligible for parole, although a state parole official was quoted in the local press as saying that technically he could be freed in about half that time.

The forty-two-year-old serial sex slayer was unhappy with the sentence, which permitted him to avoid the Texas state prison system's death row at Huntsville. He insisted that he wanted either commitment to a mental institution where he could be treated for his homicidal obsession, or the death penalty. Law-enforcement authorities in Nevada, which has a reputation for meting out swift, stern, and sure justice to killers, were anxious to help the sex strangler realize his ambition to be executed. They filed murder charges against him, initiated extradition proceedings, and prosecutors announced that they would seek the death penalty.

Despite his grisly confessions to serial murder in five states, no one else indicated much interest in prosecuting him.

Authorities in San Diego said the bodies of the women Cole admitted killing there would be too decomposed to reexamine. Earlier examination had turned up no evidence of suffocation or strangulation, a spokesman pointed out. But another official conceded that it would be possible to smother someone who had been drinking heavily without leaving telltale marks. It would be especially possible if the victim was asleep or unconscious, he added.

In Casper, authorities said they had concluded that Cole could not have committed the murder he claimed there.

Oklahoma City police conceded that they were still carrying some unsolved dismemberment cases on the books that occurred in early 1976, during the time Cole said he was there. But they were equally adamant about their plans not to follow up on his appalling confession.

One of the cases involved the slaying of a young blond woman whose nude body was discovered with a rope around her neck in February inside an abandoned van behind a truck and auto-repair shop. The woman was buried in the city's Resurrection Cemetery under a borrowed name, and it was almost a year after her death before she was identified as

Donna Lea Laughton. Age twenty when she died, she was from a small town in New Hampshire and had been a chronic runaway, hitchhiker, and drifter since she was twelve.

The other slaying was discovered on April 1 when the head and various scattered remains of Arley Bell Killian were found in a vacant house.

But a spokesman for the police department's homicide unit said that Cole wasn't considered to be a suspect in either of the crimes because he was in federal prison when they occurred. And the Laughton woman wasn't killed in the manner that Cole described to police.

Despite Nevada's determination to send Cole to the executioner, because of a bureaucratic mix-up in paperwork it was nearly three years before he was extradited to face trial. And the delay provided Deputy Public Defender Scott Bindrup with an opportunity to argue in pretrial motions that the murder charges should be dismissed because the state waited too long to extradite. The prosecution countered that three years was not an inordinate length of time for a delay and pointed out that Cole himself did not exercise his right to a speedy trial until a few months earlier.

The dismissal motion was eventually denied, and after another ruling finding the defendant to be legally sane, Cole entered guilty pleas to two charges of first-degree murder before District Judge Myron Leavitt. At Cole's request, he was permitted to represent himself in court, although two standby attorneys were appointed to assist him with legal advice if he asked.

Cole declared that he deserved to be executed and

asked that instead of a jury, Leavitt and two other district-court judges selected by the state supreme court be appointed to determine the penalty for his crimes. He reasoned that he would have a better chance of receiving the death penalty with a panel of judges than with a jury.

Tom Pitaro, one of the attorneys appointed to assist Cole, declared that the admitted serial killer was attempting to commit legal suicide. He objected to the court's decision permitting Cole to plead guilty, remarking, "I don't think society can do what an individual cannot [legally] do—kill."

Frank Cremen, the other defense attorney, said of the defendant, "I'm not sure he knows what he's doing."

Psychiatrist William O'Gorman, who interviewed Cole, testified that the defendant told him he wanted to be executed because he didn't have the courage to commit suicide. He quoted Cole as saying he may have killed thirty-four or thirty-five women in various states, and did not want to kill again. "This is the first time I know what I am doing," the psychiatrist said Cole told him of his desire to be executed.

Dr. Franklin Master, another psychiatrist who examined Cole, submitted a report to the court advising that the defendant told him he wanted to be executed because he didn't want to spend the rest of his life in prison. "He states that he is not really afraid of death but is afraid of taking the last walk to the death chamber," the psychiatrist reported. Master quoted Cole as admitting he had no remorse over his crimes, and knew that he would kill again if given an opportunity.

The two psychiatrists agreed after their examinations of the defendant that he was sane and competent to make the pleas.

Over the objections of the defendant, who complained that his rights were being violated, Pitaro was permitted to appear on his behalf during the penalty phase of the hearing as a friend of the court. Pitaro referred to Cole as a "death-wish defendant" and insisted that he didn't have a right to determine his own punishment.

But Cole persisted that he didn't want to be saved. "There's not anything good about me," he said. "I just believe in capital punishment, and I believe it's warranted in this case," he said.

Pitaro declared, however, that society must listen to both sides before imposing capital punishment and insisted that people cannot be permitted to commit what he termed "legal suicide" at a whim.

Despite Cole's determination to die, his chances of being sentenced to execution were cut in half when the three-judge panel ruled that Kathlyn Blum was murdered in 1977, before the new death-penalty law was adopted in Nevada. But Marie Cushman was slain two years later, and her killer could legally be executed by lethal injection. Nevada used the gas chamber to carry out thirty-three executions over approximately fifty years before the law was changed.

At the penalty hearing, the prosecution presented a barrage of evidence tied to Cole's violent past, including information about the murders in Dallas and the strangulation attack on the eleven-year-old girl in Missouri.

When Judge Leavitt announced that the three jurists had decided Cole should be executed for the Cushman murder, the defendant greeted the sentence with a smile. "Thanks, judge" was Cole's only comment. A life sentence was ordered for the Blum slaying.

But pronouncing a death sentence and carrying out the order are two different things. Even when a convicted killer is eager to keep his date with the executioner, appeals can drag on for years. And Cole had a determined court-appointed attorney who was ready to investigate every possible avenue of legal recourse he could think of to keep his reluctant client alive.

Prosecutors were equally bent on seeing that Cole paid the ultimate penalty for his crimes and never had an opportunity to continue his macabre crusade against barflies. They pointed out that he had a record of escapes, and that he said time and again that he knew he would continue killing if given an opportunity.

He told one prosecutor: "I was drunk, but that was no excuse. But I am not sorry for the killings. I have no remorse, and I know I am going to go on killing if I get out of jail."

He told another that his execution would send a message to serial killers that they face death for their crimes.

Although Pitaro and others struggled during the appeals process to save his life, without Cole's co-operation they had little chance of winning. Inexorably he moved closer and closer to the death chamber, and in 1985 an execution date was set for December 6. Predictably, Cole refused to appeal. "I messed up my life so bad that I just don't care to go on," he said.

Even though Cole never wavered in his determination to die, he continued to talk with news reporters about his compulsion to kill and about other serial slayers. "Things are getting so bad out there, people going around killing people. And I just don't believe in that. I never did, even though I did that. With me, it was something that got completely out of hand," he said during a final telephone interview from death row that was carried by the Associated Press.

Cole suggested that a telephone hotline should be established for serial killers, so they could call someone for help in controlling their murderous urges or to confess.

"I wonder how many other people are out there doing the same things and their crimes going undetected?" he asked.

He also stuck to his story blaming his mother for his unholy compulsion to kill, claiming he was emotionally warped by beatings she gave him as a child and by what he said was her boozing and back-alley romancing.

But it was too late for blame or hotlines for Cole. Even three fellow death-row inmates who filed suit seeking a stay for him from the Nevada Supreme Court couldn't prevent his execution.

The last-ditch effort by the inmates was denied, and on December 5, Cole was served the last meal of his choice: fried jumbo shrimp, french fries, salad, and clam chowder.

Shortly after 2 A.M. on December 6, guards strapped him onto a padded table in the converted gas chamber at the maximum-security prison in

Carson City. Relaxed with the help of sedatives administered in his holding cell, he nodded and smiled at a television reporter as he lay down.

One at a time, three lethal chemicals were pumped into catheters leading to both his arms by a team of executioners. As the drugs entered his body, his lips quivered, his eyes closed, and his stomach began to heave. Six minutes later he was pronounced dead. Although the early-morning execution was set to discourage demonstrations, twelve men and women protested in the frigid darkness outside the prison, praying and holding lighted candles.

Cole was the first person in Nevada to be put to death by lethal injection, and the fiftieth person executed in the United States since 1977, when capital punishment was restored. Lethal injection had become the most popular way of executing the nation's worst criminals, with fifteen of the thirty-eight states employing capital punishment using that method.

Pitaro expressed his bitterness at the execution when he told journalists: "Here was an easy guy to kill and so we said, 'Let's kill him.' He got what he wanted all his life. Now he's a big shot."

Cole had given permission for removal of his brain, for examination by scientists researching criminal behavior; about an hour after his death the organ was lifted from his skull by a neurosurgeon at a Carson City mortuary. There were no lesions, cuts, or signs of disease—no evidence of anything that may have prompted his lethal rage against women.

6 ◆

THE CONRAIL KILLER
Rudy Bladel (?–1978)

Someone was killing the men who worked the trains that swept through the towns and cities of southern Michigan and northern Indiana.

For fifteen blood-soaked years, a deadly marksman was looming out of the darkness of the rail yards, picking off trainmen one, two, and three at a time. He rarely wasted a shot.

The reign of terror began shortly after midnight on the sweltering evening of August 3, 1963, in Hammond, Indiana, at the huge rail yards servicing the busy steel mills and oil refineries that dominated industry in the Calumet area before it became part of the nation's rust belt.

In 1963 the mills were still producing a good share of the nation's steel, and the yards were busy day and night with diesels being hooked up to form monstrous trains of fifty cars and longer.

As Virgil Terry walked through the smoke- and ash-tinged gloom of the yards that typified the gray factory towns ringing the southern tip of Lake Michigan, there seemed to be nothing to distinguish the humid midsummer Saturday night from any other. Hulking black shapes of massive engines and cars loomed out of the darkness like metallic dinosaurs from another age. They stood in stark outline against the shimmering red-tinged glow of the blast furnaces silhouetted farther away against the skyline as Terry swung easily up onto a softly humming diesel.

Inside the cab, two other veteran trainmen waited. They were Roy Bottorff, the sixty-year-old engineer, and Paul Overstreet, the forty-five-year-old fireman. Bottorff had been a railroader for forty-three years. Overstreet had twenty-two years on the job.

It took the trio almost an hour to finish coupling onto the fifty-five-car freight and pull it to the far end of the yards, where Terry hopped off. As his companions waited inside the cab, he ambled to a switchman's shanty to call the tower for a clearance to move the train to the Calumet City yards just across the state line in Illinois.

He was instructed by the man in the tower that there would be a short wait for another train to move on, and a few minutes later he received an all clear. Throwing the switch to the main line, Terry waved his lantern in the classic switchman's signal for the engineer to pull his train ahead.

There was no reply to his signal, no indication

from the darkened cab of the diesel that the men inside had seen the swing of his lantern. So Terry began walking toward the engine, continuing to wave his lantern in a go-ahead pattern for the engineer.

Heat lightning flickered in the darkened sky as the switchman approached the engine and the configuration of the engineer's head slowly emerged from the darkness. It was stuck part way out of the side window of the cab. When Terry reached the engine, he climbed onto the machine and moved into the cab, touching the silent engineer on the arm.

It was then that he noticed the blood on Bottorff's face and neck. Shocked, he glanced across the cab at Overstreet. The fireman's face was also smeared with blood. The two trainmen were dead, each shot twice in the back of the head—execution style.

Terry leaped from the engine and ran to a yard speaker, shouting for the yardmaster to immediately send for an ambulance and to notify police and railroad officials that there had been a shooting.

No one had seen the attack. And no one in the busy rail yard, filled with the sounds of humming diesels, the crash of coupling cars, and the rumble of heavy wheels on rails, had heard the shots.

Baffled police investigators would quickly strike out in efforts to come up with a motive for the double murder. There was no indication of a robbery attempt, and there was nothing in the backgrounds of the victims to lead detectives to believe that either of the men had a personal enemy who hated enough to kill. Bottorff was a quietly introspective man who wrote poetry and was a former student at the Moody Bible Institute in Chicago. His fellow crewman was known for relaxing after the noise and activity of his hours aboard the huge locomotives by gardening. Both were married, with four children each. The men were well liked by other railroad employees they had worked with through the years.

About the only solid evidence police were able to gather were four .22-caliber shell casings, two found on the floor of the cab, one inside the engineer's open overnight bag, and one on the ground near the diesel.

Because the trains crewed by the victims were scheduled to cross state lines, they were engaged in interstate commerce—a fact that permitted the Federal Bureau of Investigation to quietly enter the case. But the crack federal agents were no more successful in coming up with leads or motives than were local lawmen.

One of the few things that seemed to add up for the investigators was a suspicion that the mysterious killer was or had been a railroader. The timing of the attack during the few minutes the two victims were alone and unobserved seemed to be too knowledgeable to have been accidental.

Whether or not their suspicions were correct, at that time the investigators were unaware that the double murder marked the beginning of a bizarre odyssey of horror that repeatedly, over a decade and a half, would eventually claim the lives of seven railroaders assigned to the passenger trains and freights that plied some two hundred miles of track between the Chicago-Calumet area and a sprawling complex of rail yards in Jackson, Michigan, to the east.

But it was five years after the trainmen died in

Hammond before the phantom of the rail yards killed again. This time the mysterious gunman selected the Robert Young Rail Freight Classification Yard in Elkhart, Indiana, some ninety miles almost due east of Hammond, to continue his gory vendetta.

A fifty-one-year-old fireman from Niles, Michigan, a picturesque town of about fifteen thousand just across the state line from South Bend, Indiana, was the third railroad man to die.

It was about 4:30 in the morning on August 6, 1968, and John W. Marshall had just completed a trip from Chicago to Elkhart. He signed in at the diesel house and was returning to the locomotive to pick up a duffel bag when the hulking form of a huge man loomed out of the predawn darkness carrying a .12-gauge shotgun. The gunman fired both barrels, and Marshall dropped to the crushed-stone ballast along the tracks with his head smashed by two slugs. Two more slugs had torn into his stomach and into his side.

Alerted by the sound of gunfire, witnesses rushed outside the diesel house in time to see a stocky man wearing overalls and a railroad cap hurriedly walk to a car parked on nearby U.S. Route 33, climb inside, and drive east toward the city.

Again, puzzled police from both local law-enforcement agencies and the railroad had no motive. And no one, apparently, thought to put together the inexplicable attack with the earlier double murder at the Hammond yards.

Then, on April 5, 1976, in the same rail yards at Elkhart, someone murdered James ("Tiny") Mc-Crory. The victim was seated at the controls of his locomotive, parked just west of the engine house, at a few minutes after 1:00 A.M., when he was shot in the head with a deer slug from a .12-gauge shotgun. Fragments of the slug were removed from his head during an autopsy at Goshen General Hospital and were sent, with other undisclosed evidence gathered at the scene, to the FBI Laboratory in Washington, D.C., for analysis.

The fifty-year-old Conrail engineer had been waiting for his fireman, whom he was instructing as a student engineer, to complete paperwork in the engine house before leaving on a run to Blue Island, Illinois, in Chicago's southern suburbs. The fireman discovered McCrory's body lying on the floor of the cab and alerted the dispatcher to call an ambulance.

No one among several railroaders in a nearby diesel shop, and elsewhere along the tracks, heard the shots or any sign of a struggle. Police and fellow employees theorized that McCrory was taken by surprise, because he was a big and powerful man who could have put up a fierce struggle for his life. McCrory lived in Niles, and was a married man with two sons and two daughters.

Faced with the second murder of a train crewman in their city's sprawling Robert Young yards in eight years, police in Elkhart began comparing an intriguing string of additional similarities in the two slayings. They learned that not only were the locations the same but that both victims had lived some twenty miles from Elkhart, in Niles.

Then, during questioning of a railroad-union official, the union man recalled that when he was at the controls of a train in the Hammond yards a few years earlier, his fireman had mentioned the murder of two crewmen there in 1963. The union official said that he recalled having a vague recollection of the killings, but had no reason to attach any special significance to the conversation at the time.

Investigators were suddenly aware that there was a deadly pattern of homicides claiming the lives of railroaders who worked the busy lines in northern Indiana and southern Michigan.

Asked to identify the fireman who brought up the subject of the slayings in the Hammond yards, the former engineer replied that it was Rudy Bladel. The name immediately struck a responsive chord in the mind of Elkhart Police Sergeant David Keck. The police investigator realized that Bladel had once been involved in a shoot-out with another railroader—in the Elkhart yards.

Pulling Bladel's file to refresh his memory, Keck found that the burly train crewman had been convicted of shooting a locomotive engineer in an ambush that carried startling similarities to the string of homicides that had been plaguing the railroads. There were a few major differences between that shooting, however, and the others in Elkhart and Hammond. This time the victim of the surprise assault was not killed and in fact managed to shoot and wound his attacker with the assailant's own gun.

Louis John Sayne had just polished off a steaming cup of coffee at an all-night restaurant and was reporting for work at the roundhouse a few minutes before 4 A.M., on March 30, 1971, for a run aboard a Burlington Northern freight engine to Chicago when a huge man loomed from the pitch-black shadow cast by a large storage tank. Without a word, the stranger began firing at him with a gun, later discovered to be a .357 magnum.

Although Sayne was struck twice in the back and hip, miraculously, it seemed, he was not killed by the two slugs from the high-powered weapon. He was later quoted as saying that his first thought was to run, but he realized that he couldn't outrace bullets, so he whirled and grappled with his attacker. When the gunman tripped over Sayne's overnight bag, the engineer sprawled on top of him, grabbed the gun—and shot him.

The sounds of the shooting and violent struggle brought other railroaders running to help, and the wounded men were transported to a nearby hospital for treatment. Despite the fearsome reputation of .357 magnums, neither of the men was critically injured, a factor credited by authorities to the bullets. They were not professionally made, but were fabricated from a welding rod and coated with wax. If the gunman had gotten away they would have been difficult, if not impossible, for police to trace.

As doctors worked over the pair in the emergency room, Sayne realized that his attacker was a surly, ill-tempered man who had once worked on a train crew with him as a fireman. Sayne recalled Rudy Bladel as a man who sat quietly at his station on the left side of the engine cab, staring straight ahead and rhythmically clapping his knees with his hands in time with the rattle of the wheels on the rails. He didn't chat.

"Why did you shoot me, Rudy?" the five-foot five-inch, 155-pound engineer asked his powerful attacker.

The six-foot three-inch, 270-pound fireman's reply was unemotional and direct. "I did all I could to get the Niles men out of Elkhart."

The somewhat cryptic reply made sense to detectives when they recalled recent railroad history. In 1959 the New York Central moved most of its area rail-yard activities from Niles to the newly expanded yard in Elkhart. Consequently, crews in Niles were cut from twenty-two to five, calling for the layoff of about seventy-five men. Predictably, the crewmen from Michigan objected, complaining through their union and the courts that they had been treated unfairly and that employees from the Elkhart yards should share in the job loss and reductions in job classifications.

When the smoke cleared some fifteen months later, the courts upheld the contractual rights of Michigan workers to follow their jobs to Elkhart. The ruling stipulated that 52 percent of the employment needs at the expanded yards should be filled by men from the Elkhart area, and the remaining 48 percent of the jobs were to be allotted to men from the Niles area.

Railroad men from both yards lost jobs or were reduced in job classifications, according to a formula based on the court-imposed percentages and seniority. Bladel and many other Elkhart railroaders who didn't lose their jobs outright were reduced in job classification and pay or subjected to periodic layoffs. The layoffs not only created a financial burden for Bladel, but were emotionally shattering. He had grown up in a railroad family, and the romantic man's world of steam and diesel engines, the crash of coupling and uncoupling cars, and the clatter of heavy metal wheels on track were his life. His father, Holgar, was a career railroader who was employed by the Chicago, Rock Island, and Pacific Railroad.

Born on Chicago's blue-collar South Side in 1932, Rudy took automotive shop courses at Chicago Vocational High School, and immediately after graduating in 1951 he went to work as a fireman for the same railroad as his father. Although diesel engines had already been introduced to railroading, many steam locomotives were still in use, and as a fireman the burly young man quickly learned what shoveling coal was all about.

But the Korean conflict was raging, and after a few months on the job Bladel joined the Army. He became an Army engineer and was assigned to the job he loved—working with locomotives—in a roundhouse in South Korea. He also became an expert marksman in the Army.

After his enlistment expired, Bladel returned to the Rock Island, gradually advancing in seniority over the years. He was a loner, and when other, more genial crewmen played poker or rummy while waiting for assignments, Rudy would disappear for a short walk by himself. Occasionally other employees would see the hulking giant with his head down, muttering to himself and shambling in his curious gait that slightly favored one leg. His limp was the result of a motorcycle accident shortly after he returned from Korea.

He didn't marry, and if he dated he didn't talk to his coworkers about it. And he wasn't a heavy boozer or gambler. His only interests other than his job appeared to be reading—he was a voracious reader of novels—and tinkering with various inventions and experiments, especially with the use of steam as a power source for automobiles. It was not a new concept and had been tried before, for the most part unsuccessfully. But Rudy seemed convinced that there was a bright future for steam-powered automobiles.

Railroading was the overpowering interest of his life, however, and he had nineteen years in the business by 1971. That was the year he shot Sayne—who was from New Buffalo, Michigan, some twenty-five miles due west of Niles, and thus, in Bladel's mind, part of the hated Niles gang. It was also in 1971 that Rudy was fired from the railroad and went to prison.

Charges of attempted murder were lodged against the sullen trainman, but in a plea-bargaining agreement, he was permitted to plead guilty to a reduced charge of aggravated battery. On New Year's Eve, December 31, 1971, he was sentenced to a one-to-five-year term at the Indiana State Prison in Michigan City. He was released in 1973, after serving eighteen months.

One of the first things he did was try to win his old job back. During a union hearing on his appeal, Bladel explained of his shooting of Sayne that he "only wanted to dust his pants off." That day he also approached his victim, shook his hand, and blandly explained that the attack shouldn't be taken personally—it was just that Sayne was one of the Michigan men.

Bladel didn't get his job back, but he refused to stay away from the railroads. He stalked the tracks and rail yards along the Indiana Harbor Belt, New York Central, and Conrail lines that looped from Hammond at the tip of Lake Michigan through northern Indiana and southern Michigan all the way east to Jackson. He would show up in Hammond and Elkhart in Indiana, or in Kalamazoo and Battle Creek in Michigan, where his menacing figure could be seen and recognized by trainmen, sometimes leaning from an overpass as a train passed underneath. The crewmen were familiar with his bearlike, hulking shape, and they knew his reputation.

Fear among the Michigan men escalated, especially after McCrory's death. Railroad wives began to worry when their husbands left home for work, afraid they might never see them alive again. A few of the railroaders started to quietly carry handguns.

After Keck learned of the 1963 murders and realized there was a pattern of attacks on railroad crewmen in northern Indiana that reached back several years, detectives in Hammond reopened the case there. And a witness was turned up who recalled seeing a big man hanging around the yards, who "walked like a farmer behind a plow, looking down at the ground."

Keck immediately recognized the description of the walk as fitting Bladel's head-down, gorillalike shamble.

Review of the Marshall slaying showed that witnesses had described a similar man—whose husky build and peculiar gait also matched Bladel's.

Law-enforcement authorities put the evil-tempered ex-trainman under close surveillance, and there was more than one sigh of relief when he was arrested on January 6, 1978, for violating federal law—ownership of a firearm by a convicted felon. He had purchased a .357 magnum in South Bend, and police there notified the federal Bureau of Alcohol, Tobacco, and Firearms. This time he drew a one-to-five-year term at the federal penitentiary at Sandstone, Minnesota. He served less than a year and was released on November 16, 1978.

When Keck learned that Bladel was free again, the police officer requested that full-time surveillance be resumed. He was advised that neither area law-enforcement agencies nor private railroad police had sufficient manpower.

Bladel loomed as a solid suspect in the deadly attacks on railroad crewmen, but to suspect him of the killings and to charge and convict him were two different things. The hostile onetime railroader had picked up enough knowledge to police ways during his earlier brushes with the law and his time in prison that he was going to be a tough nut to crack. Even before his troubles with the law, Bladel was a close-mouthed loner who didn't volunteer information. If Keck and other officers were going to get the goods on him so that he could be charged with the slayings at the yards in either Hammond or Elkhart, they would have to work for their information—or there would have to be new shootings and new evidence.

On New Year's Eve, December 31, 1978—exactly seven years after Bladel was first sentenced to prison—two trainmen were warming up in the crew's locker room at Conrail depot in downtown Jackson, Michigan. Fifty-year-old William Gulak, a conductor from the Detroit suburb of Lincoln Park, was writing in a notebook. Forty-two-year-old Robert Lee Blake, a flagman from Southgate, also a Detroit suburb, was relaxing and leaning back in a chair. They had just brought a freight into the yards and were waiting for brakeman Gregory McGowan to return from a restaurant before catching a train for Detroit. Earlier, Gulak had gone to the Amtrak office to get tickets for the three crewmen to catch rides home; McGowan decided he was hungry and asked Blake to go with him to get a cheeseburger. But the flagman decided to wait for Gulak to return, and McGowan left by himself.

Several passengers were in the terminal a few yards away waiting for the 7:15 P.M. Detroit-to-Chicago Amtrak passenger train as the third crewmen relaxed in the warmth of the locker room. Outside, a driving, frigid rain had begun to settle in when a burly man burst into the crew's quarters cradling a .12-gauge shotgun and began blasting away at the startled pair. In seconds the trainmen were crumpled on the floor, their heads shattered by slugs from the shotgun.

Thirty-two-year-old fireman Charles Lee Burton, of Jackson, had the misfortune to be just outside the depot on his way to help crew the run to Chicago when Gulak and Blake were shot. Moments later Burton became victim number three. The killer fired the first burst into the unsuspecting crewman through the crack in the door. Then he fired another shot—execution style, at point-blank range—into the head of the helpless man as he lay sprawled in a pool of blood on the station platform.

A ticket agent alarmed by the commotion in the crew's quarters was luckier. It was almost exactly 6:30 P.M. when he rushed to investigate the noise and was just in time to see a huge individual in a hat and three-quarter-length coat crossing the tracks and walking hurriedly away, carrying what appeared to be a large bag. The ticket agent was two hundred feet or more from the rapidly receding figure, and his vision was obscured by the rain and blackness of the night. Asked later if the person he saw was Bladel, he was unable to make a positive identification. He couldn't tell if the figure was a man or a woman, or black or white.

A neighborhood resident who was a bit of a law-enforcement buff was watching television when he heard a report of the shootings broadcast over his police scanner. He looked out his window just in time to see a bulky man carrying a large case and wearing a three-quarter-length coat walking away from the depot. The householder couldn't see the man's face, but continued watching until the stranger reached the nearby Adams Hotel, unlocked a door, and disappeared inside.

Blake didn't die immediately, but appeared to have little chance of surviving. A Jackson police detective leaned over the mortally injured man in the emergency room at Foote Hospital East as he was being prepared for transfer to the University of Michigan Medical Center in Ann Arbor. As gently as he could, the lawman explained to the injured railroader that he was so seriously hurt that he might die, and asked if he could speak. There was no response. The detective then asked Blake to squeeze his hand three times if he could hear. The injured man squeezed the officer's hand.

Could the assailant have been a woman, the detective asked? There was no response.

Was the gunman a man, he then asked? He got three squeezes—for yes.

Was the gunman a white man? Again there were three squeezes.

Was there only one attacker? There were three more squeezes.

Then the flagman raised one finger and waved it weakly in the air. That was the end of the interview. Blake died about an hour later in Ann Arbor.

Keck was at his home that same night when he learned of the Michigan massacre. His immediate advice to the police officer who called him: "Find out where Rudy Bladel is."

Bladel had been out of prison six weeks, and he was in Jackson. He had checked into a downtown hotel only a short walk from the train depot, on New Year's Eve. Early the next morning he saw his name mentioned in a newspaper story as a man police were seeking to question about the triple murder at the depot. He checked out a few minutes later, and Jackson police caught up with him carrying his suitcase and walking to the Greyhound bus station to return to Elkhart. When officers inspected the contents of the luggage, they found a can of gun oil—and a newspaper clipping about the slayings.

If police had hoped for a confession from the dour, uncommunicative ex-convict, they were disappointed. Bladel appeared to become nervous after detectives told him that a big man matching his description had been seen leaving the depot shortly after the shootings. But he had a ready answer when he was asked why his fingerprints were found in the crew room where the railroaders were slain. He had stopped there to use the toilet before returning to his hotel room, he claimed. The restroom story was good enough, because, in fact, his fingerprints were not found in the depot. Detectives made up the story in an unsuccessful attempt to panic him into making a confession.

And when he was asked if he was the gunman who shot down the three train crewmen, he refused to either confess or deny the crime. Instead, he coldly replied to his interrogators with a two-word challenge:

"Prove it!"

Bladel said little else to his interrogators, except that he had been in the city and checked into the Adams Hotel while he looked for work, but decided to leave after learning that he was being sought for questioning by police. "I figured I don't know what's going on here, but I'd better get the heck out," he muttered.

Scuba divers plunged into the ice-cold Grand River behind the train depot, and helicopters hovered low over nearby buildings as police officers scanned the rooftops. Other officers spread out around the rail yards in a careful search of sidewalks, curbs, yards, garbage cans, and every other location they could think of where a weapon, blood-stained clothing, or other evidence may have been discarded or lost. A single shotgun casing had been retrieved near Burton's body, but no weapon was found. The shell casing was sent to the State Police Laboratory in Lansing, Michigan's state capital, for tests.

Shortly after the shooting the press reported that a police dog had tracked the killer to a location near the depot where he was thought to have been picked up by a waiting car. Lieutenant Ronald Lowe, chief of the Jackson Police Department's detective bureau, quickly scotched the report as false. A canine officer and dog were indeed on the scene, but there were no tracks followed to a location where the killer might have been picked up by a car. Lowe pointed out that the shooting occurred during a driving rainstorm, and the dog handler couldn't ascertain with any certainty whether or not the dog had picked up any scent at all.

Bladel's clothing was stained with what appeared to be human blood, and he had no ready explanation for its presence. But the blood couldn't be matched to that of any of the shooting victims, and forty-eight hours after he was taken into custody, Bladel was released without charges. He returned to Elkhart, where he worked intermittently delivering trucks and mobile homes for a dealer there, and as a dishwasher, riding a bicycle back and forth to his job.

Bladel lived at the Faith Rescue Mission for homeless men, and during his free time spent hours quietly browsing through newspapers, magazines, and books at the Elkhart Public Library. His reputation at the mission was the same as it had been all his adult life, that of a quiet loner.

The mission was where Louis Mumford, an energetic veteran reporter assigned to the Niles bureau of the South Bend *Tribune*, found him. Mumford telephoned the mission and left a message requesting Bladel to telephone him collect, in Niles. The reporter later confessed to being mildly surprised when Bladel complied and said that he would be happy to talk with Mumford in Elkhart.

"He was a frightening man," Mumford later recalled. "I think I was most impressed by his eyes—they looked dead. And he seemed to be completely

emotionless when he talked about all the killings of
railroad men. When I asked him if he was responsible for any of the murders of railroaders, he just
looked at me with those cold eyes and said, 'I'm not
going to admit to that.' "

But when Mumford continued to press for a statement about the string of shootings, Bladel commented, "They should have thought of that before
they took the jobs away from the Elkhart men." The
down-and-out ex-railroader readily admitted that he
held a grudge against his old employers and the
union because of layoffs tied to the 1959 realign-
ments. But he denied that his anger stemmed from
actions bumping him from engineer to fireman. He
wasn't even examined to become an engineer until
1965, he explained.

"But the men at Niles were hired to work Elkhart
jobs," he complained. "We were put out of work. . . .
The Michigan men pretty much had our jobs all the
way down the line."

While being careful not to indicate that he had
anything to do with the shootings, Bladel said he
believed the 1968 murder of Marshall was prompted
by an effort to emphasize the resentment over the
manner in which jobs were shuffled as a result of
the rail-yard merger. He admitted that the job shuffle
led to his shooting of Sayne in 1971. And he acknowledged that he had fabricated the bullets used
in the shooting, because he was seeking only to draw
attention to the flap over the job situation. "I didn't
want to kill him," he claimed.

Bladel firmly closed the door on any chances of
making a similar confession to the shootings in
Jackson, however. "They asked a bunch of questions,

but they got no answers," he said of his brush with police in Jackson. "They're not about to cooperate with me, nor me with them. It's all right for them to do their job, but not for me to do my job."

The interview was disquieting for Mumford. "He had a completely cold, detached manner that I've never seen in anyone in his circumstances before," the reporter recalled. It was an attitude and manner that had been noted before—by police in two states.

Approximately three weeks after the Jackson slayings, Lieutenant Lowe met in Indiana with a dozen police officers from Hammond, Elkhart, and the Elkhart County Sheriff's Department to compare information about the railroad murders. When the two-hour session broke up, the consensus was the same as it had been at the beginning of the conference: All seven of the railroad murders carried enough similarities that they seemed to point to the same killer. But no one had sufficient evidence to make an arrest.

On March 10, Bladel boarded a bus in Elkhart and rode back to Jackson. Police were waiting for him, and followed him closely while he wandered some twelve miles of city streets. Eventually, he abandoned his seemingly aimless walkabout and returned to Elkhart.

Eight days later Jackson residents found pieces of a broken .12-gauge Remington shotgun in some brush under melting snow in Cascade Falls Park. A young woman and a friend were riding a motorcycle when they spotted part of the weapon lying half hidden in some bushes. A pedestrian found the other piece a short distance away. At one time during

Bladel's curious walk around Jackson, he had come to within about a mile of the park, but no closer.

A trace of the weapon's serial number identified it as a shotgun purchased by Bladel in an Elkhart gun shop on New Year's Eve in 1976—exactly two years to the day before the triple slaying in Jackson.

The day after the shotgun was found, a policeman returned to the park and picked up a green parka lying near a fence. It was sent to the Michigan State Police Crime Laboratory in Lansing for tests.

A warrant was issued by Judge Robert Crary in Thirteenth District Court in Jackson, naming Bladel on three counts of first-degree murder. A few hours later he was apprehended by Conrail security officers as he walked along a downtown street in Elkhart looking for a job. The Conrail officers, who had been keeping Bladel under surveillance, held him until city police arrived and took him into custody on the warrant.

Bladel waived formal extradition proceedings in court and agreed to leave Elkhart with two Jackson police officers, who escorted him back to Michigan. Unshaven and shackled at the waist, hands, and legs, Bladel nevertheless mugged for the cameras and smiled and waved at reporters he recognized when he was escorted into Jackson police headquarters. He was jailed without bond.

Once he was in custody, the usually taciturn suspect was surprisingly talkative to the press, and in an interview with a Jackson newspaper reporter he said he had wrapped his shotgun in a parka and thrown it away in the rail yard. Someone else must have recovered it and used it to kill the three trainmen, he suggested.

He continued to make news when police announced a few days later that they had uncovered an escape plot in Bladel's cell block, and moved him to an individual cell where he could be kept under closer surveillance. Although they couldn't connect the accused killer of involvement in the breakout scheme, officers said, they thought it would be best to move him.

During his arraignment in Jackson County Circuit Court Bladel stood mute, and a plea of not guilty to the three counts of murder was entered for him. He indicated to the court that he was practically penniless and wanted a court-appointed attorney to represent him. Three days later—before a defense attorney could be appointed and meet with him, however—he confessed in his jail cell to the triple slaying at the depot. Asked by detectives if he wanted an attorney before talking with them, he replied: "I don't need an attorney." He also signed a form waiving his right to have an attorney present, before making the confession.

Testifying at a hearing in Jackson County District Court approximately three weeks after Bladel's arrest, Lieutenant Lowe read what the detective chief said was a handwritten statement by the defendant. It read:

"On December 31, 1978, I walked into the hot room at the Jackson Depot and shot three men to death. I then went back to my hotel room and got rid of the gun. The reason I shot the men is that the railroad took my job and other Elkhart [Indiana] men's jobs."

Lieutenant Lowe testified that Bladel had also made a verbal confession on March 26 during ques-

tioning by police. The written statement was prepared after Bladel was confronted with specific scientific evidence linking him to the murders, Lowe
said. The detective chief identified that evidence as
metallic particles found in the shotgun and in Bladel's suitcase and clothing when the burly trainman
was picked up in Jackson on New Year's Day.

Lowe said that Bladel told him and Sergeant Richard Wheeler that he left his hotel room in Jackson at
about 6:15 P.M. on New Year's Eve carrying a suitcase
containing the shotgun. Continuing to read from
the written statement, Lowe quoted Bladel as confessing: "I went down on the platform, set the suitcase down, walked in the door at the right, and shot
the man sitting by the door [Blake].

"Then I shot the man at the picnic table [Gulak].
I shot each twice. Then the other man [Burton] came
to the door and I went out and shot him. I walked
out and shot him in the head."

Bladel said that he then returned to his hotel
room, and got rid of the gun.

The forty-six-year-old Bladel was ordered to stand
trial on three charges of first-degree murder. At a
pretrial hearing Jackson Circuit Court Judge Russell
E. Nobel ruled that the confession could be used.
The ruling placed a devastating piece of evidence
firmly in the hands of prosecutor Edward J. Grant.

When the trial itself got under way less than four
months after Bladel's arrest, it was held some two
hundred miles upstate from Jackson, in rustic Gaylord, Michigan, a small town of about three thousand. Judge Nobel had agreed to a change of venue
after considering a motion by Douglas L. Williams,
Bladel's defense attorney, who complained that the

heavy publicity in the Jackson area following his client's arrest would prevent a fair trial there.

By the time a jury was ready to begin listening to evidence, Bladel had recanted his confession. He said that he consented to make the statement only after caving in to police pressure. "Two guys grilling me like that. I about cracked up," he whined.

The confession, nevertheless, had been ruled admissible, and loomed as a key component in the prosecution's case. The presence of the shotgun, which had been so conclusively traced to Bladel and which laboratory tests had shown to be the murder weapon, was another telling element of evidence against the burly defendant. And it took a jury only ninety minutes of deliberation at the conclusion of a weeklong trial to return guilty verdicts against Bladel on all three counts of first-degree murder.

A young woman juror told reporters that she thought the huge bespectacled ex-trainman looked like a killer. "He did look like he could have done it," she said. At first, before fully reviewing the evidence against him, she and two other jurors were a bit unsure of his guilt, she admitted. "I had a couple doubts in my mind," she said. "But we went back over it, and the evidence just was enough to prove to me he was guilty."

A few weeks later, Judge Nobel announced the mandatory penalties according to Michigan law at that time for conviction on three counts of first-degree murder—three life sentences in prison, to be served concurrently without parole. In pronouncing sentence, the judge declared: "Those killings were senseless, but not without motive. They were the result of a long-standing, festering resentment against the railroad. You chose to avenge yourself by brutally killing three and probably would have killed more, if they happened to be present—defenseless and innocent railroad employees."

Judge Nobel recommended that Bladel never be considered for executive clemency. Individuals convicted of first-degree murder in Michigan were not eligible for parole, and sentences could be commuted only by action of the governor, according to the law at that time. Bladel was sent to the State Prison of Southern Michigan in Jackson, only a few miles from the depot where the three Conrail employees were shot.

Bladel and his attorneys began working on the lengthy round of appeals that invariably follow capital murder convictions. The appeals centered on claims that he had involuntarily waived his right to consult an attorney during questioning by the Jackson police. And in order to obtain a confession, it was claimed, he was forced to wait four days before consulting a lawyer.

Six years later the Michigan Supreme Court reversed Bladel's convictions and ordered a new trial. The high court ruled that his confession was improperly obtained because he was questioned before being allowed to consult with a court-appointed lawyer after requesting at his arraignment that he be provided with legal representation.

The court wasn't impressed by the waiver Bladel signed, or his verbal statement rejecting his right to have an attorney present when he met with police the day he made his confession. "It makes little sense to afford relief from further interrogation to a defendant who asks a police officer for an attorney but permit further interrogation of a defendant who makes an identical request to a judge," it was noted in the decision.

Earlier, the Michigan Supreme Court ordered the State Court of Appeals, which had upheld the convictions, to take another look at the case. The second time around, the appeals court voted to reverse the conviction—and that ruling was upheld by the Michigan Supreme Court.

The prosecution was shaken by the development, and indicated that it would be difficult to obtain a new conviction without the confession. "At best, we have only a very circumstantial case. The only eyewitness was killed at the scene. A gun purchased by Bladel several years earlier was found in the city after the shootings and the markings on the cartridges at the scene matched the gun. But whether it will be enough to convict him again or not," a spokesman confessed, "I don't know."

But he vowed to carry on with a new trial. "We are not going to allow him to slip out in the middle of the night."

Before settling in for a new trial, however, the prosecution filed an appeal of the Michigan high court's decision with the U.S. Supreme Court. The Jackson County prosecutor argued that the U.S. Supreme Court had ruled in earlier cases that confessions obtained under similar circumstances were permissible.

The U.S. Supreme Court voted several months later by a six-to-three margin to uphold Michigan's high-court decisions voiding the confession. "If police initiate interrogation after a defendant's assertion, at an arraignment or similar proceeding, of his right to counsel, any waiver of the defendant's right to counsel for that police-initiated interrogation is invalid," wrote Justice John Paul Stevens in the court's majority opinion.

Dissenters on the panel asserted that the court was going too far in protecting the rights of the accused. "There is no satisfactory explanation for the position the court adopts in this case. The court lacks a coherent, analytically sound basis for its decision," Justice William H. Rehnquist wrote. He was joined in the dissent by Justices Sandra Day O'Connor and Lewis F. Powell. Chief Justice Warren E. Burger and Justices William J. Brennan, Thurgood Marshall, Harry A. Blackmun, and Byron R. White joined Stevens for the majority.

Although siding with the majority, even Chief Justice Burger wasn't totally happy with the decision. "At times," he wrote, "it seems, the judicial mind is in conflict with what behavioral—and theological—specialists have long recognized as a natural urge of people to confess wrongdoing."

Nevertheless, Bladel's conviction had been effectively and finally overturned, in a decision that broadened a far-reaching 1981 ruling in which the court prohibited police, prior to arraignment, from questioning suspects who had asked for an attorney.

Even then the tortuous legal jockeying continued to delay a new trial, and led to another court decision that appeared to cripple the prosecution's case. Judge Nobel, who again had been picked to preside at the new trial, ruled that much of the evidence against Bladel had been obtained illegally. The important fibers linking the defendant's suitcase and the shotgun could not be used in the new trial, the jurist declared. Consequently, the only admissible evidence left linking Bladel to the shotgun were papers he signed when the weapon was purchased.

It seemed that the odds had shifted dramatically— and the changes weren't in favor of the prosecution. Grant, who had again been designated to prosecute the case, remarked that the state had lost about 80 percent of its evidence, and gloomily admitted that it seemed doubtful if—under the circumstances—a new conviction could be obtained for the triple killings.

The picture changed one more time, however, when the Michigan Court of Appeals ruled that Jackson police had indeed had probable cause to take Bladel in custody in New Year's Day 1979, with the result that more evidence, including the suitcase with the telltale fibers, was admissible.

Grant conceded to Mumford that chances of another conviction had taken a definite turn for the better. "I'm a little more optimistic—but it's still a toss-up," he said.

At last the case had completed its circuitous path through the higher courts, and both sides were ready for the new trial. It was scheduled to be held in Kalamazoo, Michigan.

A bustling manufacturing city and college town of approximately eighty thousand, Kalamazoo is due east across the state from Jackson and almost exactly midway between Detroit and Chicago. The city where the man some police officers and court watchers were now irreverently referring to as "Shotgun Rudy" was to be tried a second time for the murders of three trainmen was also a railroad town. And it's only about sixty miles northeast of Niles.

This time the gray-haired defendant, a prison pallor visibly showing after eight years behind bars, was represented by Wendell Jacobs, of Jackson. Jacobs confided to Mumford that he planned to argue that the prosecution's case was circumstantial and the state could not prove to the jury that Bladel was guilty beyond a reasonable doubt. Bladel would not testify, and his attorney did not plan to call any defense witnesses.

In his opening statement, Jacobs compared the case against his client to a jigsaw puzzle. And he promised the jury, "You'll find there are pieces missing."

Since the first trial, in 1979, three of Grant's witnesses had died, but he was able to introduce transcripts of their testimony as evidence. And he took full advantage of the renewed admissibility of the green plastic or vinyl flakes found in the suitcase confiscated from Bladel.

Detective David Townshend, from the Michigan State Police Crime Laboratory in Lansing, testified that the flakes taken from the suitcase were similar to others found in the shotgun. The firearms expert also stated that tests had shown that markings on one of the spent shotgun shells found at the scene of the triple slaying showed positively that it had been loaded into the magazine of the weapon recovered from the park.

Earlier witnesses called by Grant reestablished that Bladel was in Jackson the night of the slayings. Turning to New Year's Day, after Bladel was picked up by officers, Detective Gerald Rand, of the Jackson Police Department, testified that Bladel told him he had come to the city two or three days before to look for a job. (The questioning occurred before Bladel's arraignment, when he indicated a desire for an attorney.)

"I told him that it was odd for a holiday weekend," Rand stated. "He said he intended to stay until the second [January 2, 1979], but a newspaper story that outlined the shooting mentioned him by name and he decided to leave."

Rand said that when he told Bladel that one of the victims was survived by a widow and four young children, the burly ex-con replied: "They should have thought of that before they took my job."

Bladel's defense attorney suggested that someone else may have killed the train crewmen during an aborted robbery attempt. "It's possible someone was there committing a robbery and was caught by Burton," Jacobs said. "They may not have had time to take the wallets." Police had ruled out robbery as a motive early in their investigation, and concentrated their efforts on Bladel and his resentment of the Michigan railroaders.

During closing arguments, Grant reminded the jury of that resentment and of the fact that the defendant's anger had apparently not softened over the years. The prosecutor said that Bladel mailed a letter to the railroad only about five months before the beginning of the trial in an apparent bid to get his former job back. The letter expressed the same bitterness Bladel had expressed in earlier communications with the railroad.

The jury deliberated only two hours at the conclusion of the four-day proceeding before returning with unanimous verdicts of guilty to three counts of first-degree murder. Unflappable as he had been when he heard the guilty verdict eight years earlier, Bladel indicated reluctant acceptance of his fate, mumbling: "I guess I'm all done. . . . It's over with." But when he was pressed by reporters to tell them if he had, indeed, murdered the three crewmen in Jackson, he shook his head no. Ever hopeful, he suggested, "Maybe I've got an appeal."

Judge Nobel again sentenced Bladel to three mandatory life terms in prison, without parole. He is serving the sentences in the State Prison of Southern Michigan at Jackson.

Despite the efforts of police to clear up the railroad murders in Indiana after his earlier murder convictions, Shotgun Rudy was no more helpful then than he was after the guilty verdicts in Kalamazoo.

Sergeant Keck said he believed Bladel owed it to the families of the victims of the earlier murders to confess if he was guilty. But there was no confession to Elkhart police, or to detectives from Hammond who had also asked, before the Gaylord convictions were set aside, for Bladel's help in clearing up their railroad murders. A Hammond officer was later quoted in the press as telling the shooting suspect when they sat down in prison together to talk, "Look, Rudy, you're doing life. What have you got to lose?"

Bladel grinned at him, folded his beefy hands on his stomach, and challenged: "You're a cop. Prove I did it!"

No one ever has—but there have been no more of the railroad killings since Bladel's arrest following the Jackson slayings.

As of this writing, no one has been charged in the murders of the four trainmen killed in Hammond and Elkhart. Consequently, Bladel must be presumed innocent of those slayings.

7 ◆

THE STOCKING STRANGLER AND THE FORCES OF EVIL

Carlton Gary and
William Henry Hance
(1977–1978)

Wynnton was the Old South, a comfortable, sheltered community of stately mansions, tree-shaded streets, colorful, well-tended azaleas, and the genteel company of pleasant neighbors who could be thankful they lived there instead of down the hill in other, busier, brasher neighborhoods that make up the sprawling West Georgia city of Columbus.

Even before Columbus became a city, Wynnton existed. Named for Colonel William L. Wynn, who settled in the area in 1834, it became the community where people of substance lived, ladies and gentlemen who could appreciate their isolation from the raucousness and frontier violence that whirled around them.

Violence finally caught up with Wynnton in 1977, though, when a savage and merciless killer began an eight-month reign of terror that changed the community forever.

Seven women—widows and spinsters ranging in age from sixty to eighty-nine—died in a vicious rape-murder spree blamed on a single killer whom the press, and eventually the police, referred to as the Stocking Strangler. And in a curious instance of evil sparking evil, a second killer emerged to take the lives of younger women in acts that he claimed were retaliation for the Stocking Strangler's murderous rampage. He called himself the Forces of Evil.

Mrs. Ferne Jackson was the first to die. It was late morning on September 16 when a relative discovered her body in the bedroom of her single-story brick home. The youngest as well as the first of the victims, the sixty-year-old widow had been savagely beaten, raped, and strangled in her bed with one of her own silk stockings.

Investigators with the Columbus Police Department quickly determined that a sliding glass patio door had been forced open, apparently by the killer. Palm prints were found on the glass door, but there were few other clues.

As officers fanned out through the neighborhood to question area residents about anything suspicious they might have seen or heard, the body was examined by the Muscogee County coroner. Strangulation was confirmed as the cause of death, and samples of pubic hairs and semen were forwarded to the Georgia State Crime Laboratory in Atlanta for tests. There was no indication that valuables were stolen from the home, although Mrs. Jackson's car was taken and abandoned several blocks away. The vehicle was towed to the police garage, where crime-scene technicians went over it for fingerprints, but only those of the owner showed up.

The victim was a highly respected public-health educator who was well known in the community for helping to teach thousands of Columbus teenagers about sexual development and family planning. She was responsible for initiating courses on those subjects in the public schools, and had conducted a health-education program at a local church just two nights before her murder.

The vicious rape slaying was a shocking crime. But it was just the beginning.

Eight days after Mrs. Jackson's death, a neighbor looking for Jean Dimenstein to share coffee and conversation stepped onto the scene of another savage murder. Like Mrs. Jackson, the seventy-one-year-old retired clothing-store owner had been brutally beaten, raped, and strangled with one of her own stockings. Miss Dimenstein had lived by herself, only twelve blocks from the first murder site. And again, a window was forced by the intruder to gain entry. Her car was also stolen, and abandoned near the location where Mrs. Jackson's vehicle was dropped off.

On October 1, Columbus police were called to the home of Beatrice Brier. The fifty-five-year-old woman had been beaten, then stabbed to death. As alarm spread through Columbus, police were faced with the question of whether or not her murder was the latest in what seemed to be shaping up as the ugly handiwork of a depraved serial killer.

Although there were some similarities between Mrs. Brier's slaying and the two earlier homicides, there were important differences that indicated more than one killer might be at work. The Brier woman didn't live in Wynnton, and she wasn't strangled with a stocking as the other two victims were. There were other differences, as well.

Within twenty-four hours after Mrs. Brier's body was found, police arrested Jerome ("Duck") Livas, a slow-witted man who had dated her. The next day, Columbus Mayor Jack Mickle appeared on a local television broadcast, where he revealed that police had a suspect in the Stocking Stranglings. The news media quickly focused on Livas, and at a press conference police officials confirmed that he was a suspect in the serial killings. The twenty-five-year-old man was safely behind bars, and people in Columbus, especially older women who lived alone in Wynnton, began to relax.

Then a shocked relative found Mrs. Florence Scheible murdered in her duplex apartment. The oldest of the victims at eighty-nine, the frail widow used a metal walker to get around, was almost totally blind, and had been completely defenseless when the killer climbed through a window to beat, rape, and strangle her with a silk stocking.

The old woman was in her bed, sprawled on her back with her dress pulled up over her hips, the stocking still twisted around her neck. Her head and face had been smashed with heavy blows from a fist or blunt object, and the bedding was blood soaked. Investigators collected semen samples and pubic hair, which were sent to police laboratories. A single thumbprint that appeared to be that of a man or woman much larger than the victim was lifted from the bedroom door. An autopsy and other information developed by the investigative team indicated that Mrs. Scheible was probably attacked around noon.

Although the leading suspect in the horrifying serial murders was in jail when she was strangled, rumors circulated throughout the city that her death may have been a copycat killing inspired by the earlier slayings or by efforts of friends of Livas to throw investigators off the track.

Police, however, were quickly able to discount those theories because their investigation of Mrs. Scheible's death uncovered too many similarities to those of the Jackson and Dimenstein women. One, which only they and the killer knew about, was the distinctive knot used to tie the stockings around the victims' throats. Livas may have been the killer of Mrs. Brier, but he was not the Stocking Strangler.

Extra police cars were assigned to patrol Wynnton at night. Some older women who had relatives and close friends in the area moved in with them. And all over Columbus, but especially in Wynnton, people began to beef up personal security around their homes. So many new locks were sold and installed in private homes that local locksmiths couldn't keep up with the demand. Some locksmiths whose success had been marginal later admitted the Stocking Strangler was personally responsible for keeping them from going out of business.

One of the Wynnton residents who put in a new lock was sixty-nine-year-old Mrs. Martha Thurmond, who lived alone and had occupied herself with her own quiet pursuits since retiring a few years earlier from teaching school. But the new dead-bolt lock was installed backward, and only four days after Florence Scheible died so horribly, Mrs.

Thurmond was found dead. A neighbor who dropped by to see why she didn't answer her telephone found the front door ajar and the bolt mechanism dismantled and hanging out.

Like the others, the former teacher was beaten, raped, and strangled with a stocking. The county medical examiner later remarked that her skull was so badly shattered by the beating that she resembled victims of airplane crashes or car wrecks.

Investigators found a sheet of paper with a seven-digit number scrawled in large letters taped to the wall over the victim's telephone. It was the number of the Columbus Police Department.

As usual, the murderer left few clues behind, except for a single fingerprint on a bathroom window frame. Police found traces of peppercorns and coffee grounds along what they believed to have been the escape route, an apparent effort to eliminate his scent and confuse tracking dogs. Police were using bloodhounds around the slaying sites.

Newspapers and radio and television reports were filled with stories of the phantomlike marauder who materialized out of the night to rape and murder, then quietly faded back into the protective darkness, leaving hardly a clue behind him. As the fear spread and Wynnton residents shared their terror and their torment, churches held special prayer services, both for the dead and for the safety of the living.

The Reverend William Hinson, who was then pastor of the Wynnton United Methodist Church, later remembered the period as a time of terror. "It was a nightmare for the whole community," he said. "I saw warm, friendly people become suspicious and closed. I saw little ladies carrying pistols in their purses."

Utilizing information from a neighbor of Mrs. Thurmond who reported seeing a suspicious young black man near the house, a police artist developed a composite drawing, which was released to the news media and circulated by officers.

And a local newspaper ran a jailhouse interview with Livas, in which he confessed that he had assassinated Presidents John F. Kennedy and William McKinley, as well as kidnapped the Lindbergh baby and murdered the long-missing Manhattan judge Joseph F. Crater. By that time, law-enforcement authorities had long since ruled out even the slightest possibility that Livas was the Stocking Strangler.

Columbus police were looking elsewhere for suspects, while adding scores of officers to the case to help with hundreds of interviews and other elements of the rapidly burgeoning investigation. They announced a fifteen-thousand-dollar reward for help in bringing the killer to justice, and called on the expertise of the Georgia Bureau of Investigation, which entered the case.

Shortly before Christmas, the mayor announced at a news conference that police were forming a special Stocking Strangler Task Force to coordinate the work of the various law-enforcement agencies and to organize and make use of the vast amount of information collected in the case.

Three days after Christmas, the body of seventy-four-year-old Mrs. Kathleen Woodruff was found in her Wynnton home by a housekeeper. The maid arrived for work about 10:30 A.M. and noticed that the light was on in Mrs. Woodruff's bedroom, but assumed she was merely sleeping late and began to prepare breakfast. After a half hour and still no indication that her employer was getting up, however, the maid walked into the bedroom and discovered the body on the bed.

The widow of George C. ("Kid") Woodruff, a millionaire Columbus industrialist and former University of Georgia football coach, the victim had been beaten, raped, and strangled. This time the strangler had not used a stocking, but instead killed with a red University of Georgia scarf. A chair was overturned in the sitting room, and Mrs. Woodruff's car was stolen.

A latent left palm print and a print from a little finger were found on a window screen and the sill where the intruder broke into the house.

The next day, Mayor Mickle announced that a veteran Columbus police officer, Detective Ronnie Jones, would head the Strangler Task Force. Jones said that a strangler hotline was being established, which citizens with tips could use to call investigators anonymously. Task Force officers would also disseminate information to citizens about how they could protect themselves.

A psychiatric profile of the killer was developed by doctors and criminologists, who decided that the Strangler was probably a young male about fifteen to twenty-five years old and at least five feet, ten inches tall. Psychiatrists believed he was likely a quiet person, possibly even withdrawn, a loner who rarely displayed anger, especially with girls. Largely because of the age of his victims, they suspected that he may have been raised by a grandmother, an aunt, or another elderly female relative.

Theories were bandied back and forth by investigators, the news media, and private citizens smarting under the mantle of fear that had settled over the city. Was the killer a gerontophobiac, who hated but lusted for the elderly? Or was he merely a cowardly, sex-mad prowler who sought out the weakest, most vulnerable victims he could find for rape and murder?

Some speculated that the killer was a young white man who grew up in Wynnton and had recently been released from prison or a mental institution. There was even talk that police or city officials knew who the killer was but were covering up information and protecting him because he was from a prominent family.

There were other suppositions. One psychologist suggested that the killer may have worked in Wynnton, possibly as a yard worker or delivery man.

Information from the medical examiner and pathologists disclosed that the Strangler's blood type matched that of about 20 percent of the population, and both his hair and sperm were normal. Impressions of footprints found at one of the murder sites indicated that he probably wore a size-ten shoe. Evidence was slowly accumulating, despite the killer's best efforts to hide his tracks.

But the new year dawned without either another murder or an arrest.

Then, on February 12, an intruder broke into the home of Ruth Schwob, a prominent Columbus woman known throughout the city as a wealthy patron of the arts. The husky young burglar loomed over her in her bedroom and attempted to strangle her with a stocking. But the spunky seventy-four-year-old widow fought off her attacker by slamming his head with a heavy bookend. Then she pushed a bedside alarm button to alert a neighbor. The neighbor telephoned police, and within two minutes a squad car pulled up in front of the Schwob home and two policemen sprinted inside. Mrs. Schwob was sitting up on the bed, dazed, with a silk stocking looped around her neck.

In less than ten more minutes, some thirty law-enforcement officers had spread through the neighborhood looking for the attacker. Some of the officers were dog handlers with bloodhounds. But it seemed that the masked intruder had vanished into thin air.

A few hours later the body of Mildred Dismukes Borom was found in her home, barely two hundred yards from the Schwob house; she had been beaten, raped, and strangled. This time the death weapon was a cord from a venetian blind. Frustrated police speculated that the wily killer may have hidden in the Schwob home while they searched the neighborhood, then slipped out to find and murder the seventy-eight-year-old widow just a short distance away. A few days before her death, a relative of Mrs. Borom had sent a workman to her house to screw shut her windows as a protection against intruders.

It was dark when Mrs. Schwob was attacked, and she was fighting for her life, so she didn't get a good look at the burglar. She was able to report only that he was masked and wearing dark clothing.

But after reading about the attack on Mrs. Schwob, a woman who had seen a man behaving suspiciously the day of Mrs. Scheible's murder telephoned police. She said she had just returned home and parked her car when she saw him walking quickly by and glancing worriedly over his shoulder. The woman, who lived only four blocks from the Scheible home, described the stranger as a rather tall black man with chin whiskers. She said he was dressed in a black turtleneck sweater, knit cap, and dark green suit that was so dark it was almost black.

Three days after Mrs. Borom was killed, the coroner revealed at a press conference that pubic hairs found at the scenes of the rape murders were Negroid. All the victims were white. Until then, authorities anxious to avoid fanning racial animosities had been soft-pedaling the probability that the Stocking Strangler was black. But too much evidence had been accumulating that indicated there was an interracial aspect to the killings, and now the story was out.

Black clergymen and politically liberal spokesmen erupted with a barrage of criticism, charging that the disclosure would further racism and devisiveness in the troubled city. Law-enforcement officials responded that there was no racial motivation at all. They insisted that they had no choice, and had to get as much information about the killings and suspected killer to the public as possible if they wanted the public's help in stopping the dreadful massacre.

Police also came in for strong criticism from civil-rights spokesmen for stopping and questioning black males spotted in Wynnton, and city officials were accused of selective enforcement. But whites who attracted the attention of police for no more reason than that they were joggers, meter readers, or deliverymen were also stopped for questioning.

Many delivery and repairmen, both white and black, refused to enter Wynnton at night. Some of the more cautious workers wouldn't even make calls there during the day unless residents met them on the street to escort them.

Despite some local protests and the fears of horrified city fathers already worried about the tense racial situation, members of the Ku Klux Klan began patroling the neighborhood in private vehicles.

As the controversy raged in the city's press, a superior-court judge in Columbus was quoted in the Washington *Post* as saying he had lost confidence in the ability of local police to solve the case. The only way the Strangler would be caught, he said, was "if he runs a traffic light." Columbus was under siege, and seemed to be shattering into opposing camps. A single elusive killer was bringing a proud southern city of some 180,000 residents to its knees—and one of the most bizarre developments in the tragic story was still to come.

The Forces of Evil was added to the troubles of the already shaken community.

On March 31, letters were received by the police department and the Columbus *Ledger* newspaper, threatening that black women would be the next to die if the murders of the elderly white victims weren't solved soon. The letter writer claimed to be chairman of a terrorist group called the Forces of Evil, and demanded a ten-thousand-dollar ransom to stave off the new killings.

They were the first in a series of ominous notes composed in carefully drawn block letters that were sent to Columbus police, newspapers, and authorities at Fort Benning, the U.S. Army's huge advanced infantry training center that sprawls along the southeast edge of the city. The letter writer threatened to kill a black woman every thirty days until the stranglings stopped. In one of the letters, written on Army stationery, the author claimed to be holding prisoner a woman identified as Gail Jackson, and another only as Irene. Both would be executed, he threatened, if the demands weren't met.

The author of the semiliterate mailings, which were filled with misspellings and grammatical errors, described the FOE as being composed of seven members including a chairman, cremator, executor number one, executor number two, male secretary, contractor, and seek-out man. The seek-out man was named as the individual who contacts the chosen victim.

Identifying himself as the chairman, the letter writer claimed the group came to the area from Chicago to carry out justice. In the second letter, he wrote that the FOE was "pratrolling [sic]" the "Wynonton[sic]" area. "You just don't know us," he said.

Referring to the coroner's revelation that pubic hairs found on or near the victims were identified as Negroid, the FOE author wrote: "Since that coroner said that the strangler is black, we decided to come here and try to catch him or put more pressure on you. I see now, more pressure is needed. . . . This is the break that we have been looking for. Tell that coroner, thanks a lot. From now on, black women in Columbis, Ga., will be disappearing until the strangler is caught."

After police failed to respond to the first letter, the chairman wrote again, warning that he was the only member of the FOE who was keeping the woman identified as Gail alive, and that the others wanted her executed.

The Georgia Bureau of Investigation asked the FBI for help, and a team of profilers with the Behavioral Science Unit at the agency's academy in Quantico, Virginia, went to work. A few days later the team, popularly known as the Mind Hunters, reported that their psychological profile indicated that the FOE was not a group, but instead was a single black male, twenty-five to thirty years old. They said he was probably an Army enlisted man who was a military policeman or artillery man stationed at Fort Benning. The experts added that he had a schizoid personality.

Clues in the letter that the team found useful included the syntax of the message, which when compared with previous analysis of similar letters indicated that the writer was black. Terminology and format, such as writing a date as "1 June 1978," instead of the more common civilian usage "June 1, 1978," pointed to a military man.

Meanwhile, a few days after the first letter was received, the decomposed remains of a black woman believed to be a prostitute were found buried in a shallow grave just outside the huge military base. The victim had been bludgeoned to death, and was identified through fingerprints as twenty-one-year-old Brenda Gail Faison, also known as Brenda Gail Jackson. She was last seen by friends with a soldier at the Sand Hill Bar and Club, a popular tavern just outside the Army base.

Military and civilian law-enforcement authorities were worried that the Forces of Evil may have already claimed other victims. Two more women, both

black, were missing. They were thirty-two-year-old
Mrs. Irene Thirkield and twenty-four-year-old Karen
Hickman. Private Hickman was a soldier from
Omaha, Nebraska, and had been missing from her
assignment as an Army cook and clerk at Fort Benning since the previous September. The other
woman had been missing only a few days. If they
had been slain, as feared, it appeared almost certain
that their killer and the murderer of the Faison
woman was a GI. Two Columbus detectives were
assigned to work with military authorities on the
cases.

With revelation of the new slaying of a young
black woman and the ominous disappearance of two
others, the already-strained race relations in Columbus threatened to flare out of control. It appeared
that an ugy force of white racists was targeting black
women for murder in retaliation for the Stocking
Strangler's attacks on elderly white females.

Then officers with the Army's Criminal Investigation Division (CID) at Fort Benning found the
soldier who had been seen drinking with the Faison
woman shortly before her disappearance. Specialist
Fourth Class William Henry Hance was named as a
one-man Forces of Evil and the killer of the prostitute. Hance was a twenty-six-year-old ammunition
handler for the artillery and former Marine from
Lexington, Virginia—and he was black. He fit the
Mind Hunters' profile almost exactly.

Columbus Police Chief Curtis McClung called a
press conference to announce Hance's arrest in the
Faison case. A few hours earlier, Army MPs had also
recovered the nude body of Irene Thirkield. The
mother of four was found buried on a seldom-used

rifle range on the post after an anonymous telephone tip to MPs. (A telephone tipster had also led MPs to Miss Faison's remains, covered lightly with pine straw and leaves.) Like Miss Faison, Mrs. Thirkield was bludgeoned so savagely that portions of her skull were crushed.

At the press conference, Chief McClung went on to say that he believed the Thirkield slaying was related, although he stopped short of pinpointing the soldier as her killer. But he did his best to lay to rest any further fears about the Forces of Evil. "We will say he is involved with the Forces of Evil," Chief McClung stated. "There is no evidence to indicate there are any other members of the FOE."

After a marathon interrogation by the CID that extended over two days, Hance confessed to the murders and led agents to the battered body of Private Hickman. The nude remains had been disposed of in a ditch alongside a highway on the post. All three of the murdered women were known to have hung around the same bar near Fort Benning.

Hance was charged in Columbus with murder and theft by extortion for the Faison slaying. Because the bodies of the other two victims were found on the Army post, military authorities had jurisdiction and announced they were withholding filing of charges until the civilian proceedings were concluded. They pointed out that there was no statute of limitations for murder in U.S. military law.

FBI agents also began investigating the possibility that Hance was connected with the death of yet another young woman, Gabrielle Badger, whose body had been found about six months earlier in a wooded section of the Army post. The twenty-two-

year-old estranged wife of a Fort Benning sergeant,
she had been beaten in the head with a blunt instru-
ment.

Hance had been in trouble before for beating
women with blunt instruments. He was sixteen
when he was indicted for beating a woman in his
hometown with an iron pipe. Although he was a
juvenile, he was certified as an adult by the court
and placed on indefinite probation. The charge was
dismissed in 1971, when he joined the Marines.

Even before he gave up his sergeant's stripes in the
Marines and joined the Army, the soldier seemed to
be almost constantly involved in troubles with
women. He was the divorced father of a preschool
daughter in Williamsburg, Virginia, and at the time
of his arrest was carrying on various affairs, including one with a woman who was the mother of his
baby boy. Another of his lovers was the divorced
mother of two children, who later described herself in court as "a known prostitute" and Hance's
fiancée.

Although relatives and neighbors in Hance's
hometown in Virginia recalled him as a quiet boy
who stayed out of trouble, his ex-wife said that he
beat her. "He was a violent person. He used to beat
me for no reason. He used to throw me around a lot,
but he really beat me out-and-out about two or three
times," she was quoted as saying. Hance was small
in stature, but he fought on Army boxing teams and
was strong and scrappy.

"To tell you the truth, I really think he could have
done it," his ex-wife said of the Gail Faison (alias
Gail Jackson) killing. "It could have been that he was
trying to get revenge on me because I left him."

But suspicions that Hance might be the Stocking Strangler as well as chairman of the Forces of Evil were quickly laid to rest by police. Alibi witnesses and other information gathered by investigators convinced them that he couldn't possibly have murdered the women in Wynnton. He was cleared in the slaying of the Badger woman as well.

Hance rejected efforts by family members to hire an attorney for him, and insisted on acting as his own defense counsel in his civilian trial in Muscogee County Superior Court for the Faison slaying. But attorney Richard Smith was appointed by the court as his cocounsel.

In an approximately hour-long opening statement District Attorney William J. Smith told the jury that Hance murdered Miss Faison and wrote the blackmail letters threatening to kill her unless ten thousand dollars was paid. Hance, the DA declared, was the chairman and lone member of the mythical FOE.

In a much briefer statement, Hance told the jury of five women and seven men that he was innocent and had been nowhere near the scene of the crime. "The DA's evidence is hearsay. I killed no one," he declared.

Hance and his cocounsel objected strenuously when prosecutors presented witnesses who testified about the death of the Thirkield woman. Smith objected that the Faison and Thirkield cases were separate and that testimony about the slaying of the older woman was inflammatory.

But prosecutors insisted that the murders were related and that it was necessary to provide details illustrating the link. "The proof of one tends to prove the other. They show exactly the same mode

of operation," the district attorney argued. Judge
Kenneth Followill ruled that the defendant's conduct in similar incidents at the same time was
admissible, and allowed the testimony.

The most dramatic moments in the trial occurred,
however, when Hance accused a military investigator of forcing him at gunpoint to sign confessions to
the slayings. He insisted that he was innocent and
claimed that experts who testified that he was the
author of the FOE letters and that his fingerprint
was found on one of the notes were mistaken.

Hance declared that he was set up by the CID
because he had refused to help investigators arrest
some drug dealers at Fort Benning. It was shortly
after his refusal that a CID agent pulled a pistol and
held it to his head, forcing him to sign the statement, he asserted.

In the confessions, which were read into evidence,
Hance admitted that he bludgeoned Brenda Faison
and Irene Thirkield after each of them had propositioned him in bars. The women were reportedly
knocked unconscious with karate blows to the temple as they were taking off their clothes in his car,
then beaten about their heads with a blunt instru-
ment. The Faison woman was bludgeoned so savagely with an automobile jack that her brain and
part of her skull were missing when her remains
were recovered.

CID agents and detectives from the Columbus
Police Department testified that the defendant vol-
untarily signed the confessions and waived his rights
at least four times during the two days of questioning.

Among witnesses called by Hance in his defense

were a former fiancée, who said he was the father of her ten-month-old son and that he had never been violent toward her. During jury selection, another young woman disrupted the proceedings after she was instructed to leave the courtroom because she might be called as a witness. She was permitted to stay after screaming, "I ain't gonna' be no witness against my fiancée." The woman, who told a reporter she was the mother of two and was "a known prostitute," was not called to testify.

The jury deliberated slightly over an hour before returning a guilty verdict on both the murder and extortion charges. Judge Followill ordered Hance to be executed in Georgia's electric chair. A five-year prison sentence was ordered on the extortion conviction.

Hance's confessions also figured prominently in his military trial for the murders of the two women whose remains were found on the base. At a preliminary hearing on a defense motion to dismiss the charges, he again argued that a CIA investigator ordered him to sign a confession at gunpoint. The former investigator, who at the time of the trial was a civilian working as a deputy sheriff in Alabama, took the stand to deny the charge. Lieutenant Colonel Kevin McHugh, the military judge presiding at the hearing, ruled that the confessions to the murders were "a product of a free and unconstrained choice by their maker," and thus admissible.

At the court-martial, Army Prosecutor Captain Walter Hall read the confessions to the murders, including that of Brenda Faison. In the statements, Hance said he killed the women because they were prostitutes. "Whenever a woman offers her body for money, she gets me upset," he was quoted as saying. "She has no business being around."

The description of Private Hickman's death was especially gruesome. Hance was quoted in his confession as claiming she propositioned him in his car and started to take off her clothes, leading him to knock her unconscious with a karate blow. Then he bludgeoned her with a tree limb before driving her to a wooded area of the base, where he propped her against a tree and twice rammed her body with the car. Finally, he drove over her.

The former CID agent had testified earlier that Hance told him it was the job of the Forces of Evil to rid the world of prostitutes.

In this closing argument, defense counsel Captain Arthur Dumas admitted that Hance had written the Forces of Evil letters, but claimed the only motive was publicity. And Dumas observed that the letters "got a heck of a lot of publicity."

The military proceeding had barely gotten under way when the highest-ranking member of the court-martial panel was dismissed after reporting that he had received three mysterious early-morning telephone calls since being publicly identified as a juror. The callers did not say anything, but special security was established around the officer's house.

The nine-member military panel deliberated for six hours before returning verdicts of guilty on both counts of murder. The prosecution had not sought the death penalty, and Hance was sentenced to two life terms in military prison.

In 1981, however, both convictions were overturned by a board of military review. Military prosecutors chose not to try him on the charges again.

After the U.S. and Georgia supreme courts each twice upheld Hance's conviction in the Faison slaying, the Eleventh U.S. Circuit Court of Appeals threw out the death sentence on the grounds that the district attorney had improperly made an emotional appeal to the jury during the sentencing phase of the trial. Although the conviction stood, a new trial on the sentencing was held in 1984, and a new Muscogee County jury again imposed the death penalty. As of this writing, Hance was on death row in the Georgia State Prison in Jackson.

Livas was also convicted of murder in the Brier slaying, and sentenced to life in prison. Charges of rape were dismissed.

But even though by early 1978 the Forces of Evil killer and Livas were both safely behind bars, the Stocking Strangler would continue to elude justice for another six years. And the killing wasn't yet over.

It was April 20 when he struck again. It had been sixty-seven days since the last Stocking Strangler murder, and this time the victim lived outside the Wynnton area.

Mrs. Janet T. Cofer, a sixty-one-year-old first-grade teacher, lived in a ranch-style brick home about two miles from Wynnton. Her body was found in the rear bedroom of her locked home after the principal of the Diamond Elementary School went there to find out why she hadn't shown up at work. One of the first things he noticed was a torn front-window screen.

When the principal and a police officer entered the house they found the woman's partially nude body with a stocking wrapped tightly around her throat and a pillow over her face. She had been strangled, appeared to have been raped, and there were teeth marks on her left breast. An autopsy later confirmed the rape, and indicated that Mrs. Cofer was murdered between 6 and 7 A.M.

A neighbor and fellow teacher said the gentle widow had played the piano during choir practice at the Wynnton United Methodist Church the previous night. Like scores of other older women in Columbus, Mrs. Cofer had had a buzzer installed in her house after the stranglings began, but it hadn't been used.

Georgia Governor George Busbee signed an executive order increasing state reward money in the case to seventy thousand dollars to ten thousand dollars for each victim. Although authorities weren't aware of it at the time, Mrs. Cofer would be the Strangler's last known victim.

The horror was over at last, but the citizens of Columbus had undergone a nightmare ordeal that would never be forgotten. Direct costs of the massive investigation topped one million dollars, and with the state's contribution the reward fund had grown to one hundred thousand dollars, more than five thousand people had been questioned, and leadership of the city administration and the police department had changed. Detectives with the Strangler Task Force even traveled one hundred miles north to Atlanta, another city that had been held in seige by a serial killer, and interviewed Wayne Williams. Although Williams was eventually convicted of killing two young adults who died during Atlanta's infamous string of child murders in the early

1980s, he was cleared of any connection with the Columbus killings.

Despite outward signs that might have indicated there was not much progress in the case, law-enforcement authorities had continued to stubbornly pursue every lead they could get their hands on, and years after Mrs. Cofer's death their efforts at last began to pay off. Unknown to the press and the general public, by early 1982 investigators had settled on a strong suspect. The big problem was, they couldn't find him.

Carlton Gary was a Columbus native and cunning career criminal who was as mean as an oil-field bully and as elusive as a snake. The thirty-two-year-old suspect had been in almost constant trouble since he was seventeen, and had blazed a trail of thievery, violence, and misery in at least six states.

His rap sheet and other records disclosed arrests that began with charges of stealing from an automobile and escalated to burglaries and arson in Gainesville, Florida, and assault on a police officer in Bridgeport, Connecticut.

He had his first legal brush with a murder case in the early 1970s when he was arrested in a rape and robbery in Albany, New York, in which an eighty-four-year-old woman was killed. Retired schoolteacher Nellie Farmer was raped and strangled in her room in a retirement hotel, then covered from her face to her toes by her bedclothes. Gary admitted that he was there, but blamed the rape and murder on a friend. Based on Gary's statements, the friend was charged with murder, but was found innocent.

Gary was given a ten-year prison sentence on a charge of first-degree robbery. He was out in five, but only four months after parole to authorities in Syracuse, New York, he was in trouble again. He was accused of third-degree escape, resisting arrest, and violation of parole and was returned to prison, where he served another nine months.

In January 1977 a woman in Syracuse was awakened in her bed by a man straddling her and attempting to strangle her with a scarf. She fought him off, but he escaped before she could get a look at him good enough to make a later identification possible. Gary was arrested, however, and he had a watch taken from the woman's dresser. He was sent to prison for possession of stolen property, after claiming that he had been only a lookout and had stayed outside while a friend entered the house to do the dirty work.

Gary, it seemed, just couldn't avoid bad companions and stay out of trouble. During other periods of intermittent freedom, charges of assault and of resisting arrest were filed against him. He was in the Onondaga County Correctional Institute in Janesville, New York, awaiting trial after one of his brushes with the law when he escaped and returned to Columbus. Ferne Jackson died just twenty-four days later.

Gary's years in prisons and jails, on the run, and on the street had helped him become a seasoned, cagey criminal who was difficult to track down and catch. He learned the value of aliases, how to acquire and use false identification, how to support himself through thievery and other people's weaknesses, and how to lose himself by fading into the street life of the nation's black ghettos.

Gary's lust for fast money led him back to armed

robbery, and in late 1978 and early 1979 a string of restaurant stickups occurred in Columbus and in Greenville, South Carolina. There were so many, they were so professional, and the modus operandi was so similar in each that police and the press began referring to the bold gunman as the Steakhouse Bandit.

The MO was always the same: A tall black man with a red plastic bag over his head would barge into a steakhouse and at gunpoint herd all the employees and customers into walk-in freezers, where he would lock them up after robbing them. Then he would clean out the till.

The stickups ended when Gary was captured for a restaurant holdup in Gaffney, South Carolina, and sentenced to a long prison term.

Ironically, Columbus police traveled to South Carolina to talk to Gary about the robberies and he confessed to four stickups in their city. No one thought to ask the confessed stickup artist about the murders of old women in Columbus. He wasn't considered a suspect.

After a brief trip back to New York State, where he pleaded guilty to the escape charges, Gary was returned to South Carolina to serve his sentence on the armed-robbery conviction. His behavior at the high-security Kirkland Correctional Institution was so impressive after nearly five years that he was transferred to the minimum-security Goodman Correctional Institution in Columbia. He learned barbering there and became a trusty, a position that permitted him much more freedom. Two weeks after he was awarded trusty status, he finished trimming the hair of a fellow convict, put away his comb and shears, and strolled unmolested out of the barber-shop and out of the prison. Stocking Strangler investigators just missed him.

Tall, dark, and lean, Gary was a high-stepper, a flashy dresser who always seemed to have plenty of money and kept on the move. He sometimes played the saxophone or drums at small but jumping night spots. He also liked women, and they liked him, and at times he seemed to change girlfriends about as often as he changed shirts. He was well known among the black clubs in Columbus, and just across the Chattahoochee River in neighboring Phenix City, Alabama. Twice, police would eventually learn, they talked with Gary while they were checking night spots but didn't recognize him. The second time he was actually booked on a disorderly-conduct charge, and released after posting a five hundred dollar cash bond. He was using one of his favorite aliases.

Police investigating a restaurant holdup in Phenix City showed a series of mug shots to witnesses, who pointed to a photo of Gary as the gunman. Phenix City police were notified that he was a suspect in the serial murders in their neighboring city.

Questioning girlfriends and others who knew Gary, police learned that although the Columbus–Phenix City area seemed to be his current home base, he was also making frequent trips to Gainesville, Florida, and Albany, Georgia. There were indications that Gary was moving heavily into drug dealing and using some of the women he attracted as couriers.

Tipped off that Gary was holed up in a Phenix City hotel, police surrounded it and burst into the room. No one was there, but the raiders confiscated fifteen hundred dollars in cash and a half pound of cocaine.

A court-authorized tap on the telephone of one of the fugitive's girlfriends finally enabled his pursuers to run him to ground. Detectives monitored a call as Gary phoned from Albany, Georgia, and told the woman that he wanted her to bring him a stash of cocaine that he desperately needed and had left behind.

A SWAT team of officers from the Albany Police Department surrounded the motel where Gary had hired three rooms and holed up with a girlfriend. Joined by police from Columbus, officers waited until she walked out of the rooms, and took her into custody. Then, with guns drawn, they barged into the room where Gary was lounging on a bed. He lunged for a .38-caliber revolver on a bedside table and tried to snatch an officer's gun. But when Detective James Paulk pointed a MAC-10 submachine gun at him, the fugitive wisely gave up the fight.

It was May 3, 1984, slightly more than six years since Mrs. Cofer became the Stocking Strangler's last known murder victim.

The big break in the exhausting investigation had occurred months earlier, after Columbus police were notified that a man hundreds of miles away in Kalamazoo, Michigan, had applied for a permit on a .22-caliber pistol he had recently purchased. The serial number on the gun identified it as a weapon stolen from a Wynnton home during the Stocking Strangler killings.

Detectives tracked the weapon through three states from its theft in Georgia and its sale by a relative of Gary's in Phenix City to the most recent owner in Michigan. Initially, the Phenix City man was reluctant to talk about where he obtained the gun, but after some prodding by detectives his memory improved and he recalled that he had gotten it from a relative, Carlton Gary.

Gary's name was entered in the National Crime Information Computer, which within a few seconds began spitting out a record of thievery and violence that cemented the suspicions of investigators. He was the hottest suspect yet in the serial killings that had paralyzed Columbus with fear.

Gary's mother had once worked as a maid in several Wynnton homes, and he admitted he was familiar with the neighborhood.

Cocky and arrogant even though he was manacled and flanked by two burly officers, he sauntered into Columbus police headquarters after his arrest and the trip from Albany as if he didn't have a care in the world. He went out of his way to give the appearance of confidence.

Despite his long record and experience with police, he rattled off a torrent of words on the drive back to Columbus and during a tour of Wynnton that detectives took him on before delivering him to police headquarters. On the drive around the neighborhood, Gary pointed out the homes where the women were killed. But he was careful not to admit he had committed any of the crimes, and framed his comments so that it seemed he was merely calling on common knowledge to trace the bloody path of the shadowy figure known as the Stocking Strangler. He also pointed out several homes where other non-violent unsolved burglaries had occurred.

Gary insisted that he wasn't the Strangler, but said that he knew the man who was. He pointed the finger of guilt at a thirty-four-year-old friend he had known since childhood, who had driven through the South with him after the murders, during the holdup spree.

Investigators didn't buy the story, and it was Gary who was indicted by a Muscogee grand jury on charges of burglary, rape, and murder in each of three of the seven slayings. He was ordered to be held without bond. Gary's court-appointed attorneys filed motions protesting the no-bail ruling, and complained that he was being held in what amounted to solitary confinement, with no opportunity to venture outside his cell or exercise. In response, the Muscogee County sheriff pointed to Gary's record of escapes, and added that he was also concerned with the prisoner's personal safety. There had been threats to kill Gary before he could be taken to trial.

District Attorney Smith wanted Gary alive for trial and the appeals process only. He announced that he would ask for the death penalty for the Scheible, Thurmond, and Woodruff murders, which evidence had pinpointed as the prosecution's three strongest cases.

While attorneys pleaded his case in preliminary courtroom procedures, Gary was busy in his cell. Jailers reported that he tried to commit suicide and failed when they found bedsheets tied to a wall fixture. Then he was caught after ripping off one of the legs on his bunk to use in digging mortar out of the concrete-block wall of his cell. He had covered the hole in the wall with a piece of cardboard used

to mount family photographs on. Security around
the prisoner, already tight, was tightened even more.

A hearing before a specially selected jury charged
with determining if Gary was mentally fit to stand
trial and assist in his own defense accounted for one
of the major delays in the case as it wound its
tortuous way through the courts. His attorneys complained that he had become paranoid and irrational,
had suffered loss of memory, and had deteriorated
physically during the two years in jail awaiting trial.
One of his attorneys said Gary's suicide attempt was
evidence of poor mental health. Another read from
a statement by the accused Strangler that seemed to
indicate Gary might be suffering from a split- or
multiple-personality disorder. In the statement, the
defendant declared, "Carlton Gary is a nice guy who
does nice things. Michael David is not." Michael
David was an alias frequently used by Gary.

Gary also claimed in the statement that he believed a former wife had placed a "root curse" on
him, a form of magical spell believed in by many
rural blacks, which caused him to do bad things.

Smith contended that Gary was malingering and
carrying out a sham to avoid going to trial. The jury
apparently agreed and ruled that Gary was competent and capable of assisting in his own defense.

But the long-awaited trial of the man accused of
holding Columbus in a bondage of fear wasn't yet
about to get under way. The extraordinarily heavy
publicity surrounding the case seemed to leave little
question that the trial would not be held in Columbus, which directly suffered the trauma of the
crimes. Attorneys nevertheless tilted in court in
Columbus for two weeks in efforts to select an

impartial jury before a defense motion for change of venue was approved. The proceedings were moved about sixty miles away, to tiny Griffin, Georgia, in rural Spalding County, for selection of a jury supposedly unbiased by the deluge of news stories about the savage harvest of old ladies' lives. The Spalding County jurors would be transported to Columbus to hear the case.

It was the second week of August 1986 before jury selection was completed and testimony in the trial got under way in Columbus, with Judge Fallowill of the Muscogee Superior Court presiding. Considered to be a patient and meticulous jurist, he was the third judge assigned to the case. The first disqualified himself after testifying at a hearing that he held a very low opinion of the integrity of police officers who investigated the series of murders. The second judge withdrew because he was the district attorney in Columbus when the murders occurred.

Smith, a former FBI agent who was appointed DA the year the Stocking Strangler murders stopped, headed the prosecution. He was noted for his calm, cool courtroom manner. Assistant District Attorney Doug Pullen, also quiet and nontheatrical, was the other member of the state's team.

A prominent Atlanta attorney and fiery death-penalty opponent, August F. ("Bud") Siemon III headed the defense. The redheaded, animated defense attorney seemed to be the exact antithesis of the prosecutors. He was given to a more dramatic courtroom style than his opponents. He had been preceded as Gary's defense counsel by two sets of attorneys since the arrest, and donated his services.

Before testimony got under way, a hearing was

conducted without the jury present to determine whether the prosecution would be allowed to present evidence not directly related to the murders Gary was on trial for. Smith was anxious to link the defendant to the other silk-stocking slayings, as well as to introduce evidence tieing him to the death of a woman in Albany, New York. The modus operandi of the serial killer who had terrorized Columbus was vitally important to the case. Judge Fallowill ruled in the prosecution's favor.

Gary wasted no time in indicating his low respect for the court when he told the judge that he was sick and asked to be excused from what he described as "this circus or whatever you call it." The judge ordered him to remain in the courtroom, and he slumped down next to his attorneys.

Smith and investigators had assembled an impressive array of witnesses and physical evidence to argue the case that Gary was the Stocking Strangler. Two fingerprints and a palm print placed him at the scene of three of the rape murders, but samples of foreign pubic hair found on some of the victims or in their heads were less damning. Laboratory technicians testified that they were not an exact match with Gary's.

Two women testified and identified Gary as the stranger they had seen in the neighborhood during the period of the killings. One was the woman who had watched him walk rapidly by her home while repeatedly peering over his shoulder on the day Mrs. Scheible was raped and strangled. "He's sitting right there at the table," she said, pointing to him from the witness chair. Gary watched impassively, his chin casually cupped in his hand.

Explaining why the tall, slender black man had captured her attention, she pointed out: "Everybody was pretty edgy in those days, and we noticed things we didn't usually notice."

The witness was nervous and visibly uncomfortable under defense questioning. At one point she fumbled in her purse, and Siemon demanded, "Why were you looking into your purse, for your glasses?"

"No," she responded. "I was reaching for my nitroglycerin."

The other woman had lived a couple of houses from Mrs. Scheible, and said she saw Gary jogging past her apartment in a running suit a couple of days before the blind widow was slain. She said she had also seen him jogging with another man as she was leaving a park near her home, and he frightened her by veering off and running toward her. She was so alarmed that she asked a motorist in the park to drive her home.

The woman explained that she did not think to mention the menacing jogger when she was interviewed by police following the Scheible slaying because the victims of the Stocking Strangler were much older women than she. "I thought he was after me," she said.

The witness testified that she finally contacted police a few months prior to the trial after she saw Gary's picture in newspapers and on television and recognized him as the mysterious jogger.

Detectives from the police department in Albany, New York, testified that they believed Gary was the killer of the woman murdered there in 1977 when he was in the area.

The prosecution also called the man Gary had

accused of being the Stocking Strangler to the stand, even though the defendant had already abandoned that story and Siemon objected that "we are not contending that this man had anything to do with the killings."

The witness, who ran a bootblack business at Fort Benning, also insisted that he had nothing to do with the slayings of the elderly women. But he testified that he drove the car during the armed-robbery spree that followed the murders, although he never personally participated in the stickups.

Siemons was also unsuccessful in efforts to prevent the prosecutors from introducing scientific testimony about blood, saliva, and semen samples taken from the victims. The defense attorney claimed the tests performed by Georgia State Crime Laboratory technicians were considered unreliable by some scientists, and pointed out they would have been inadmissible in at least two states, Michigan and California.

Smith called the scientific witnesses in efforts to show that the blood, saliva, and semen samples did not eliminate Gary as a suspect in those rape murders.

One of the most dramatic moments of the trial occurred when the defendant's mother, a rotund, gray-haired woman who had faithfully attended every day of testimony, fainted and had to be carried out of the courtroom.

During summation, Siemon pleaded with the jurors to have mercy on his client. "What's the difference between retribution and revenge?" he asked. "If we're going to take vengeance, let's call it what it is and not sugarcoat it with words that mean the same thing. You don't have to kill anybody, no matter what you believe the evidence was," he said.

But when all the drama, theatrics, and legal manipulating were over at the end of twelve exhausting days of testimony, the jury took only three hours of deliberation before returning with verdicts of guilty on all three charges of first-degree murder, three counts of rape, and three counts of burglary.

There was another day of argument before the jury was asked to determine whether Gary would be allowed to live or ordered to die by execution. Smith used the opportunity to point out Gary's long criminal record of armed robberies and escapes, recapped much of the evidence, and talked of the horrible deaths of the victims. In order to justify a sentence of death, according to Georgia law, the jury was required to find that at least one of the murders was committed under aggravating circumstances. The prosecutor argued that the rapes and burglaries preceding the murders of the women constituted sufficient aggravating circumstances.

Siemon suggested that his client may have been framed by police. But the jury had already decided on the defendant's guilt or innocence and, after deliberation, returned a recommendation of death.

Judge Followill sentenced Gary on each of the three murder charges to execution in Georgia's electric chair. He ordered long prison sentences for the other crimes. Gary stood facing the judge as the sentence was pronounced, hands on his hips, chewing gum and with an insolent half smile on his face.

Today Columbus' Stocking Strangler remains on Georgia's Death Row, waiting out the lengthy appeals process.

8 ◆

DEATH-ROW GRANNY

Margie Velma Barfield
(1971–1978)

Margie Velma Barfield was a Jekyll and Hyde granny who posed as a loving daughter, wife, and mother. She worked hard caring for the elderly and infirm, taught Sunday school—and murdered the people who loved and trusted her the most.

And the murderer of at least five people became the darling of worldwide forces opposed to capital punishment during nearly six grueling years on North Carolina's death row.

They called the gentle-appearing woman—who knit baby booties and found new religious meaning in her life in prison—Sweet Velma. Law-enforcement authorities and grieving relatives of some of her victims called her a cold-blooded murderess and a modern-day Lucrezia Borgia whose poisoned victims died writhing in agony.

Velma's early life was quietly normal and not untypical for a North Carolina girl raised in the far southeastern part of the Tarheel State, where a large portion of the residents commonly looked to the huge textile industry for employment.

The second of nine children and the oldest girl, from infancy she was called by her middle name. Accounts of her childhood differ. Velma claimed that her father, Murphey Bullard, was an ill-tempered bully who worked night shifts at local textile mills, kept his family in a state of terror, and raped her when she was thirteen. Some family members, however, claimed that their father was a good, hardworking man who did his best to provide them with the best life he could and who would never have sexually abused one of his children. At least one of her siblings agreed with Velma about their father's reputed forbidden lusts.

Whatever the truth of the matter, Velma insisted that she had a miserable childhood. She was barely seventeen and in her third year of high school when she ran off from her home near the flyspeck village of Parkton, in Robeson County, to South Carolina with her boyfriend to get secretly married.

Her young husband, Thomas Burke, was an eighteen-year-old high-school senior. He quit school and got a job in a textile mill, as the couple settled down in the Parkton area to married life. Thomas treated his bride well, and built a little house for them. Near the end of 1951 they became parents of a son, Ronald. The young mother was nineteen. Nearly two years later, a daughter, Kim, was born. Velma ushered her little family to services at the Parkton

Baptist Church. She especially loved the music and vigorously joined in during the hymn singing.

The couple's married life apparently began to go wrong in the mid-1960s, when Thomas started to drink heavily. The relationship between husband and wife deteriorated further after Velma arranged to have her husband committed briefly to the Dorothea Dix State Hospital in Raleigh for evaluation and treatment of his drinking problem. He checked himself out three days later, and according to Velma and others he never forgave her.

Early in 1968 Velma collapsed and passed out with a nervous breakdown. Her father drove her to a hospital in nearby Fayetteville, and as part of her treatment she was given tranquilizers. Her first experience with the prescription drugs was the beginning of a rapid descent into hell that Velma later blamed for turning her into a helpless pill addict and merciless serial killer.

As Thomas's drinking continued and Velma found herself increasingly unable to cope with the pressures of her life, she began taking more and more pills. She started to obtain prescriptions from multiple doctors, and took handfuls of such drugs as Butisol, Librium, and Valium. She got tranquilizers, muscle relaxants, and analgesics.

The drugs began to rule her life until her world became a fuzzy haze, shimmering and unreal. Thomas's life was no more satisfying. Only his drug of choice was different.

On April 19, 1969, he came home late from the midnight shift at one of the nearby mills and dropped into bed. He had been boozing heavily. It was late morning, and Velma went to the coin laundry with her mother and a niece. When Velma returned home about two hours later and walked into the house, it was filled with smoke. Firemen carried Thomas from the bedroom, and he was pronounced dead on arrival at the local hospital. Velma agreed when she was told that her husband had probably accidentally caused his own death when he passed out or fell asleep while smoking and set the bedclothes on fire.

A nurse administered a shot of tranquilizer to help the new widow cope with the grief.

Velma's life was revolving around what she referred to as her "medication," and she was working at a big department store in Lumberton when she met Jennings Barfield. A big man a dozen years her senior, he had retired early from farming because of emphysema and diabetes. His wife, Pauline, was one of Velma's closest friends at the department store.

When Pauline died of cancer, Jennings and Velma began going out together. Despite Jennings's condition, he continued to smoke heavily and was in such bad shape that he had to keep oxygen at his home to help him breathe, so their dates were quiet affairs. Usually they just went out to eat. One night after finishing dinner, Jennings asked Velma to marry him. She agreed.

Jennings's health continued to deteriorate after their marriage, and a few times Velma had him rushed to the hospital after he passed out because of difficulty breathing. She was frustrated and angry because, regardless of how ill he became, he continued to smoke and refused to watch his diet.

She had her own problems with her nerves and her medication, and only a few weeks after her remarriage she took so many pills that she overdosed and had to be rushed to the hospital to save her life. A few months later she overdosed again.

Velma was disgusted with the way her life was going, and she blamed a lot of her troubles on the farmer she had married. She was sick and tired of taking care of him, when she had so many troubles of her own. So she bought a bottle of ant and roach poisoning. Later that day, as her husband struggled desperately for breath, he began to vomit as well. Velma had him rushed to the hospital, where he died the next day.

Her husband was a sick man when she married him, and no one raised any questions when doctors decided he had died of a heart attack. People talked of poor Velma's efforts to save Jennings by having him rushed to the hospital, and of how she had been such an attentive and loving nurse during his illness.

Velma's medication was so totally in control of her life that she frequently was unable to make it to work. Even when she did show up she was listless and moved like she was in a daze. Eventually she was fired from the store.

After her second husband's death, she moved back into the house Thomas had built, but she was so preoccupied with her constant need for more drugs and functioned in such a daze that she let the mortgage payments lapse. She lost the house and moved in with her parents. Velma got a job at a knitting plant in nearby Raeford.

Her father had been seriously ill for months, and his ailment was eventually diagnosed as lung cancer. He died after a long stay in the hospital. There was nothing suspicious about his death.

Velma quit her job in the knitting plant and went to work at a textile mill in the same small town. But she had no interest in her work. By her own later admission, all she cared about or could think about was her "medication." One day she swallowed so many pills at work that when the driver of the car she was riding in left her off in front of her mother's house, she fell flat on her face, unconscious. Her son drove her to the hospital in Lumberton, where they kept her for two weeks.

Her next job was in another department store, but it lasted only a few weeks. Velma obtained and lost jobs in department stores and textile mills one after another, and she had more overdoses. She worked fitfully, holding on to a job only as long as she absolutely had to in order to pay for her medication.

She moved out of her mother's house, then in again. Her mother was suffering from heart trouble, and the two women bickered and quarreled. Lillie Bullard was worried about her daughter's frightening dependence on pills, and pleaded with her to leave them alone. Velma responded that it was merely medication, and she had to have it for her nerves.

Velma's inability to hold a job had left her broke, and by the fall of 1974 she knew that if she didn't get some money somehow she wouldn't be able to pay for her doctor visits and prescriptions. She borrowed one thousand dollars from a loan company in Lumberton by forging her mother's signature and putting up the family home as collateral. The money disappeared rapidly, and it wasn't long before she borrowed another thousand dollars.

It seemed there was no way Velma could pay the money back, nor was there any way to prevent her

mother from learning about the loans. So she bought
another bottle of ant and roach poison.

Lillie Bullard began to vomit, her body was
wracked with diarrhea, and she was doubled over
with stomach cramps. Velma telephoned a doctor,
and he called in a prescription to a local drugstore.
But the seventy-four-year-old woman got worse, and
Velma called a brother, who sent for an emergency
unit. Mrs. Bullard was rushed to the hospital and
admitted to the intensive-care unit, where she died
a short time later. Velma was advised that her
mother expired of a massive heart attack. And she
readily consented when she was later asked to agree
to have an autopsy performed.

It was months before the family received the autopsy report. There wasn't a word about ant or roach
poison, or a fatal amount of arsenic in her system.

Velma had begun writing bad checks on a closed
account before her mother died, and she continued
to do so after moving in with other relatives. She
always kept the amounts of the checks under fifty
dollars, but it wasn't long before sheriff's deputies
stopped to see her and warned her to pay the money
back or face the dismal prospect of going to jail.

She took a deliberate overdose of a combination of
pills. When she passed out and hit the floor, she
broke her collarbone. Relatives rushed her to the
hospital. She stayed three weeks. A few days after
her release sheriff's deputies arrested her, and she
was lodged in the county jail on the check charges.
Nobody bothered to search her, and she swallowed
another handful of pills in her cell. She passed out
again and was rushed to a hospital, where her stomach was pumped.

A few days later Velma pleaded guilty to the check charges and was given a six-month sentence at the North Carolina Correctional Center for Women, in Raleigh. She told a doctor there about her need for medication, and was given enough tranquilizers to keep her from serious withdrawal problems.

Four months after Velma walked into the prison, she walked out. Two months were cut from her sentence for good behavior. On her first day of freedom she stole a check from a relative, cashed it after forging his name, and put in a supply of pills by refilling an old prescription.

Then she got her first job as a live-in companion and housekeeper for an old woman. A few months later, after the old woman was institutionalized, Velma took a new job with Montgomery and Dollie Edwards, an elderly couple in Lumberton. Montgomery Edwards was ninety-three, an invalid, and blind. His wife was about ten years younger, and did most of the cooking. Velma bathed and fed Mr. Edwards, gave him his medication, and helped with other work around the house. She was paid seventy-five dollars per week, which she spent on doctor visits and prescriptions.

About a year after Velma began working for the couple, she met their nephew. Stuart Taylor was a tobacco farmer who was separated from his third wife. And according to his aunt, he was also an alcoholic, a binge drinker who could go for weeks without a taste of booze, then set off on a two- or three-week tear. Velma and Stuart went out together a few times for seafood and barbecue dinners before he suddenly stopped coming around to see her. Velma heard that he had gone back to his wife.

Mrs. Edwards was getting on Velma's nerves. They disagreed over how to care for the old man, and they bickered about the housekeeping. But Velma kept her job at the house even after Mr. Edwards died a natural death early in 1977, even though her association with Mrs. Edwards didn't improve. Their relationship seemed to get worse, in fact.

It was March when Velma went to the store and picked up another bottle of ant and roach poison. Two days later, after wracking stomach pains, diarrhea, and vomiting, Dollie Edwards was dead.

There are always many elderly or infirm people who need someone to help them with housework and unskilled nursing care, and Velma had no trouble finding a new job. This time she moved in with eighty-year-old John Henry Lee and his gray-haired wife, Record. Mrs. Lee had recently broken a leg.

The couple didn't get along well and constantly bickered. Velma couldn't stand all the fussing, but she needed the job to pay for her pills. She had also taken a cut in pay when she went to work for the Lees, however, and was getting only fifty dollars a week, which wasn't enough to pay for the medication and doctor visits to obtain new prescriptions. So she stole one of Mr. Lee's checks, forged his name, and cashed it.

But once she had her pills, she began worrying about what would happen when he got his bank statement and discovered the fifty-dollar theft. She bought some more ant and roach poison, and John Henry Lee died in terrible agony. He had a history of angina, and the medical report on his death listed heart trouble as the cause.

Taylor began to drop in on Velma again after his

uncle's death, and they resumed their dinner dates. He explained that he and his wife were finally getting a divorce.

Velma continued to date the tobacco farmer after she left the Lee household, moved into a trailer, and got herself a job as an aide in a Lumberton nursing home. She also began to learn firsthand about her boyfriend's binge drinking. Despite his heavy boozing, however, they usually got along well and soon started to talk about marriage. Taylor's binges seemed to be occurring with less frequency since he and Velma had become serious about each other. She even got him to attend church regularly.

Then he found some letters written to her while she was in prison. He was furious because she hadn't told him about her troubled past, and he brought it up every time they quarreled.

Their relationship took an even more serious downturn when he learned that she had stolen one of his blank checks, forged his name, and cashed it. They had a terrible argument, and he threatened to turn her in to police, but somehow she weathered the storm. And later that year, after she underwent breast surgery, she moved in with him.

It was a mistake. They quarreled bitterly. But worst of all, Velma, who had no income during her period of surgery and recuperation, forged another of Taylor's checks. This time the amount was three hundred dollars.

Just as she had known when she stole and forged other checks, she knew that she faced certain exposure once Taylor received his bank statement. She was waiting for a prescription to be filled when she bought another bottle of ant and roach poison.

Taylor's daughter, Alice Taylor Storms, had been ill, and he and Velma dropped by at the young woman's house to visit. For a time the little family group sat on the floor looking at old photographs, and Velma held Taylor's three-month-old grandchild on her lap. No one except Velma realized that the deadly ant poison was in her purse. And Taylor's daughter was unaware that she would never see her father alive again.

That night Velma sprinkled ant poison in Taylor's beer and iced tea. Then she left with him to attend a Christian revival meeting featuring the evangelist Rex Humbard. Both Velma and her boyfriend loved the rich knee-knocking, hand-clapping gospel music of revivals. But the service was barely under way before Taylor became so sick that he had to leave. He waited outside in the car while Velma sat through the rest of the service.

Taylor seemed to be even worse when they got home, and Velma telephoned his daughter. She told Mrs. Storms that Taylor was ill, and she would sit up with him. The next day he was so sick with vomiting and diarrhea that Velma drove him to a hospital emergency room, where doctors treated him for the flu and sent him home. As she had done with the others, Velma fussed over him, cleaned up the mess from the vomiting and diarrhea, and put fresh bedclothes on the bed.

On the third day after Taylor was poisoned, he was returned to the hospital. He died an hour later. Doctors scheduled an autopsy.

Taylors' children raised four hundred dollars and gave it to Velma because they believed she had cared for him as best she could. At the funeral, Velma held the hand of Taylor's daughter and gently assurred her that her father was at peace in Heaven. And she prayed and sang. Velma was always good at funerals, as she was at deathbed vigils.

Nearly six weeks later a detective from the Robeson County Sheriff's Department knocked on the door of Velma's home and said he wanted her to ride with him to headquarters in Lumberton to talk about Taylor's death. As usual, although it was mid-afternoon, Velma was groggy from drugs, but she climbed unsteadily inside the police car.

There she was read her rights and advised that the autopsy indicated Taylor had died of arsenic poisoning. And she was advised that authorities believed she was his killer.

Somehow Velma made it through the interrogation without confessing or breaking down, and she was returned home in time to report for her late-night work shift. She spent the weekend in a drug- and fear-induced haze before admitting to her son that she had sprinkled ant poison in Taylor's drinks. Her son drove her back to Lumberton for another confrontation with investigators. Before leaving, she fortified herself with a devil's brew of four different tranquilizers and pain relievers. This time, when she was asked point-blank if she had poisoned her boyfriend, she confessed that it was true.

But she didn't mean for him to die, she insisted. She just wanted to make him sick.

When she was asked if there were others, she replied that there were. Velma admitted poisoning Taylor's Aunt Dollie, John Henry Lee, and her mother. But she denied killing Jennings Barfield, and declared that her first husband's death in the fire was purely an accident.

A sheriff's deputy whom she had known since they attended school together in Parkton showed up in the interrogation room and joined in the questioning. Gently, he probed for more information. When it was time for Velma to be photographed and fingerprinted, he led her through the routine. And he drove her to the Robeson County Jail.

She was charged with first-degree murder in the death of her fifty-six-year-old fiancé. But no charges were filed in the deaths of the others she confessed to poisoning, even though their bodies all disclosed traces of arsenic when they were exhumed.

Jennings Barfield's body showed traces of arsenic as well, and in the book *Velma Barfield: Woman on Death Row*, which she collaborated on with the writer Cecil Murphey, she admitted poisoning her second husband.

But except for Taylor, all the victims were killed during a period when the death penalty was in limbo across the country as a result of a U.S. Supreme Court ruling. North Carolina's death-penalty statute was declared unconstitutional in 1975 as a result of the ruling. Only Taylor's death occurred after a new capital-punishment law adopted by the North Carolina state legislature went into effect in 1977. The most serious penalty available for a murder conviction in any of the other deaths would have been life imprisonment. And the prosecution wanted the death penalty for the lethal granny.

District Attorney Joe Freeman Britt headed the prosecution team, and Velma couldn't have drawn a more capable, determined, and imposingly ominous adversary. Britt was already well on his way to a listing in the *Guinness Book of World Records* as America's "deadliest prosecutor." He would eventually be credited with winning more than forty death sentences—more than any other prosecutor.

A striking six feet, six inches tall, Britt used an overpowering, theatrical courtroom style, waving the bloody clothing of victims before jurors, shaking the Bible at them while quoting Scripture, and word-painting grisly images of the dead.

"You've got to use every argument in your arsenal because you never know what's going to convince a jury," he was once quoted as saying in a news interview. But for all his flamboyance, he was a stickler for preparation and facts. When Britt obtained a conviction, it stood up on appeal.

Velma's court-appointed defense attorney, Robert Jacobson, was less well known. In fact, Velma's defense marked his first capital-punishment case. But he dug in with a vengeance, determined to do his best for his client.

Already religious before her arrest, Velma claimed to have undergone a deep spiritual experience one night in 1978 while she was locked up alone in her cell at the Robeson County Jail. Coming down from her near decade-long drug binge, aware that she had killed some of the people she cared for the most, and faced with a first-degree murder charge that could lead to execution, she was at a low point in her life. Then, she said, she heard a Methodist preacher on a religious radio program one of the guards was listening to. "Yes, somebody loves you and his name is Jesus! He loves you tonight no matter where you are or what you've done," the minister said.

According to the story Velma related in numerous news interviews after that, she felt that the minister was reaching out directly to her, and she prayed for forgiveness for her sins. She claimed she underwent a religious conversion and was born again, with all her sins washed away.

But religious conversions are not all that uncommon in prison, particularly among convicts facing capital murder charges and the possibility of execution. Being born again might help her in the next life, but it wouldn't guarantee rescue from a more worldly retribution for her sins in this life. Especially not when the cigar-chomping Britt would be lined up against her in the courtroom.

Because of extensive publicity surrounding the case in the Lumberton area, the venue of the murder trial was moved a few miles east, to adjoining Bladen County. Velma pleaded not guilty due to insanity, and she chose to testify at the trial.

As she had done before, she claimed that her mind was so addled by drugs that she didn't know what she was doing. And she insisted that she hadn't meant to kill anyone. Instead, she said she poisoned her victims a bit at a time, only in order to make them sick long enough for her to cover up theft of the checks and money from the forgeries. When Britt pointed out on cross-examination that she hadn't stolen from Dollie Edwards before poisoning her, Velma said she couldn't explain.

"I put some in her cereal and coffee," she said of the poison. Then she confessed, "I figured it would kill her when I gave it to her."

Taking advantage of Velma's confession to poisoning her mother, Mrs. Edwards, and John Henry Lee, Britt repeatedly brought up their deaths during questioning and stressed the cold-blooded pattern to the murders.

Britt once asked an ambulance attendant to illustrate the pain that Taylor was in during his last minutes, and the witness threw back his head and filled the courtroom with a blood-curdling scream.

Velma also apparently hurt her own case by refusing to take her attorney's advice and show remorse on the stand. He reportedly told her to cry if she felt like it. Instead of crying or otherwise indicating her regret, she quarreled with Britt. She even applauded sarcastically when he concluded his summation.

The jury deliberated about three hours before returning a unanimous verdict of guilty to first-degree murder. In accordance with the recommendation of the jury, Velma, still dry-eyed, was sentenced to death. The execution date was set for February 3, 1979.

In North Carolina at that time, accused killers were given a macabre choice of the manner of execution: deadly gas or lethal injection. Velma opted for lethal injection. But no one expected the sentence to be carried out for years, if at all, because of the cumbersome state and federal appeals process in capital-punishment cases.

Velma's ordered execution would be fought especially hard and draw worldwide attention, because no woman had been put to death in an American prison since individual states had begun reinstituting capital punishment following the 1975 U.S. Supreme Court decision. Elizabeth Ann Duncan, who hired two workmen to murder her daughter-in-law and was executed in California's gas chamber in 1962, was the last woman put to death in the United States. And North Carolina hadn't executed a woman in nearly forty years.

Velma had spent most of her time since her arrest in jail in Lumberton before being moved to the lockup in Elizabethtown for the trial. But once the trial was over, she was moved to the state Correctional Center for Women in Raleigh, where she had previously served time on the bad-check charge. This time she was a celebrity prisoner. And instead of being assigned to an open unit with some freedom of movement, she was locked in a somber cell built of concrete walls and bars that served as a one-woman death row.

As she settled down to wait out the appeals process she began to develop a reputation as a gentle, caring soul who devoted much of her time to comforting and counseling other prisoners—especially younger women. When a frightened fifteen-year-old girl who was sentenced to thirty years for involvement in a savage murder was moved into the next cell, Velma reached through the bars and held her hand all night. The girl eventually became so attached to her that she called her "Mama Margie." (Unlike people on the outside, prison authorities and other convicts used Velma's first name.)

Although Velma couldn't see other prisoners, they could talk with them. She also became involved in Bible studies with volunteer ministers who came to the prison, and developed a friendship with the wife and daughter of the evangelist Billy Graham.

As one appeal after another was rejected by the

courts, journalists from throughout the Western world trooped to the prison to talk with Sweet Velma, the quiet-spoken, crocheting grandmother on death row. She was interviewed by writers from Britain and France, and from newspapers and magazines in several major U.S. cities, and appeared at different times on network television shows. Her attorney of four years, James D. Little, of Raleigh, made a point of sitting in on the interviews. Most of the stories were sympathetic.

Finally, the U.S. Supreme Court refused for the third time to hear an appeal of her conviction and death sentence. She was scheduled to be executed on August 31, 1983. Velma was moved to the Central Prison in Raleigh in the middle of June. Her new cell was next to the execution chamber.

Britt was quoted on television's *CBS Morning Show* as remarking, "Velma Barfield is a sweet little old lady in appearance, and underneath she is a cold-blooded, merciless killer." She was "a dangerous woman who should die and get it over with," the hard-bitten prosecutor declared. The furor over Velma's death sentence had become a major world media event.

Velma's attorneys, civil-rights activists, clergy, family members, and others sympathetic to her worked frantically to get the execution date set aside. They formed a Margie Velma Barfield Support Committee. A Roman Catholic nun, Sister Mary Teresa Floyd, who worked in the prison for seven years, joined the committee in preparing a petition to North Carolina Governor James B. Hunt seeking a commutation to life imprisonment without parole.

But just a few months earlier the governor had rejected an appeal for executive clemency on behalf of James W. Hutchins. The killer of three police officers, Hutchins became the first person put to death by the state of North Carolina since 1961 when he was executed by lethal injection on May 8.

The governor met with the clemency group, as well as with relatives and friends of some of the people who died at Velma's hands and who urged him to deny the appeal. The prodeath group, organized by Margie Pittman, whose eighty-year-old father was one of the dead, called themselves the Victims of Barfield.

"She stood over daddy and watched him writhe and twist in pain and she said nothing," Mrs. Pittman said of Velma during a news interview.

The commutation forces argued that the death-row grandmother had become a born-again Christian who befriended and helped other female inmates. And they insisted that she was so addicted to prescription drugs when the murders were committed that she didn't know what she was doing. "If they execute my mom, they're executing someone who did not commit those murders," her son declared.

But opponents of commutation argued that she was faking and would murder again if she got the chance. Taylor's daughter, Alice Storms, told journalists as she left the governor's office: "A serial killer does not want help. They enjoy killing. And Velma Barfield enjoys killing. She enjoys watching people suffer and die, and then watching the families as they suffer with the agony of their loss of their loved ones." Velma, she bitterly charged, was "an outstanding liar."

Velma didn't meet with the governor, but she said in an earlier interview that she wanted to live so she could be with her family and friends and "see my grandchildren grow up."

On July 2, almost two months before her scheduled execution, Velma was returned to the Correctional Center for Women. She had received another stay, this time from Chief Justice Warren E. Burger, pending action by the full U.S. Supreme Court. The court was planning to rule soon on another precedent-setting case that could possibly reflect on Velma's conviction and sentence.

The old execution date passed, but the Supreme Court denied the petition for rehearing. A new execution date was set for November 2.

In mid-September Governor Hunt ruled on the appeal for clemency. In a prepared statement, he announced: "After carefully looking at the issues, I don't believe that the ends of justice or deterrence would be served by my intervention in this case."

He added: "Death by arsenic poisoning is slow and agonizing. Victims are literally tortured to death. It has been a tragedy for an entire community as well as our state."

Appeals and time had finally run out for Velma. She had been on North Carolina's death row longer than any other inmate. In the six years since her conviction and sentencing in 1978, her case was reviewed by eight courts and twenty-one judges. She had received five postponements of execution. But the courtroom circus was over at last, and she was transferred back to a death-row cell at the Central Prison. Late on the night of November 1, 1984, she said good-bye to her family and to her lawyer. Her attorney gave her two red roses.

She refused a final meal, and shortly before it was time to leave her cell she changed from her brown prison dress into pink cotton pajamas. Then the plump, bespectacled, matronly little fifty-two-year-old woman with the freshly curled, gray-flecked brown hair was strapped, faceup, to a steel gurney and wheeled the eighteen steps to the execution chamber. Only the embroidered collar of her pajamas showed beneath a blue-green sheet that had been pulled over her.

In a brief final prepared statement to Warden Nathan Rice and others, she apologized for the terrible things she had done: "I want to say that I am sorry for all the hurt that I have caused," she said. "I know that everybody has gone through a lot of pain, all the families connected, and I am sorry, and I want to thank everybody who has been supporting me. . . . I want to thank my family for standing with me through all this and my attorneys and all the support to me, everybody, the people with the prison department. I appreciate everything—their kindness and everything they have shown me during these six years."

North Carolina law provided three options to the warden for carrying out an execution. He could do it himself, select from staff members at the prison, or rely on volunteers.

Witnesses seated in darkness behind a double-glass window watched silently as Velma's lips moved, as if she was muttering a prayer. Her eyes fluttered as intravenous tubes attached to both her arms were connected to equipment behind a tan curtain.

At exactly 2 A.M., three executioners selected from the staff stood behind the curtain and injected fluid into the equipment leading to the intravenous tubes. One of the injections carried sodium thiopental to induce sleep. Then a double dose of procuronium bromide, a powerful muscle relaxant, surged through the tubes, stopping her heart. None of the executioners knew which of them had injected the fatal dose.

Velma was quiet when a doctor approached the gurney and placed a stethoscope to her chest. Then he checked the pupils of her eyes. At 2:15 A.M., he pronounced her dead.

Outside the prison, death-penalty opponents cried and sang "Amazing Grace," Velma's favorite hymn. Another group of people across the street from them cheered and waved signs supporting the death penalty.

One final macabre note was added to the bizarre saga of Velma Barfield when a team of organ-transplant surgeons fought desperately for forty minutes to restart her heart so that, along with her lungs, kidneys, and liver, it would be in suitable shape to transplant.

The team received the body at the prison's hospital exit and, in efforts to get her heart pumping blood to the other organs so they could be saved, immediately injected her with a cardiac stimulant. But it was too late.

One doctor complained that if the team had received her body ten minutes earlier her kidneys and liver may have eventually saved someone's life.

And doctors were careful to explain that they were not trying to bring her back to life. She was brain-dead and could not be revived. They were merely attempting to temporarily restore heartbeat so the usable organs could be preserved until they were removed.

♦

THE BOY KILLERS

Dean Corll,
Elmer Wayne Henley, Jr.,
and David Brooks
(1971–1973)

Summers in and around Houston, Texas, tend to be hot and sultry. And as policemen in any big city will tell anyone who cares enough to inquire, when the heat and the humidity climb, murder rates and other forms of random and planned violence go up right along with the temperatures.

So when an officer at the Pasadena Police Department on the outskirts of Houston picked up the telephone shortly before 8:30 on a bright and hot early August morning, he paid serious attention to the startling confession he heard: "Y'all better come right now. I killed a man. The address is 2020 Lamar."

Carefully drawing out the owner of the shrill, frightened voice, the officer learned that he was Elmer Wayne Henley. And he got Henley's easy promise to wait right where he was until a police-man arrived to investigate.

A few minutes later, a uniformed officer arrived at the green-and-white wood frame bungalow to in-vestigate. A late-model Ford van was parked in the driveway. Three shaken teenagers, two boys and a girl, were sitting quietly on the front steps. In addi-tion to seventeen-year-old Henley, there was six-teen-year-old Timothy Kerley, and fifteen-year-old Rhonda Williams. The kids appeared lethargic and moved slowly. They were uncoordinated, as if they had been up all night—or had been doing some heavy doping or boozing.

Henley identified himself, then produced a .22-caliber pistol. He said he used the weapon to kill his older friend, Dean Corll, the owner of the house.

The officer found the stocky body of Corll sprawled facedown on the hallway carpet. He was naked, and six bullets had been fired into the sallow, flabby flesh of his shoulder and back. A telephone cord was caught between two of his toes. The patrol-man radioed for help.

Within minutes the bungalow was alive with uni-formed and plainclothes policemen. As the body was photographed and prepared for the trip to the morgue and crime technicians spread throughout the house, the teenagers were loaded into squad cars and driven to Pasadena Police Headquarters for ques-tioning. Officers noticed that Rhonda was limping as she walked to the squad, and it was later learned that she had broken some bones in one of her feet when she caught it between two cars. She had been sitting on the hood of one of the vehicles.

Inspection of the littered, sparsely furnished bun-

galow was barely under way before officers realized
that the owner had not only had been an extremely
poor housekeeper but also must have had some
strange hobbies.

The investigative team found a copy of *Human
Sexuality* among a handful of books in the house,
several curious thin glass tubes—and a gigantic,
seventeen-inch, double-headed plastic dildo. The
truly intriguing belongings, however, were in the
bedroom.

The bedroom rug was covered with heavy sheets
of clear plastic. A hunting knife was lying on one
end of the plastic, and a short distance away there
was a can of acrylic paint in a brown paper bag. A
military-type gas mask had been discarded near the
bed.

But the most outlandish item of all was a thick
seven-by-three-foot length of rough plywood. Holes
had been drilled at each corner. Separate sets of
handcuffs were fastened to two sets of holes, and
lengths of strong nylon cord were threaded through
the others. A small pillow and another length of
cord were at the top of the board, and a third set of
handcuffs was on the floor a few inches away.

Inspection of a locked shed in the backyard turned
up equally ominous signs of strange goings-on. The
most intriguing object in the shed was a large plywood box approximately three feet high, two feet
wide, and two and a half feet deep. Air holes had
been drilled in the sides and a hinge provided for
opening and closing it from the front. A few strands
of human hair were found inside.

The box was just large enough for a person to
crouch or kneel in, but it was obvious that it would

take only a few minutes of such treatment for the pain to become excruciating. Adding up discovery of the book, the sex toy, the board, and the box, it seemed logical to conclude that someone at the bungalow had learned to achieve sexual pleasure from pain, either their own or—more likely—that of others.

If there was any doubt at all in the minds of investigators at the house on Lamar that they were looking at the implements of a sadist, they were dispelled after a few minutes of conversation at headquarters between the teenagers and detectives. The youngsters were talking, and Henley especially was full of information that he appeared anxious to share with police.

Henley identified Corll as a thief, sadist, homosexual rapist, and serial killer. He himself had lured some of the young male victims to the house for Corll's rape and torture sessions, he admitted. The voluble youth said that he and his friends would probably be dead if he hadn't shot the older man.

The interrogators of the trio of teenagers settled down for a long day of talking and, more important, listening.

Piecing together events at the bungalow early that morning, detectives learned that Henley had shown up at about 3 A.M. with Timothy and Rhonda. Timothy had been lured to the house with the promise of dope and booze. The girl had been having family troubles and was running away from home. Henley was fond of her and took her along because she had no place else to stay.

But Corll was furious when he saw her. He began swearing and flew into a rage. "You weren't supposed to bring any girl," he screeched. "Goddamn you, you ruined everything!"

Somehow, Henley managed to get his friend calmed down, or so it seemed. Eventually, now that the host's good nature had apparently returned, the teenagers began sipping moonshine whiskey and passing around the can of acrylic paint with the brown paper bag. They took turns spraying quick bursts of paint into the sack and inhaling the intoxicating fumes. Corll's eyes narrowed into pleased slits as he watched the huffing party, and as, one at a time, each of the youngsters slumped unconscious onto the rug.

The starlit Texas night had given way to daylight when Henley painfully regained consciousness. His ankles were securely trussed together, and Corll was snapping handcuffs on his wrists. Corll was mean again! He was still mad about Rhonda's presence and was threatening to make Henley pay for crossing him. Rhonda and Tim had already been tied up, and the boy was naked.

"I'm gonna kill you all," Corll snarled. "But first I'm gonna have my fun."

Henley was dragged into the kitchen, where Corll jammed a .22-caliber pistol into his belly. Eyes bulging in fear, the boy pleaded for his life, babbling about their long friendship and promising to do anything at all that the older man wanted. He swore he would even torture and kill his friends if that would please him.

Gradually Corll calmed down, moved the pistol aside, and loosened the cuffs and ropes from Henley. Moving on shaky legs, the youth allowed himself to be pushed back into the bedroom, where Corll handed him the hunting knife and ordered him to cut off Rhonda's clothes.

Then Corll began flinging off his own clothes, before securing Tim facedown, spread-eagled, and naked on the plywood board. He told Henley to take the girl, while he raped the boy. Both the younger teenagers were still heavily under the influence of the paint fumes and booze, and were unaware of what was going on. Rhonda moved her head and moaned slightly.

That was enough for Henley. He didn't want to hurt Rhonda. He told Corll that he wanted to take her out of the room. Corll ignored him, so Henley grabbed the gun from a night table and pointed it at his friend. The party was over.

Corll blew up. Rolling off Tim, the naked man lumbered toward Henley, his face flushed and contorted in anger. "Kill me, Wayne. Kill me," he taunted.

Henley pulled the trigger, and he continued firing until the gun was empty.

His mind addled by the chemicals and by the trauma of the past few minutes, Henley shakily pulled at the ropes and shackles holding his friends until they were free. Then he made the telephone call and joined the others on the front porch to wait for police. A few minutes before officers arrived, Henley matter-of-factly remarked that he could have sold Kerley for fifteen hundred dollars if they hadn't been such good friends.

Corll had paid Henley to bring him young boys before, although never an amount anywhere near fifteen hundred dollars. Sometimes he didn't pay at all, and at other times Henley was rewarded with five dollars or ten dollars or with worthless IOUs, the interrogators learned.

Some of the boys were apparently murdered and buried under a boat shed on the southwest side of Houston after the husky sadist was through with them, the chatty teenager told his interrogators. As Henley talked, he seemed to relish his moment in the spotlight. He basked in his feeling of self-importance.

Police don't believe everything they're told. But they had a dead man who was apparently a homosexual sadist and child molester, a houseful of torture implements, and three frightened teenagers on their hands. They also had a story pieced together from the trio that was holding up amazingly well, considering the sort of night the youngster had just experienced.

Equally as interesting, however, there had been a worrisome series of disappearances of early-teenage and preteen boys in the Houston area. More than a fair share of the missing youngsters were from a generally run-down area of about six square blocks known as the Heights, just northwest of the central downtown district. Predominantly white, the Heights sheltered mostly hardworking blue-collar families. The residents were, for the most part, lawabiding, patriotic, and devoted to their families, but many were underemployed or underpaid. And the neighborhood, one of the oldest in Houston, seemed to sag, as if dispirited and worn out.

Initially police had written off most of the missing boys from the Heights as runaways. But the unsettling possibility that something more ominous was responsible had suddenly been raised. Pasadena police notified homicide detectives in Houston that they were working on an investigation that might be of mutual interest. They also passed along identification of a couple of boys named by Henley as possible victims: David Hilligiest and Charles Cobble.

If Houston homicide detectives had been inclined not to show much interest in the babblings of an aimless teenager who was admittedly coming down from an all-night huffing party, the names of Hilligiest and Cobble ensured immediate attention. The parents of both boys had been pestering police for help in locating their lost sons. Unfortunately, people from the Heights had neither the wealth nor the political pull that would attract high-priority attention to their problems from local authorities. Several other boys had also been reported missing, but worried families were unable to generate much interest from police, who chose to regard the youngsters as runaways.

Now the phenomenon of disappearing Heights teenagers had taken on a frightening new perspective.

Police had first become aware of David Hilligiest shortly after dawn on Sunday morning, May 30, 1971, when his distraught mother, Dorothy, telephoned to report that the thirteen-year-old schoolboy was missing. He hadn't been seen since about 2 P.M. the previous day, shortly after telling her that he thought he would join two of his brothers at a nearby pool.

Despite Mrs. Hilligiest's pleas, and her assurances that he wouldn't deliberately stay out all night on his own, police refused to launch a search for him.

An officer told her that David would be listed as a runaway.

The Hilligiests continued their search on their own, scouring the neighborhood, checking factories and vacant houses, and talking to boys, girls, and adults who might have seen their son. Late Sunday, they learned that the previous afternoon he had been with an older neighbor boy, sixteen-year-old Gregory M. Winkle. But Gregory, the oldest of two sons in a fatherless family, had also dropped from sight. Both he and David were wearing only their swimming trunks, hardly the kind of clothing they would have chosen if they were running away.

When Mrs. Winkle informed the Hilligiests that her son had telephoned her late Saturday night and told her that he was sixty miles away in the little Gulf Coast village of Freeport with a group of his buddies, the adults drove there looking for the two boys. The effort was fruitless. They had no better luck when they searched other seaside towns and beaches and checked hospitals and the police department in Galveston.

Eventually the Hilligiests began to consult psychics, and for a while they hired a private detective—until the money ran out. Elmer Wayne Henley, Jr., who lived across the street from them, helped place posters carrying David's description at local schools. But neither the Hilligiests nor Mrs. Winkle ever saw their sons alive again.

Charles Cobble was a loser whose lanky, slump-shouldered frame floated unobtrusively through the Heights with few friends but an agonizing plethora of fears. A high-school dropout like many of his contemporaries, he was afraid of just about everything and everybody. He had gone through life lonely and rejected by other youths his age until he met up with Marty Ray Jones. He couldn't have picked a worse companion.

Marty was a rootless boy with a reputation as a troublemaker and small-time dope dealer who ripped off his contacts whenever he could. And after Charles surprised everyone by bringing home a big-eyed, redheaded fifteen-year-old girl and announcing she was pregnant and they were going to get married, it was Marty whom she blamed for the breakup of their marriage a few months later. Charles refused to abandon his friend when they argued about him, and she finally moved out. Marty moved in.

Marty wasn't any more popular with others in the neighborhood than he was with his buddy's wife. One of the Heights residents he had managed to cross swords with was Elmer Wayne Henley, Jr.

But no one gave much thought to the bad blood between the two youths when Marty and Charles suddenly stopped showing up around the teenage hangouts in the Heights.

Few other people may have cared much about the boys, but members of Charles's family loved him. And like the Hilligiests, they reported to police that he was missing. Police showed no more interest in the Cobbles and their fears for their missing son than had been shown over the disappearance of David Hilligiest and other boys. So, like the Hilligiests and Mrs. Winkle, the Cobbles pressed their own search. One of Charles's uncles had experience as an investigator in the armed forces and helped in the search. But the young man, along with his friend

Marty, seemed to have dropped from the face of the earth.

Fruitless searches had been conducted for other boys as well. Johnny Delome and his best friend, Billy Baulch, were two who were missing. About a year after David Hilligiest and Gregory Winkle dropped from sight, Johnny and Billy vanished. The two buddies left the Baulch home together and never returned.

Seventeen-year-old Ruben Watson's grandmother was the last member of his family to see him when he walked out the door after she gave him money to go to the movies. Fourteen-year-old Wally Simoneaux left home to spend the night with his thirteen-year-old friend, Richard Hembree. Then both boys dropped from sight.

Billy Lawrence told his father, Horace, that he was going fishing with friends. It was five days before Horace heard from his son, when the mailman dropped off a postcard. A message purportedly from Billy advised that he was in Austin, where he had found a good job, and that he would be back home in August. There wasn't another word from the boy.

Eighteen-year-old Mark Scott had been embroiled in minor scrapes with the law for some time when he told family members a few days before Christmas 1972 that he planned to go to Mexico for a while. Then he, too, joined the growing list of missing boys from the Heights. The last his worried parents heard from him was a brief note on a postcard mailed from Austin, advising that he was going to work there for a while.

Even eighteen-year-old Frank Aguirre disappeared. And Frank was no aimless Heights teenager drifting through life in a haze of dope and indolence. He was a hardworking youngster with solid goals; not only was he determined to hang onto his job at a Long John Silver and continue his studies until he graduated from high school but he was also planning to get married. Rhonda Williams was the girl he wanted for his wife.

Yet Frank also vanished, without a word to his young fiancée. He didn't even pick up his paycheck from the restaurant, and he abandoned the five-year-old car that was his most prized possession in a parking lot. There was just no way, Rhonda and their friends agreed, that Frank would run away, leaving his car and his girlfriend behind.

Apparently no one thought to put the information together at the time, but curious unifying threads linked most of the missing boys with Corll, Henley, and another frequent companion of theirs, eighteen-year-old David Owen Brooks. The missing boys were either acquaintances of one or more of the trio, had at one time lived near one of them, or were involved in the petty drug and huffing scene that pervaded teenage society in the Heights. Some of them attended the all-male drug and booze parties that Corll hosted, first at his home in an area known as Yorktown, then at an apartment he had occupied near the Heights, and finally at the wood-frame bungalow on Lamar Street.

Strangely, Henley's closest friends weren't among the boys periodically reported missing by anxious families. Most of them weren't even invited to the parties. One of those who was, however, was Brooks. A jaunty, blond-haired, bespectacled teenager, Brooks was such a close friend of Corll's, in fact, that the pudgy electrician helped him buy a shiny green 1969 Corvette. Brooks tooled around in it, trying to impress the other kids in the Heights while bragging that Dean had given it to him.

Police were to eventually learn that he was the third and final member of a deadly trio that was responsible for the mysterious disappearances of boys and young men that plagued the Heights for two and a half terrible years between 1971 and 1973.

Henley's early-morning telephone call to Pasadena police had lifted the lid off a ghastly Pandora's box of evil that would not only shame and alarm citizens in Houston and its suburbs but send shock waves throughout the country.

Despite spirited efforts of police and community leaders to protect the city's image and defend its handling of the missing children, Houston would be sent reeling under the pressure of lurid headlines and news stories labeling it as the murder capital of the world.

But the true horror lay under the galvanized-steel boat shed in South Houston, in a humid forest in East Texas, and along a remote Gulf Coast beach where the bodies of the victims of the sadistic homosexual murder ring had been disposed of. Ever cooperative, Henley led investigators to the burial sites.

Among items stored in the boat shed were a collection of clothing sized for males considerably smaller and slimmer than Corll; a stripped-down 1971 Chevrolet Camaro later learned to have been stolen from a car lot; a bicycle owned by a missing thirteen-year-old Pasadena boy; and an empty sack that had once held quicklime.

A few minutes of industrious digging by two trusties drafted from the city jail revealed what the lime had been used for. A layer of the caustic white chemical was uncovered near the shed, a couple of inches under the dirt; and under that they found the first skull. The unmistakably putrid, sweet stench of death rose from the shallow grave, enveloping and clinging to the search team as the diggers continued at their grim task. Eventually the nude body of a young blond boy perhaps thirteen or fourteen years old was unearthed. He had been buried in a plastic shroud, and appeared to have been dead no more than a week or two.

A few inches below the body, the skeleton of another victim was uncovered. More trusties, promised a day off their sentences for helping with the ghoulish task, were brought to the shed, and as night fell the area was illuminated with floodlights so the digging could continue. A few inches from the first bodies, another layer of lime was exposed and the remains of two more teenage boys were pulled from the ghastly ossuary. One of the boys had been shot in the head, and the other still had the cord used to strangle him knotted tightly around his neck. At about 10 P.M., Henley was driven away from the site to spend the rest of the night in the austere little police lockup in Pasadena.

Four more bodies, in rotting bits and pieces, were pulled from the fetid, sandy earth before Houston Police Lieutenant Breck Porter called off the search for the night. A uniformed policeman was designated to guard the shed until the next day, when digging would resume.

The first news reports on radio, television, then in

the newspapers, began to circulate, notifying Houstonians that bodies of teenage boys or young men were being pulled from a makeshift graveyard under a shed. By daylight the grim story had flashed throughout the country and was spreading around the world.

Police switchboards were lighting up in Houston and in Pasadena with calls from fearful parents wanting to know if their missing boys had been pulled from the dreadful burying ground. And a somber David Brooks had walked into headquarters, accompanied by members of his family, to explain that he had been a close friend of Corll. He agreed to make a statement, to help, he said, in the investigation.

Brooks said he was in the sixth grade when he first met Corll. Dean was coowner, with his mother, of Corll's Candy Kitchen, a candy factory in a green tin building with a big candy cane painted on a sign on the front. The candy factory was just across the street from the Helms Elementary School, which Brooks attended. Corll knew many of the students from the school, especially the boys, and he was generous in handing out free candy as well as prized rides on his motorcycle. He became known among the boys at the school as the candy man.

Few parents were aware of Corll's unusual friendship with their sons, and most of those who were saw nothing to be suspicious of. Corll appeared simply to enjoy palling around with young boys, and he didn't seem to be the kind of man anyone should worry about. A Christmas Eve baby, Corll was born in Fort Wayne, Indiana, in 1939, and he hadn't yet started school when his parents divorced. Consequently, he and a younger brother were raised by their mother, although she remarried their father for a brief time. Then there was a second divorce and three more marriages.

Eventually, after his mother's third marriage, the family found their way to Texas and began making candy commercially. But Dean got drafted into the Army and went to a radio-repair school before he was honorably discharged after ten months and returned to Houston and the candy factory.

The young man had never shown much interest in females, although he briefly dated a girl named Wanda during a brief stay on his grandparents' farm back in Indiana. But he returned to Houston without her, and eventually dated a divorcée with two small sons on and off for five years. He also quit the candy-making business and got himself a job with the Houston Lighting and Power Company.

Even while he was dating, however, he would sometimes show up with a carload of boys. He seemed clearly to prefer the company of young boys and spent less time with his girlfriend than with his pals. Pals like Henley and Brooks.

Brooks revealed that what had at first seemed to him to be a platonic relationship gradually led to a homosexual one. He said that Corll paid him five dollars or ten dollars for each act of oral sodomy. Eventually Brooks moved in with Corll, and they lived together off and on for about three years. Brooks said that one day after he had introduced Henley to Corll, his two friends overpowered him and strapped him facedown on a bed. Then Corll raped him. But the repeated acts of rape that day didn't destroy their friendship.

Reluctantly, as the questioning progressed, Brooks admitted that he had once seen Corll abusing two young boys who had been stripped naked and tied to the plywood board. He said that Corll later confessed to him that he killed the boys. Then Corll helped Brooks buy the Corvette in return for keeping his mouth shut. The teenager provided the names of other boys that he said Corll might have killed. But he steadfastly denied having anything to do with the murders of anyone, and insisted that if killings occurred they were committed by Corll and Henley.

Brooks's interrogators had serious suspicions about his innocence in all the murders, but they were patient and willing to wait for a clearer, more believable story as they kept the teenager talking. Although Brooks came from good, hard-working people, his family had been split by divorce years before, and since then he had compiled a juvenile record in Texas and Louisiana as a thief and burglar. He was also known to keep a loaded .38-caliber revolver and had been quoted by others as warning that he could shoot any policeman who ever walked in on one of the drugs-and-sex sessions with Corll and others. He had a reputation among the kids in the Heights for being lean and mean.

Henley had been considerably more forthcoming during resumption that morning of his talks with police. He admitted that he had been involved with Corll in eight murders, and knew of at least sixteen others. He estimated that as many as nineteen bodies might be found under the floor of the shed, and others uncovered from an isolated stretch of Gulf Coast beach and from piney woods near the Corll family's summer cottage in Angelina National Forest at Lake Sam Rayburn, about 170 miles north of the city.

According to the young murder suspect, Corll killed some of his victims, and let others go after raping and sexually torturing them. Most were abused with dildoes, some had glass rods inserted into their rectums and urethras, and a few were castrated. Corll was thrilled and excited by the fear and pain he inflicted. He loved to hear the helpless young boys scream and cry out for their mothers. Henley also had a lot to say about David Brooks that stripped away the young boy's claims of innocence. Brooks was officially placed under arrest late that afternoon, and locked in a cell to await further questioning the next day.

Detectives loaded Henley into a police car and drove him to Lake Sam Rayburn to look for bodies. He talked almost all the way there. He talked about girls, and he talked about how difficult it was to strangle young boys. Sometimes it took both him and Corll together to get the job done, he said.

In one of his conversations with police he discussed the murder of Charles Cobble's friend Marty. "When I choked Marty Jones, I found out it wasn't as easy as on TV," he marveled. "I had to ask Dean for help." Then he demonstrated how he struggled to choke the Heights teenager.

He also explained how he and Corll would get rid of corpses by putting a piece of carpet next to the graves to keep the area clean, then placing boards on top of the bodies to keep them from rising.

By the time the caravan of official cars, including vehicles from the Houston and Pasadena police departments and a carload of Texas Rangers, reached the cabin near the lake, it was already midafternoon. Henley directed officers straight to a mound of earth in a small clearing and told them that a boy named Billy Lawrence was buried there. Officers found the body under a board and a streak of lime. It was wrapped in plastic and badly decomposed. Billy was not working in Austin, and he would never be back home to attend school.

A short distance away in some scraggly piney woods, again at Henley's direction, they located and disinterred another plastic-wrapped nude body.

That night Henley slept in a cell in the county jail at San Augustine, a small town near the lake. Back in Houston, digging crews mixed with jail trusties and detectives working in brief shifts had been busy at the shed. They dug up nine more bodies, some in bits and pieces, pathetic chunks of bone, hair, and rotted clothing. A pair of tiny, mud-stiffened trousers that looked like they could have fit a boy of nine or ten was one of the most pathetic discoveries. "It takes a cruel man to do this," murmured one of the trusties. "I will never forget this. It hurts when you reach in and grab a pair of pants that were for a small boy."

One of the most horrible discoveries was genitalia that had been nearly bitten in half and showed the marks of human teeth.

Some of the corpses were exhumed with the arms still tied behind their necks. One boy had the bones of his chest caved in, some had been shot, most had gags in their mouths and strong cord tightly secured around their necks. During two terrible days, seventeen bodies were pulled from the mass grave. "This guy must have spent half his time digging graves,"

murmured Detective Larry Earls, an eight-year po-
lice-department veteran.

By the time the twenty-seventh body was unearthed, police officials had had enough. They announced that all the bodies that were going to be
found under the shed floor had been recovered. Efforts to locate more bodies at that site were over.
The job of identifying the remains had already begun, but ten years later authorities would still be
trying to learn the names of some of the victims.
Police were fairly certain they knew the identities of
a few of the boys. Identification cards and hospitali-
zation cards found with the bodies of two youngsters
buried together carried the names of thirteen-year-
old Jerry Waldrop and his fifteen-year-old brother,
Donald. And Henley had provided the names of
others.

Brooks opened up the next day, dictating a lengthy
confession that detailed his knowledge of the years
of torture and homosexual abuse heaped on young
boys from the Heights by his friend Corll. Brooks
traced the progress of the onetime candy maker's
perversions from passing out sweets and paying children with money or other presents for sex, to drug,
booze, and marijuana parties, forcible rape, torture
on the board, and murder.

Once a boy was strapped to the board, Brooks said,
he was as good as dead.

Brooks said that Corll once told him of killing two
boys, but the first homicide he actually witnessed
was the murder of Ruben Watson. He also said that
he was living with Corll when the former candy
maker strangled two brothers. And he witnessed two
other separate killings—all before Henley began lur-

ing victims for the murderous sex-and-torture orgies.

The teenager told his interrogators that Henley
progressed from providing victims to taking an active part in the murders. "Wayne seemed to enjoy
causing pain," he said.

Brooks said that all three were present when Mark
Scott fought back with a knife, swinging at Corll
and scratching his skin. But the boy had one hand
tied, and Corll grabbed his knife hand while Henley
ran into another room and came back with a pistol.
Scott just gave up at that point, Brooks said, and
Henley killed him.

Henley also strangled Billy Baulch, Brooks said,
and a few minutes later shot another boy named
Johnny. He said that Henley yelled, "Hey, Johnny,"
and, when the boy looked up, shot him in the
forehead with a .22-caliber pistol. The bullet exited
from his ear. Miraculously, it appeared, the boy
wasn't dead, but when he pleaded for his life, Henley, with Corll's help, finished him off by strangling,
according to Brooks's statement.

It seemed almost as if there was no end to the
recitation of horror. Brooks talked of killings in one
home after another that Corll moved to. He talked
of walking into an apartment to find an unsuspecting boy marked for murder and of walking out again
before the killing; of bringing pizza to a small blond
boy from South Houston before he was tortured and
slain; of a murdered boy from Baton Rouge, Louisiana; of a boy "accidently" shot in the jaw by Henley
but killed later in the day with another youth; and
of a boy whose life he saved by begging Corll to let
him go. But the deadly pair went through with so

many murders that Brooks couldn't even give an accurate count of the victims.

"In all, I guess there were between twenty-five and thirty boys killed, and they were buried in three different places," he said. He admitted that he helped bury many of them under the shed, at the lake, and along the Gulf Coast beach near the sleepy seashore town of High Island. He said he was willing to help police recover the remains. He did just that, with Henley's help.

Henley and his police escort had awakened early in San Augustine and returned to Angelina National Forest, where the bodies of two more teenage boys were dug up. Then, after the remains had been hauled away in hearses, with police approval, Henley hosted a press conference.

Sitting in an unmarked police car as journalists crowded around, he confirmed that teenage boys were sexually abused and murdered by Corll, then buried in the forest. He agreed that he had been paid for luring boys to Corll's homes, although nowhere near all the money he was promised. He also claimed that he tried to talk Corll out of the mad round of sexual torture and murder, but the onetime candy man refused to stop. "He had a lust for blood," Henley shuddered.

Henley clearly didn't enjoy talking with the press as much as he liked to talk with detectives. He was truculent and brusque, and seemed relieved when a sheriff's deputy broke off the press conference. Then the cadre of officers climbed back into their vehicles, and with their prisoner drove in a car caravan south to the beach near High Island. Brooks, accompanied by two Houston detectives, joined them there.

The boys split up on the beach. Trailed by a group of officers, Brooks pointed out a shallow grave, and a few minutes later the plastic-wrapped skeleton of a teenage boy had been dug up. A short time later, this time following Henley's directions, a second body was unearthed. The remains were badly deteriorated, but long black hair still stuck to the skull, and the jaw held teeth that were spotted with gold fillings. With luck the fillings would help identify the victim. With the latest two discoveries, the body count had risen to twenty-three. A gray Cadillac hearse moved across the sand and onto the road, carrying the corpses away in black bags.

Although detectives continued to search for more than an hour, no additional bodies were found on the beach, and by late afternoon the lawmen and their prisoners piled in the cars for the return to Houston.

Monday morning after a relatively quiet weekend, the local sheriff and a posse of deputies gathered at the High Island Beach to oversee more excavation. This time a heavy-duty road grader was used to peel the top layer of sand away as the sheriff and deputy in a jeep trailed a few feet to the rear, watching for bodies, parts of bodies, or telltale lime streaks. A dozen or more journalists from television, radio, and newspapers clustered around the edges of the search area, interviewing anyone who would talk to them.

The search had barely resumed when the massive grader blade turned up what appeared to be a human leg bone and a clump of matted black hair. The grader was moved away and a party of men with shovels completed the exhumation of the body of another young man or boy. The body count was numbered twenty-four.

A few minutes later, a couple of miles up the beach just over the county line, a truck driver led a sheriff's deputy to a suspicious-appearing mound. The trucker explained that several months earlier he had come across a car that seemed to be stuck in the sand. But when he offered to help the young driver, he was brusquely told that no assistance was needed.

The sheriff's deputy stuck a long stick into the mound. Then he and the driver reeled backward, their stomachs churning from the overpowering, sweetly fetid odor of death. A digging crew exhumed the blue-jeans clad body of a young man. His hands and feet were bound, a pair of scissors hung from his belt, and several rounds of ammunition for a long gun were in his pockets. Four or five bullets had been fired into his ribs. He was victim number twenty-five.

Several hours later, victims twenty-six and twenty-seven were unearthed near the location where the first recovery of the morning had occurred. The bodies were lashed together, one atop the other.

If, as it appeared, all twenty-seven were victims of the same savage killer gang, they represented a modern American murder record. No single killer or gang of killers had even been suspected of murdering so many people in North America since the late nineteenth century, when the infamous Herman Mudgett (better known by a favorite alias, H. H. Holmes) slaughtered up to two hundred victims, mostly women, in his infamous murder castle in Chicago; and Johann Otto Hoch, also in Chicago, killed about fifty women. Both operated murder-for-profit schemes.

A Mexican immigrant and labor contractor, Juan V. Corona, had held the modern North American record for serial killers since his conviction in 1971 for the slaying of twenty-five transients and migrant workers near Yuba City, California. The victims had been robbed, and there were indications that some were homosexually raped, before burial in an orange grove.

Now, it appeared, the unenviable record had moved to South Texas. And it would remain there until late 1978, when shocked authorities in Chicago and the nearby suburbs would link John Wayne Gacy, Jr., to at least thirty-three deaths in a two-year homosexual killing spree that was ominously similar to the Houston rampage.

Calling off the search so abruptly led to severe criticism of the police department by the news media, family members of missing boys, and others who complained that there was a good possibility that additional bodies could still be located. Police were accused of being reluctant to add to Houston's grisly murder record, and with quitting too soon.

But the thoughts of police were not on murder records. Instead, they were focused on tieing up the case against the two suspects who remained alive, on identifying the victims, and in checking out the disturbing possibility that the homicidal trio may not have been involved in an isolated instance of child killing, but instead were part of a nationwide ring of sadistic pedarasts who bought and sold boys for rape and torture.

One of the nation's most industrious and notorious "chicken hawks" (men who specialize in sexually exploiting boys) was in fact caught up in the fallout from the ring's activities. John Norman had established an escort service for homosexuals called the Odyssey Foundation, in Dallas. The service offered fifteen-dollar memberships, and three-dollar catalogues with photographs and written descriptions of hundreds of boys available to pedophiles. Young escorts were recruited for the foundation with bold ads in homosexual periodicals, and reportedly by cruising bus terminals and other locations where they were likely to gather.

Norman was dragged into the murder-ring investigation after a boy staying overnight with him flipped through one of the catalogues and discovered the word "kill" stamped on the pictures of several youths. Details of the Houston-area murders were fresh in the minds of Texans, perhaps homosexuals more than anyone else, and the alarmed young man notified the editors of a gay newspaper of his suspicions that Norman might be dangerous. The editors notified the FBI, which in turn passed the information on to Dallas police.

Both the FBI and local authorities realized that the word *kill* is a printers' term indicating material that is no longer usable. Nevertheless, Norman's apartment was raided the next day and police carried away a pickup truck full of photoengraving equipment, cameras, and files containing sex literature and thousands of names and addresses. Although Norman was not linked to the murder ring, he was charged with other sex offenses—and promptly jumped bail. But fears persisted that the murders in the Houston area might still have been linked to the activities of a nationwide cartel of sadistic pedophiles.

Curiously, Norman resurfaced in Chicago, where he again got into trouble with the law for his organized child-sex activities, at just about the time police uncovered the Gacy murders.

In Houston, both Henley and Brooks had obtained legal counsel, and the youths clammed up. Any information that police obtained from here on in would have to come from other sources: interviews with family members, friends, neighbors, and acquaintances of the suspects and of the victims; collection and examination of physical evidence; ballistics tests; and forensic studies of the remains.

Twenty of the victims were identified in the early weeks of the probe, and all but three were boys and young men with close connections to the Heights. One of the others had been bicycling near Corll's house in Pasadena when he dropped from sight; another had the misfortune to meet Henley at driving school; and University of Texas student Jeffrey Konen was a hitchhiker. Brooks indicated that Konen was probably the first to die, and was killed in 1970, when Corll was living briefly in the quiet South Texas hamlet of Yorktown.

Among the missing Heights boys who were identified were Charles Cobble, Marty Ray Jones, David Hilligiest, Gregory Winkle, Ruben Watson, Billy Baulch, Johnny Delome, Billy Lawrence, Mark Scott, and Rhonda's boyfriend, Frank Aguirre.

There was also fourteen-year-old Wally Jay Simoneaux and his friend, thirteen-year-old Richard Hembree, who vanished after planning to spend the night together at Richard's house; brothers Donald

and Jerry Waldrop, fifteen and thirteen, whose bodies
were lifted from the floor of the shed; fifteen-year-
old Danny Yates; and fourteen-year-old James Glass,
who was killed while Corll and Brooks were living
together in Houston.

Then the identification process slowed, despite
the efforts of Harris County Medical Examiner Joseph Jachimczyk in Houston and law-enforcement
agencies throughout the country.

Teeth found in the remains were checked carefully
against the dental records of missing young men and
boys in efforts to identify victims through fillings,
caps, and other dental characteristics; blood types
were determined from hair, fingernails, and sometimes from bone; clothing and scraps of cloth were
inspected and meticulously studied for clues that
would lead police and medical sleuths to the identity of the owners; forensic anthropologists and forensic odontologists studied the remains; and finally, skulls were used to re-create the faces of the
victims.

Some of the remains have been unidentified for
years, leading to speculation among certain journalists and police that some parents don't want their
children named because of the homosexual overtones in the case. Other victims may have been
runaways or drifters who had lost contact with families long ago. Yet, slowly, new identifications have
trickled in.

The number of unclaimed bodies was last
trimmed in 1985, when teenager Willard K.
("Rusty") Branch, Jr., was identified through information provided by his sister as one of the seventeen
boys pulled from under the boat shed. He was from

the Heights. Two years earlier, nineteen-year-old Richard Allen Kepner was identified by his mother after she watched a television program about the slayings. She said she hadn't heard from her son since November 12, 1972, when he told her he would see her in a couple of days so they could have Sunday dinner together. At this writing, in December 1988, four bodies still remain without name tags.

But most of the bodies were identified within a few weeks, and parents of the victims were bitter and hurt. Grieving and frustrated, they struck out angrily at what they saw as the cold, inexcusable refusal of the Houston Police Department to take their pleas for help in finding their lost children as anything more serious than problems with runaway teenagers. They charged that police should have recognized a pattern in the disappearances.

Selma Winkle described her experience with the police when she reported her son, Gregory, missing as like talking to a blank wall. She quoted an officer as advising her: "Lady, we just don't have the time to chase every runaway." Police ignored her insistence that her boy wasn't a runaway.

Everett Waldrop, whose two sons who vanished in 1971, complained that police treated him "like some kind of idiot." Walter Scott said that he and other family members were disgusted with the Houston Police Department, and he indicated that police in the Texas state capital city of Austin also demonstrated a lack of concern when he twice wrote them asking for help locating Mark. They never replied.

Verne Cobble told journalists of his family's desperate search for Charles, and the boy's friend Marty, then remarked: "It's such a futile thing to go through this and not get any help from the authorities."

Houston Chief of Police Herman Short defended his department, pointing out that even when police do locate runaways, the kids cannot be arrested. If they are under seventeen, they can be returned to their parents, but police can't force them to stay. And if runaways are over seventeen, the most police can do is to ask them to notify their family.

Other spokesmen pointed out that in 1972, during the middle of the fierce kidnap-and-kill rampage, Houston police logged reports of fifty-two hundred missing children.

Meanwhile, however, with the ringleader of the killer gang already dead, law-enforcement authorities vowed to obtain murder convictions against his surviving confederates. Henley was charged with six of the slayings. No charges were filed in Corll's death; it was considered justifiable homicide.

Henley was tried first, and security arrangements were extraordinarily strict. More than thirty guards were assigned to stations inside and outside the Harris County Courthouse in Houston during pretrial proceedings. More than three hundred journalists, some from as far away as Japan, scrambled for the sixty-four seats that were set aside for the media. The media followed in equal numbers when the trial was moved on change of venue to San Antonio because of the extensive publicity in the case. A second request for a hearing on a change of venue from San Antonio, again because of heavy publicity, was denied.

All the stomach-churning evil of the events in Corll's homes—the lure of booze and doping parties, the sex, torture, and murder—were recounted in shocking detail. Investigators testified about boys who were castrated while still alive, of rape, and about Corll's offer of a two-hundred-dollar bounty for every youngster brought to him—more for "really good-looking" boys. But the horror and pain for families didn't end with the testimony.

Descriptions of the fear and pain of the victims were so vivid during the prosecution's summations that the mother of one of the boys ran from the courtroom screaming. Don Lambright, an assistant district attorney from Houston, was reminding the jurors of how Marty Ray Jones was strapped to the board and forced to watch as his friend was tortured and slaughtered when the shaken women broke for the door.

Will Gray, chief defense attorney, accused the prosecution of appealing to bias and prejudice, and attacked the testimony and reliability of the three police officers who took Henley's confessions.

"The monster is dead," he said in an apparent reference to Corll. Then he asked that the jury give Henley—whom he referred to as "this boy"—the benefit of every reasonable doubt.

An hour after the six men and six women began deliberations, they returned guilty verdicts against Henley on all six charges of murder with malice. They recommended he be sentenced to a total of 594 years in prison, the maximum of ninety-nine years on each count. Barely one week after it began, one of the most widely reported trials in the history of Texas was over.

Several days later, San Antonio District Court Judge Preston H. Dial pronounced sentence and, honoring the jury's recommendation, ordered the prison terms served consecutively. Because there was no valid death-penalty law in Texas at the time, Henley's sentence was the harshest available.

It was a sentence that Assistant District Attorney Don Lambright said he was delighted with. "I'm ecstatic the judge stacked the sentence," Lambright crowed. "Frankly, I hope he serves the rest of his natural-born life in the department of corrections."

But Henley's tearful mother vowed to reporters that she wasn't giving up on her son and would do her best to win his freedom through legal appeals. "It's not all over. It's just getting started," she declared.

She had testified earlier, as defense attorneys vainly attacked her son's written and oral statements to police, that when she visited him at the Pasadena jail he was apparently hallucinating. "I was with Wayne for about five minutes and he was incoherent," she said. "I just asked if he was all right and he said, 'Get me a lawyer and a doctor just as quick as you can.' " She said she asked detectives not to question her son again, but they refused. She quoted them as saying he didn't have to answer their questions.

Four years later, in December 1978, as investigators were pulling the bodies of boys from under the house of John Wayne Gacy, Jr., in Chicago, Henley won a new trial from the Texas Court of Criminal Appeals. But the ruling had nothing to do with the admissibility of his statements, written or oral, to police. By a six-to-three decision, the state's highest appeals court ruled that Judge Dial erred in refusing a second change-of-venue hearing after indications that the jury had been influenced by extensive pretrial publicity. The lanky convict's six ninety-nine-year sentences had been erased, and it appeared that he might eventually be freed from prison.

But Henley was retried the following June, and a jury again convicted him of six of the sex-and-torture slayings. The new jury, sitting in a Corpus Christi court, recommended that he serve six concurrent, not consecutive, life terms in prison. A few days later, Judge Noah Kennedy pronounced the sentence.

The third member of the murder trio, David Brooks, was convicted on a single count of murder, and sentenced to life in prison.

10 ◆

THE VAMPIRE RAPIST

Wayne Clifford Boden
(?–1971)

Despite the serene expression on the face of the petite young schoolteacher who looked almost as if she had merely dropped off to sleep after a few pleasant moments of romance, homicide investigators realized as soon as they saw her that they were dealing with the grisly handiwork of a murderous sexual psychopath.

Attractive twenty-one-year-old Norma Vaillancourt was dead. And the peaceful expression on her face was spoiled by an ugly purple-and-red bruise that circled her throat—and by ragged, bloody marks left by human teeth that had savaged her bare breasts. She was nude.

The teacher's macabre death marked the beginning of a ghastly sex, mutilation, and murder spree that would make headlines throughout Canada and baffle the Montreal police department's top homicide investigators for nearly four years.

And ironically, the horror that began in Canada's largest city on a hot midsummer day in 1968 would not end until the psychopath that both journalists and police called the Vampire Rapist moved more than twenty-three hundred miles away to the western province of Alberta.

Homicide detectives summoned to Miss Vaillancourt's Montreal apartment a few minutes after 1 P.M. on July 23, however, could hardly have known that they would soon be looking for a perverted serial killer with an amazing ability to exert a hypnoticlike charm over trusting young women. Like Miss Vaillancourt, most of the victims would be lured into romantic trysts that ended not in the promised glamor and excitement of a love affair but in savage mutilation and violent death.

Except for clues collected from the body itself—semen, foreign pubic hairs, and the telltale bite marks—investigators were unable to collect much helpful evidence in the victim's apartment. There were no signs of a struggle, such as overturned furniture or torn flesh under her fingernails or bruises, to indicate she may have tried to scratch and fight off an assailant. Nor was there any indication that any of her personal property had been stolen.

Detectives quickly turned to the circle of acquaintances she had formed since moving from the small town of Ste. Anne-des-Monts, along the southeast shore of the Saint Lawrence Seaway, to taste the big-city life of Montreal. She had loved the excitement of the city and was as vivacious and popular as she was pretty. Investigators quickly put together a long list of boyfriends. They learned, in fact, that she was seen with three different men on the day before her death.

After an autopsy was performed, pathologists estimated the time of death at about 10 P.M. the night before the body was discovered.

But although investigators patiently tracked down her friends and acquaintances, paying special attention to the men she had known, their efforts didn't produce a single solid suspect. Contacts with other law-enforcement agencies in Canada and in the United States in efforts to turn up reports of similar crimes were also fruitless.

The popular young schoolteacher had been dead more than a year when twenty-year-old Shirley Audette died. Like Norma Vaillancourt, she had brown hair and was petite, weighing in at around one hundred pounds. She had also had sex with a man shortly before her death, her breasts were shredded and bloodied by a series of savage bite marks, and she had been strangled.

Unlike the other woman, she was almost fully clothed, except for her brassiere, which had been forcefully ripped off before her body was found in a courtyard at the rear of an apartment complex about a block from her own. But like Norma Vaillancourt, she was a small-town girl; she had moved to the city from suburban Longueuil.

Investigators theorized that the victim was strangled and raped in one of the hundreds of apartments in the neighborhood, then dressed by her killer, carried to the courtyard, and dumped.

Questioning of acquaintances quickly turned up indications that the young woman not only had known her killer but had also suspected that he was dangerous. Detectives learned that she had confided her apprehension to a friend at the shop where she worked as a clerk. "I'm embarked on something which I'm not sure I'll be able to get out of," she had said.

The dead woman's boyfriend provided even stronger indications of her distress when he told police that he telephoned her at about 3 A.M., during his 7 P.M. to 7 A.M. shift at an area factory.

"I'm scared," she said.

When he asked her what she was frightened of, she replied that she was "just scared." She refused to elaborate.

The boyfriend was the last person known to have talked to her, except for her killer.

More than a year later, twenty-year-old Marielle Archambault was murdered. The body of the pretty jewelry-store clerk was found in her apartment at about 1 P.M. on November 24, 1969. She was sprawled on the living-room floor, partly covered with a blanket. Her panty hose were pulled down under her knees, and her brassiere had been ripped and torn down the middle.

The Vampire Rapist had left his macabre calling card on her breasts and neck. They were torn and bloodied with the marks of human teeth.

This time, however, there were signs that a minor struggle had occurred, and the killer had left behind what appeared to be a promising clue: a crumpled photograph of a handsome young man.

The photograph itself was too badly damaged to permit making reproductions with a camera, but a police artist provided a sketch that was quickly flashed to law-enforcement agencies and the news media throughout Canada. Other officers began contacting acquaintances and friends of the slain young woman for questioning and viewing of the sketch.

Her employer and other coworkers quickly agreed that the drawing resembled a young man who had twice stopped at the store to chat with Marielle on the last afternoon they had seen her alive. They said he first stopped in at about 4:30 P.M., then an hour later. She seemed to be pleased, and the second time she told him to wait, because she would be getting off work in a few minutes. He nodded in agreement, and the couple left the shop together at about 6 P.M.

The shopkeeper and his employees said that the first time Marielle talked with the young man she spoke French, then switched to English. She called him Bill.

Because her first language was French, the fact that she had called to him in English when she suggested he wait for her led investigators to believe that English was his primary language.

The mystery man was described as about twenty-five years old, five feet, nine inches tall, 160 to 165 pounds, and well dressed, with moderately long, carefully styled hair.

Delving further into Marielle's background, detectives learned that she had come to the big city from nearby Jolliette, and liked to party and have a good time with other fun-loving singles at popular local night spots.

Bill was also apparently a regular at many of the discotheques, and several young people pointed out that they frequently saw him around on the club scene. But no one was able to provide a last name,

ddress, place of employment, or any other infor-
nation helpful in leading police to the slippery man-
bout-town. And despite his obvious fondness for
ightclubs and pretty girls, he dropped abruptly
rom sight. He wasn't seen around at the discos
nymore.

But he was a hot suspect in at least three grisly
sex-and-mutilation murders, and investigators felt
almost certain that it was only a matter of time and
opportunity before the Vampire Rapist would strike
again. They renewed the public warnings to young
women to beware of strangers, no matter how
charming they might appear to be.

A new year and new decade were ushered in without incident. Then, barely three weeks later, Jean
Way died. The lovely twenty-four-year-old broker-
age-firm secretary was apparently raped and strangled in her apartment while a boyfriend stood impa-
tiently outside, ringing the doorbell to pick her up
for a date.

The date had been set for 8:30 P.M., but the boyfriend arrived about fifteen minutes early and was
surprised and disappointed when she didn't answer
the bell. He later told investigators that he just
couldn't believe she had broken their date without
notifying him.

Disappointed but not yet ready to give up seeing
the lovely secretary, he walked to a nearby tavern,
where he had a couple of beers; then he tried to
telephone her at about 9:15 P.M. When she failed to
answer the phone, he returned to the apartment.
This time when she didn't respond to the bell, he
tried the door. It was unlocked, and he swung it open
and walked in.

His girlfriend was stretched out naked on the front-room sofa with a leather belt knotted around her neck. Her clothes were lying all over the floor where they had been thrown as they were ripped from her body. Her breast were covered with bloody bite marks.

A window was open, leading police to speculate later that the killer had planned to leap from the second-floor apartment after the boyfriend's unexpected arrival interrupted the murder and rape.

Jean roomed with a nurse who worked a 4 P.M. to midnight shift at a local hospital. The roommate told detectives that she telephoned her friend at about 7 P.M., and Jean said that she was with a male friend. Jean named him, but the nurse could remember only the first name, Bill.

Detectives also learned that on the afternoon of the day before she died, Jean had stopped in a photo studio to have some film developed. When she left she pleaded to use the back door. The proprietor said she told him that she was frightened of a man outside who had been annoying her.

"I'm scared," she said.

Of four victims, she was the third who had confided to friends or acquaintances shortly before their deaths that they were afraid of someone.

An autopsy confirmed evidence of sexual intercourse between the victim and a man shortly before or at about the same time of her death. And although she had died of strangulation, the weapon was the killer's hands. The belt had apparently been looped around her neck and tightened after she was killed, to make sure that she was dead.

But the age and appearance of the victim, includ-

ng her petite build, as well as the location of the
murder and the mutilated breasts, clearly marked
the slaying as the handiwork of the same killer who
had been terrorizing young Montreal women for
nearly three years. And like the other women, Jean
Way was not a native of the city. The second of three
children of a surveyor and his wife, she was a native
of Hare Bay, Newfoundland.

Some of the most experienced homicide detectives on the Montreal Police Department had devoted two years to the investigation of the sex stranglings, and yet it seemed there was nothing they
could do to put a stop to the horror. They had few
leads to work on, and one of the most promising—
the crumpled photograph—had disintegrated when
they learned that the man in the picture had died
before the first murder in the series occurred. Police
had spent hundreds of man-hours trying to match a
suspect to the photograph.

And despite repeated warnings, naive and trusting
young women continued to fall under the evil Svengalilike spell of the bloodthirsty killer. "If the fiend
isn't a hypnotist, he has a hypnotic way about him,"
a frustrated police spokesman declared at a press
conference. "He seduces and strangles with such a
delicate touch that the victims show no agonized
expression."

Among themselves, some investigators speculated
that the killer might have selected young women he
instinctively felt were a bit masochistic and would
permit some delicate biting and strangling during
sex. But sometimes their lover would get carried
away, lose his gentle touch, and become homicidal.

Detective Lieutenant Marcel Allard, who was in

charge of the special ten-man squad working almos
full-time on the case, warned that investigators wer
certain the strangler would strike again. "We're deal
ing with a psychopath," he continued. "We've ha
dozens of psychiatrists tell us that he must hat
women, or that he hated his mother, or sister, o
wife, etc., etc. But that still doesn't help find him."

Although police weren't yet aware of it, the nightmare had in fact ended at last for the shaken citizens
of Montreal. It hadn't yet started more than two
thousand miles away, in Calgary.

Known worldwide for its famous rodeo, the annual
Calgary Stampede, the city of nearly a half million
people is broad-shouldered and brash, and peopled
by citizens who pride themselves on self-reliance
and minding their own business.

But the entire community was stunned when it
was learned that one of the most sadistic and ghoulish killers in Canada's history had apparently
shifted his nightmare activities from Montreal to
their city.

The first hint of trouble surfaced when Elizabeth
Anne Porteous, a skilled and well-liked business-
education teacher at Bowness High School, failed to
show up for morning classes or to notify her principal that she was ill. She didn't answer telephone
calls from other school employees, and she failed to
respond after the manager of the high-rise apartment
hotel she lived in was notified and knocked at her
door.

Another teacher who lived in the same building
had knocked at the door earlier on her way to work
and had gotten the same results. There was no
response.

By early afternoon, the concern of the thirty-three-year-old teacher's colleagues was turning to dread. She had a reputation for dependability and efficiency and wasn't the kind of person who would suddenly decide she needed an unscheduled day off or would leave town because of family problems without notifying her employers. The building manager was contacted again and was asked to enter her apartment to check on her.

The manager let himself in with a passkey. The apartment was a shambles. Furniture was overturned, and papers were scattered over the floor. The manager quickly retreated and called for police.

The schoolteacher was lying on her back on the bedroom floor. Her dress was ripped open and her brassiere had been violently torn from her body. Her breasts and neck were smeared with blood and punctured with the imprints of human teeth.

It was May 18, 1971, nearly a year and a half since Jean Way died in Montreal. An alert news reporter quickly recognized the ghastly trademark of the Vampire Rapist, and after confirming his suspicions with a phone call to Montreal, he passed on his information to Calgary police.

Had Canada's most-sought-after serial slayer moved to Calgary from Montreal? the media wanted to know. Or were police looking at the work of a copycat killer?

Like three, possibly four of the Montreal victims, the schoolteacher had been slain in her own apartment, and like all four, her breasts had been mutilated with bites from human teeth. And like the others, she had grown up as a small-town girl. The

only child of a banker and his wife, she was a nativ
of Dundas, in Ontario.

But despite the similarities to the Vampire Rap
ist's dark deeds, there were also several glaring di
ferences in the teacher's slaying. The condition c
the apartment and of the body left no doubt that sh
had put up a fierce fight for her life. Not only wa
the front room a shambles, but the fight had appar
ently extended into the bathroom as well. A corne
of the water closet on the toilet had been shattered
and the medicine cabinet was pulled from the wall
Bright red buttons from the victim's dress were
scattered over the floors of both rooms, like malig-
nant drops of blood. A woman's shoes, with the heel
ripped off, lay on its side in the hallway.

And there was no sign of the serene expression on
the teacher's face that had added such a bizarre
dimension to the Montreal murders. Her agonized
grimace showed clearly that she had died in terrible
fear and pain.

After police technicians had photographed the
body at the crime scene, and its location on the floor
had been pinpointed as precisely as possible, the
corpse was removed for autopsy to the morgue at
Calgary General Hospital. As the body was being
raised at the hospital to remove the shredded remains of the dress, a man's cufflink clattered onto
the metal examining table. It would become a valu-
able piece of evidence.

As expected, the autopsy disclosed that the victim
had been raped. And, true to the murder style of the
Vampire Rapist, she had been strangled: either with
the killer's hands, or from pressured applied to her
throat with his forearm.

Pathologists also discovered five fresh burn marks on her back, which they believed were inflicted with the tip of a lighted cigarette.

As news of the tragedy flashed throughout Calgary, friends and acquaintances of the dead woman began to contact police with information. A man-and-wife pair of educators told police that the night before Elizabeth's body was discovered, they had seen her with a man who appeared to be in his mid-twenties. They said they were stopped at a traffic light when she and her well-dressed companion pulled up beside them. They recalled that the car was an older-model light blue Mercedes, and it had the small figure of a steer visible in the rear window.

A description of the vehicle was disseminated to all uniform and plainclothes officers in Calgary, and they were told to be on the lookout for it. The owner, or driver, was wanted for questioning.

One of Elizabeth's friends told police that the teacher had talked to her about a date she had set up for the night of May 17. But, unfortunately, she hadn't named her escort or provided any other helpful background about him.

But another friend, a former teacher at the high school, informed detectives that they were in the nearby mountain resort town of Banff about a month earlier when Elizabeth met a handsome young man in a cocktail lounge. The good-looking stranger appeared to be in his mid-twenties, had stylishly long brown hair, and was well dressed.

While exchanging the usual cocktail banter, he had identified himself as a car salesman and said he drove a Mercedes. He said his name was Bill. Surprisingly, the couple learned, they had grown up in the same town, Dundas, Ontario.

Elizabeth was impressed with the smooth-talking stranger, and before leaving the lounge she scribbled her name, address, and telephone number on a piece of paper and suggested that he give her a call sometime.

The day after the grisly discovery of the teacher's body, a policeman spotted an older-model light blue Mercedes parked a few blocks from her high-rise apartment. A stakeout was set up, and after a brief wait a young man was apprehended as he approached the vehicle.

He readily admitted the car was his, but said he didn't know anything about the man called Bill, whom police were looking for. He said his name was Wayne Clifford Boden, he was twenty-three, and he had been in Calgary about eighteen months since leaving his native Ontario. He was a traveling salesman, and was originally from Dundas—Elizabeth Porteous's hometown.

Transported to police headquarters for interrogation, Boden conceded that he had dated the unfortunate schoolteacher, but insisted that he knew nothing about her murder. He said they had gone to a nightclub for a few drinks and dancing, and that he had her back at her apartment before midnight. She invited him in for coffee, he said, but explained that he declined because it was late and both of them had to work the next morning. He added that he heard her latch the door as he left.

"Elizabeth was alive when I saw her last," he declared.

When police interrogators showed him the cuff-ink that dropped from her dress, he admitted it was his but said he lost it at the apartment before they went out nightclubbing. They had looked all over the apartment for it, he claimed.

Despite Boden's smooth replies and repeated protestations of innocence, he was charged with first-degree murder in the teacher's slaying and lodged in jail.

But the investigation was still a long way from over. Police in Montreal were notified of the arrest and sent Criminal Investigation Bureau detectives to question Boden about the serial killings there.

Their difficulties with the bizarre case hadn't yet ended, however, and by a curious twist of fate, as the three detectives were returning to Montreal, their Air Canada jet was hijacked. They were eventually rescued, along with 115 other passengers and crewmen.

In Calgary, homicide officers spread out on a variety of assignments aimed at putting together an undeniable chain of evidence against the suspected sex strangler. Some detectives continued questioning acquaintances of the victim, and others began assembling information about Boden's background.

Checks with authorities in Dundas, and in the larger nearby city of Hamilton where Boden had also lived for a time, revealed that he had no record of trouble with police in either community. Police in Dundas, in fact, recalled him as a mild-mannered youth. He appeared to be well behaved and well liked.

A search warrant was also obtained from the Alberta courts, and police began a painstaking search of Boden's apartment. The search turned up a red button similar to those ripped from Elizabeth's dress. It had been discarded in a paper wastebasket Detectives also confiscated a cartoon book filled with drawings of women, which someone had crudely sketched over with gross exaggerations of the breasts and nipples.

A young woman who had been living with Boden as his common-law wife told investigators that they had come to Calgary from Montreal about eighteen months earlier. On the night the schoolteacher was murdered, he had told his sweetheart that he was going to a sales meeting. He returned about midnight, looking very tired.

The slender, soft-spoken salesman went on trial for the Porteous murder on February 15, 1972, in the Alberta Supreme Court before Chief Justice J. V. H. Milvain. As anticipated, both the cufflink and the button recovered from the wastebasket figured as important pieces of physical evidence.

But some of the most sensational testimony was provided by a Calgary orthodontist who confirmed that the bite marks on the breasts and neck of the victim were inflicted by the teeth of the defendant. The unique character of Boden's teeth and bite matched the wounds on the victim.

Appearing as an expert witness, the orthodontist testified that an analysis of the wounds showed twenty-nine points of similarity to the formation of Boden's teeth. Thirteen points were matched on the right breast and sixteen on the left. The minimum total number of corcordant points required by law for identification was thirteen, he told the court.

He added that his findings were confirmed by a skilled British orthodontist who was also an experi-

nced consultant on similar wounds and a respected
xpert witness.

The dental expert's testimony made judicial his-
ory in Canada, where it marked the first time such
vidence was admitted in court for the purpose of
dentifying a defendant.

A crime technician with the Royal Canadian
Mounted Police crime-detection laboratory in Ed-
monton identified a pair of men's shorts, removed
rom Boden and found to be stained with seminal
luid. The technician testified that strands of hair
found in the shorts were identical in color and
texture to hairs taken from the body of the victim.
He also identified hair taken from the rug in her
apartment as matching hair taken from Boden.

But the most startling testimony of all dealt with
a conversation Boden had at police headquarters
with his live-in lover three days after the victim's
body was discovered.

The chief of the Calgary Police Department's
homicide squad said he was present when Boden, in
effect, confessed the murder to his girlfriend. Detective Sergeant Ernest Reimer testified that Boden told
the woman he was going to plead not guilty by
reason of insanity, then asked if she knew what he
meant. He said Boden repeated the question, then
declared:

"You understand? I am the one. That is why I am
charged. I did it but I don't know why. It's not in my
character to do something like that."

Boden's girlfriend also testified, confirming the
homicide sergeant's statements about the conversation. She said that her boyfriend appeared to be

"pretty shook up" when he told her about his plan for the insanity plea.

Boden did not testify, and his defense counsel did not call any witnesses.

At the conclusion of the trial, conducted without a jury, Boden was pronounced guilty by Chief Justice Milvain of noncapital murder. He was given the mandatory sentence: life in prison.

But the young sex strangler's troubles weren't yet over. He was still wanted in Montreal, where he was suspected as the Vampire Rapist who had terrorized the city for more than two years.

Although he had previously denied being the killer, he waived extradition to Ontario, then gave statements to police admitting three of the Montreal slayings. Police learned that he had known and dated Jean Way for about a year before she was killed. He had also lived in an apartment near Shirley Audette's home, and he hung around the same discotheques as Marielle Archambault.

When he appeared before Justice Jacques Ducros, in the Court of Queen's Bench in Montreal, Boden disregarded the advice of his court-appointed attorney and pleaded guilty to the three murders. He admitted that he had strangled Shirley Audette, Marielle Archambault, and Jean Way.

But he denied that he was responsible for murdering Norma Vaillancourt, the first victim in the shocking string of sex-and-mutilation slayings on Montreal's West End that had been blamed on the Vampire Rapist.

Despite the best efforts of the Montreal Police Department's homicide investigators, Crown prosecutors determined that there was insufficient evi-

ence to convict Boden of the Archambault killing,
so he was not charged and brought to trial in that
case. Officially, the murder was left unsolved.

Boden, however, was sentenced to separate life
prison terms for the other three slayings that he had
confessed to.

The Canadian justice system hadn't yet heard the
last of him, however.

Barely more than twelve years after he was sentenced to four life terms behind bars, he walked
away from an unarmed guard in downtown Montreal
while he was on an authorized strangler's day off
from a federal maximum-security prison. The prison
arts-and-crafts teacher assigned to accompany him
on his daylong holiday gave him permission to go to
the washroom in a hotel restaurant by himself—and
he never returned.

Instead, the onetime Vampire Rapist who had held
the city hostage to a nightmare more than a decade
earlier not only left his escort without a prisoner to
return with but also stuck him with the dinner bill
as well. Then he looked up an old friend he had met
in prison, and they went out on the town together.

Police caught up with Boden the next evening
when patrons at a bar where he was drinking recognized him from the old days and turned him in. He
was sitting quietly in the artificial twilight of the
bar, wearing dark glasses, and casually sipping a
beer.

According to his ex-convict pal, Boden had spent
a good part of the previous evening drinking with a
woman he met at another hotel bar in the same
neighborhood he roamed when he had held the city
hostage to a nightmare of sexual assault, mutilation,

and murder. He financed his spree with three hundred dollars in prison earnings and with a credit car
he had been issued while behind bars in 1977.

Police and citizens were apprehensive and out
raged when they learned that the Vampire Rapis
had been allowed to so casually resume his ol
barhopping habits. When Louis Way, the father o
one of the Montreal victims, was contacted by
newspaper reporter, he was shocked: "What's the
world coming to when you have people like tha
prowling the streets?" he asked. "As far as I'm concerned, they should bring back the death penalty."

But the thirty-six-year-old killer was convinced
that it was he who had been wronged, and when he
appeared before Sessions Court Judge André Chalous
he complained that he pulled off the high-profile
escape merely to get media attention. He was angry
that he had been kept in prison so long without
parole.

"I want someone to go to Ottawa and find out why
I have been put off for thirteen years," he complained.

"You killed three people in Montreal," the judge
sternly reminded him.

Boden was returned to the federal government's
Laval Correctional Development Centre, with a new
one-year prison sentence to serve for escape. He had
fled the same prison during the second of two out-
ings allowed outside the walls.

Asked about future security measures for the notorious Vampire Rapist, a corrections official told
newsmen that it would be "a good while" before he
was awarded another day on the town.